I0083753

A Life Adrift

A Life Adrift, the memoir of balladeer-political activist Soeda Azembō (1872-1944), chronicles his life as one of Japan's first modern mass entertainers and imparts an understanding of how ordinary people experienced and accommodated the tumult of life in prewar Japan. Azembō created *enka* songs sung by tenant farmers in rural hinterlands and factory hands in Tokyo and Osaka. Although his work is still largely unknown outside Japan, his poems and lyrics were so well known at his career's peak that a single verse served as shorthand expressing popular attitudes about political corruption, sex scandals, spiralling prices, war, and love of motherland. As these categories attest, he embedded in his songs contemporary views on class conflict, gender relations, and racial attitudes toward international rivals. Ordinary people valued Azembō's music because it was of them and for them. They also appreciated it for being distinctively modern and home-grown, qualities rare among the cultural innovations that flooded into Japan from the mid-nineteenth century. *A Life Adrift* stands out as the only memoir of its kind, one written first-hand by a leader in the world of *enka* singing.

The Author
Michael Lewis is Professor of History at Michigan State University.

Routledge Contemporary Japan Series

A Life Adrift

Soeda Azembō, Popular Song,
and Modern Mass Culture in Japan

Introduced, annotated,
and translated from the
Japanese by

Michael Lewis

Routledge
Taylor & Francis Group

LONDON AND NEW YORK

Transferred to digital printing 2010

First published 2009 by Routledge
2 Park Square, Milton Park, Abingdon, Oxon OX14 4RN

Simultaneously published in the USA and Canada
by Routledge

Routledge is an imprint of the Taylor & Francis Group, an informa business

© 2009 Michael Lewis

Text designed by Hannah Cohen

All rights reserved. No part of this book may be reprinted or
reproduced or utilised in any form or by any electric, mechanical
or other means, now known or hereafter invented, including
photocopying or recording, or in any information storage or retrieval
system, without permission in writing from the publishers.

British Library Cataloguing in Publication Data
A catalogue record for this book is available from the British Library

Library of Congress Cataloging in Publication Data
A catalog record has been requested for this book

ISBN10: 0-7103-1337-3 (hbk)
ISBN10: 0-415-59216-0 (pbk)
ISBN10: 0-203-88621-6 (ebk)

ISBN13: 978-0-7103-1337-9 (hbk)
ISBN13: 978-0-415-59216-1 (pbk)
ISBN13: 978-0-203-88621-2 (ebk)

Contents

In Memory of Iwasaki Shigetoshi

Acknowledgements

I first encountered Soeda Azembō as a lone voice happily singing bitter songs about modernity's mixed blessings. In the years since I began learning about the life behind the lyrics, my solitary relationship with Azembō's as subject for historical study has made for many friendships with people who have helped me come to know him better. Azembō was a prickly character, a pessimistic humanist and popular entertainer with a reclusive streak. I sometimes wonder how he might have felt about his individual poetic voice providing an opportunity to engage so many collaborators in assaying his place in Japanese history. I am still unsure how to answer that, but suspect that Azembō, ever the performer, would probably be pleased to once again be in a new public's gaze. From what I have learned about his willingness to give credit where it is due, I am more confident that he would approve acknowledging the players whose efforts make it possible for the 'mute cicada' to be heard again after such a long silence.

I am especially appreciative of the librarians and archivists at Waseda University, Sophia University, and the Kanagawa Museum of Modern Literature Research (Kanagawa Kindai Bungaku Kan) who guided me to sources of information about Azembō's life and times. The Kanagawa Museum additionally facilitated the use of photographs reproduced in this volume. Professors Anzai Kunio at Waseda and Kate Wildman Nakai at Sophia provided entrée to their campus libraries and shared their thoughts on Azembō's historical significance.

I received help from many quarters in translating *A Life Adrift*. Iwasaki Shigetoshi, an independent scholar and the person to whom this book is dedicated, taught me much about finding the meaning for ideas and expressions from an historical context that is no more. Iwasaki Sensei, at times bemused about one of Azembō's arcane references, looked forward to reading how I would finally render *Ryūsei-ki* into English. I regret that the translation was not completed before he passed away. I trust that Iwasaki Yuko, who also became involved in this project, will appreciate how some of the puzzles of translation have been worked out in his final version, thanks to her and her husband's guidance.

Several friends and colleagues read the completed translation and introduction that accompanies the text. I am especially grateful to Andō Emi for assisting in finding resources, textual and human, relating to Azembō's life and times. Gary Jung and Mie Lewis deserve thanks for reading the manuscript in its entirety and making valuable suggestions for revision. Fellow historians E. Taylor Atkins, Jim Huffman, and Roy Hanashiro shared their expertise to help improve both the content and presentation of Azembō's story. Jan Bardsley, ever enthusiastic, proved true to form in her unflagging support.

Finally, gratitude is owed to Michigan State University's Office of the Provost and Office of the Dean of International Studies and Programs for providing funding and time away from campus to research and write this study. Lou Anna K. Simon, John Hudzik, and Jeffrey Riedinger are the individuals responsible for the institutional support which proved essential to completing this project.

I apologize for overlooking any one who offered encouragement and advice. Many supporters means some are bound to be missed. I sincerely appreciate the generous help I have received. All who have contributed are of course absolved from any mistakes in fact or interpretation that may appear in this work despite their good advice to the contrary. Final responsibility for remaining errors rests with me.

Michael Lewis, 2009

List of Illustrations

Measures and Money

Japanese Terms and U.S. Equivalents

Japanese	U.S.
Land Area	
1 *chō*	2.45 acres
Volume and Weight	
1 *shō*	half-gallon (approx 1.8 litres)
Length and distance	
1 *ri*	2.44 miles
1 *chō*	0.67 miles
Money	
1 *ryō* (widely used pre-1868; equaled 1 yen after 1871).	$0.75
1 yen (*en*)	$0.50
100 *sen* = 1 yen	
100 *rin* = 1 *sen*	

Introduction

A Life Adrift (Ryūsei-ki)

Soeda Azembō (1872-1944) begins his memoir, *A Life Adrift*, in a downtown Tokyo junkyard, a wartime center for recycling used goods for the 'sake of the nation.'[1] It is a fitting place because Azembō himself is seeking resurrection. After climbing from the anonymity of the day laborer's work camp in the 1880s to the peak of popularity as Japan's best-known singer-songwriter during the first decades of the new century, he all but vanishes into the obscure hand-to-mouth life of a wandering recluse during the 1930s. Towards the end of that decade, he resurfaces briefly as a chronicler of Tokyo's demimonde amusement district, Asakusa. Now, writing in the early 1940s, he has found temporary sanctuary as extra help at the junkyard. But the harbor is impermanent, merely a resting spot where he is tolerated more for reasons of friendship than usefulness. His memoir, *A Life Adrift*, is another attempt to rise once more and move on.

Finding a new start is not easy for Azembō. Not only is he well past middle age, his artistic reputation as a leftist writer of wildly popular satirical songs of social and political criticism is a liability in wartime Japan. He is suspect in the eyes of officials who decide what can and cannot be published during the current national emergency. To skirt this obstacle, Azembō begins *A Life Adrift* with his personal paean to the state. Just as junk dealers salvage paper and old clothing for the 'sake of the nation,' a set phrase to justify every wartime sacrifice, Azembō recycles a long patriotic poem, one that he originally wrote for an army magazine, to begin his life story.

The poem praises the 'New Order,' a system mandated by Premier Konoe in 1940 to create a militarized centrally controlled economy at home and an empire abroad. As poetry, 'Advance! New Order, Advance!' is not very good. Its form is flat and mechanical; its meaning, formulaic and uninspired. In short, it is noticeably different from Azembō's earlier satires that overflow with wit, lively images, and uninhibited criticism of officialdom, big business, and well-fed 'high collar' classes.

This poetic beginning of *A Life Adrift*, as well as other chapters in which he professes a newfound conservatism, is, at least in part, Azembō's attempt to meet the state more than halfway. In his memoir Azembō, whose sobriquet means 'the mute cicada,' hints that this compromise is a way to regain his voice and his public. If this was the intention, it worked.[2] The verse of the opening poem, filled with clichés that praise state power, in the end satisfies the censors who permit publication.

Yet, although some critics consider Azembō's compromise as merely stylistic, it was in fact more than that. The poem and sections of the work it prefaces, express Azembō's profound love for 'Japan,' an abstract love for an even more abstract entity that is ever present in his poetry, songs, and prose. It was a love that was matched by his concrete disdain for specific government officials and their flawed policies. The combination was one captured by Mark Twain in his observation, 'Loyalty to the country always. Loyalty to the government when it deserves it.'

Wartime exigencies, his country's and his own, convinced Azembō that the state deserved his support more than ever. His use of the 'Advance! New Order, Advance!', a poem devoid of his characteristic humanism, reveals this willingness to forsake social criticism and satire for the greater good. Ever aware of his own needs, he also uses slavish nationalism for his own sake. Eulogizing the 'New Order' assures that his voice will be heard. It is a way to tell his life story and retail *A Life Adrift* under wartime conditions, while fulfilling his duty to 'Japan.'

Such compromises, superficially selfless but at bottom self-serving, were hardly rare among Japanese artists (and are perhaps common to professional artists anywhere and always).[3] Yet, Azembō's refurbished heroic image in postwar Japan has been at odds with the mix of self-interest and patriotism, self-promotion and deprecation, social criticism and strategic silence that we actually encounter in *A Life Adrift*. The contradictory mixture is far closer to his career than that of undiluted saint or martyr. Although *enka* songwriters and singers are selectively remembered as Meiji rebels who embraced the pure cause of Liberty and Popular Rights, even Azembō implicitly recognized the gap dividing rhetoric and reality. In *A Life Adrift*, he acknowledges his own variableness, yet does not seek the reader's forgiveness of his political inconsistency or personal inconstancy. The genuine contradictions in Azembō's life evident throughout *A Life Adrift* are left standing on their own, largely unexplained.

The absence of self-explanation gives a refreshing honesty to the story, but does not mean that Azembō is above dissimulation. His shift from subversive satire to super patriotism obviously reflects his attempt to write with one eye toward the censors. He had to satisfy, at least superficially, those publication gatekeepers who appreciated militaristic twaddle such as 'Advance! New Order, Advance!' but were suspicious about the author's reputation and earlier work. Writing in wartime makes Azembō even more prone to the self-conscious and self-serving obfuscation inherent in autobiographies. In places, it seems that he is quickly moving his hands to cover some exposed part of the body of his story. In places, those sudden movements also work to draw our attention to what he seeks to hide.

The dissimulation is especially evident in his abbreviated history of the late Meiji and Taishō years, from the 1890s to the late 1920s. This was the period when Azembō was most active in the socialist movement and least restrained in attacking the state and the social and economic injustices he attributed to it. Unfortunately, it is these chapters that are among the shortest and most clipped in *A Life Adrift*. Thanks to postwar reprinting of original versions of Azembō's poems and lyrics, some of the sections that he left out of his memoir are now available. I have included fuller versions of lyrics in this volume in the Notes section to fill in the gaps resulting from Azembō's self-censorship.

Although Azembō selectively edits his memoir, it is valuable as the only existing first-person account of the life and times of a prewar *enka* singer.

As a musical style, modern *enka* was among Japan's very first mass cultural forms. It predated, but only barely, sound recordings, movies, and radio in its sway over a national audience. Relying on modern printing methods and distribution through a new and more tightly meshed transport and communications network, Azembō's songs, both authorized and bootlegged versions, circulated widely throughout Japan.[4]

After the turn of the century, Azembō also wrote lyrics and accounts of the lives of *enka* singers as workers in an emerging music industry for urban newspapers such as the *Commoners' Press* (*Heimin shinbun*) and magazines, including *Reconstruction* (*Kaizō*). Although his popularity may have originally depended on live street-corner performance, his fame grew alongside Japan's rapidly expanding and technologically modern mass media. During the 1920s, gramophone records, movies, and radio broadcasting, along with ever changing popular tastes in music, spurred newer *enka* forms to grow from older roots. The politically charged Meiji-Taishō songs gave way to the modern 'popular songs' (*kayōkyoku*) predominant among *enka* down to today. The break was not sufficiently hard or fast to negate the ties connecting Azembō's songs to those that followed. Themes and forms from earlier styles echoed in later songs. In fact, *kayōkyoku* artists, singers such as Shōji Tarō, covered versions of Azembō's music decade in and decade out in a manner reminiscent of Western rock musicians adopting and adapting songs from earlier blues and rock and roll performers. The comparison with blues artists is also useful for understanding how the modern music business worked in Japan. *Enka* writers and singers in Japan, like blues artists in the West, often failed to profit from their contributions to popular music and wound up down and out despite their one-time social prominence.

In Azembō's case, his decline as a performing artist was matched by his rebound as a frontline chronicler of life as a member of Japan's underclass, a life that was as culturally rich and dynamic as it was materially poor. His account of life in Tokyo's Asakusa district provides a window on Tokyo's vibrant mass culture, a unique sense of time and place, that might otherwise be lost to us.[5] The downhill side of Azembō's career, the years spent adrift in the Japanese countryside, provide a view that contrasts with life lived in Tokyo. Personal encounters with the *tekiya*, petty grifters and pitchmen who worked local festivals, and his life on the road with begging pilgrims making the circuit of Shikoku in the 1930s, capture experiences ethnographically rich in detail.

The delight in Azembō's account, however, is not just in the details. He also witnessed firsthand the broader changes that transformed his times. He saw sweeping social and industrial reforms remake the way Japanese people lived their lives from the mid-nineteenth century through the 1940s. He observed life from the ground-level perspective of the down-and-out Tokyo slum dweller. At times outraged by what he witnessed, he attempted to influence the making of a new political system, one that held out the possibility of greater economic and social equality. He also experienced Tokyo's phenomenal expansion as Japan's premier city and survived its fall in earthquake and fire. At the time he wrote *A Life Adrift*, the Japanese empire had expanded to its fullest extent throughout Asia. By the time of his death, signs clearly indicated that Japan was edging ever closer to utter defeat in the Pacific War. Azembō's presence at the creation and at the destruction of so many real and figurative landmarks in Japanese modern history makes his memoir a valuable source for grasping how life was lived, triumphs savored, and hardships endured by people living at Japan's lower depths during the prewar years.

Azembō's identity as a performer of indigenous music and commoners' advocate has revived interest in his music in postwar Japan. Today, his songs have been rearranged by new groups of young, countercultural artists. They exalt Azembō for his advocacy of social and economic justice for the Japanese poor, while tending to overlook his jingoistic songs and poetry in praise of empire abroad and the New Order. This new audience's selectivity, taking the good and ignoring the bad, would probably have met with Azembō's approval. His own life demonstrated a preference for the pragmatic, at times at the expense of the principled, as a way to survive in a hostile world.

The Prewar *Enka* Repertoire: Songs of Parody, Romance, and Protest Politics

Today, popular *enka* are usually songs of nostalgic loss, usually for a lost love and sometimes for one's rural roots. Azembō's *enka* carried the seeds that developed into the contemporary form. But from the 1880s through the 1920s, the period of Azembō's stellar rise, the *enka* themes were far richer and diverse than sentimental songs of longing, whether for a lost love or one's hometown.[6] During the prewar years, the form flourished as popular poetry widely appreciated for its sharp political and social satire and humorous commentary on current events and the human condition.

The roots of *enka* chronologically lie in medieval Japan and can be traced to the Asian mainland.[7] The modern form sung by prewar *enka-shi* composer-singers began to flourish in the 1880s alongside the Liberty and Popular Rights movement for expanded political rights. This early form was less singing than chanting in which the sole instrument was the chanter's voice. The typical performance, usually carried out on an urban street corner, featured one or two male singers wearing kimono, tall wooden sandals (*geta*), and oversized straw hats. They carried thick sticks that they tossed back and forth as they rhythmically recited their 'songs.' The rap-like chants usually carried a political commentary attacking people and policies associated with the new Meiji government.[8] The songs also called for opening a national assembly, reducing taxes, implementing social reforms, and revising unequal treaties. These Meiji *enka* became so closely associated with political activists that the genre is known as activist songs (*sōshi bushi*).[9]

The *sōshi* singers' garish costumes helped draw a crowd while the rhythmic chanting made the message easily accessible as these Meiji street artists performed guerilla theater on behalf of the Liberty and Popular Rights movement. Unlike speakers at more formal political rallies, *sōshi* singers did not need a podium and could easily shift from one street corner to another to evade the authorities. The performer's messages were also hard to suppress. Satires and lampoons spread by word of mouth found easy acceptance even among people unable to read. Some songs also relied on sex and double entendre— which of course made them even easier to remember and repeat— to make a political point. One such early *enka* went:

> Her age, seventeen,
> The peak time of connubial ripeness
> At twenty-three, without doubt, the bloom will be off her rose
> But her old man is a difficult and won't allow a teenage marriage
> Ah well
> What the hell
> I'll just wait 'til she's twenty-three.

On the surface this appears to be just a song of frustrated teenage lust. But the message behind the licentiousness was about Ōkuma Shigenobu, a Liberty and Popular Right's leader who proposed the opening of the national assembly in Meiji 17, or 1884, only to be booted from the government and forced to wait until Meiji 23.[10]

Historians of *enka* usually maintain that *sōshi* singers tried to skirt the law by claiming that their songs were merely entertainment and thus not subject to the oppressive ordinances intended to limit the campaign for popular rights.[11] There is little evidence that insisting on this legal nicety actually deterred police or prosecutors.[12] It became even more difficult to defend the singers' claims that their performances were just apolitical good fun when activists began selling crudely printed song sheets or booklets that put lampoons in print. The ties binding singers and opposition politicians became explicit after the founding of formal political parties in the early 1880s, when singers also came to live in clubs (*kurabu*) directly subsidized by these organizations. Azembō describes life in the most famous of these, the Seinen Club located in central Tokyo, as a place where activism finally eclipsed art as singers became indistinguishable from political hooligans routinely used as shock troops to promote a particular candidate or harass party rivals.[13]

From activist songs, which even Azembō described as angry shouting more than singing, the form quickly diversified. A new generation of singers emerged trained in singing styles introduced in primary school choral groups. These young people were more interested in melodies than in forcing the music to fit the words. The waning of the Liberty and Popular Rights movement, the opening of the Diet in 1890, and the dissolution of the Liberal Party (*Jiyūtō*) in 1898, also worked to dilute *enka*'s antigovernment content and make space for singers of largely apolitical student songs (*shōsei bushi*).

The student singers, with their tales of romance in the big cities, became known as the first *enka* specialists (*enkaya-san*). They had few if any ties to political clubs and took as their mission entertaining for pay. They also relied more on musical instruments such as the reed-less bamboo flute (*shakuhachi*) and violin. Around 1910, domestically produced violins could be had for as little as three yen; a few years later accordions manufactured in Japan also became affordable. These novel instruments helped spur an extraordinary increase in students and bogus students keen on singing their way to fame and fortune.[14] Their regular appearance on city street corners and in vacant lots of Japan's growing cities established the *enka* artist as a socially recognized category of Meiji period professional performer.

Although the student singers were the first acknowledged modern professionals, their predecessors also wrote and sang for money.[15] As depicted in *A Life Adrift* and other histories, the singers survived and in some cases flourished from what they earned selling song booklets. Eventually, the booklets were offered for retail sale in stores, but more often were sold directly by the singers to audience members. *Enka* fans might be found anywhere in Japanese cities, but more often gathered at informal but widely recognized sites. Entertainment areas such as Asakusa in Tokyo or Dotonbori in Osaka were among the first of these semi-fixed venues. The first *enka* singers preferred places such as Asakusa, with its close association with a major Buddhist temple, because religious institutions drew crowds.[16] Singers also performed at more profane sites in the heart of red light districts throughout Japan. Azembō worked the famous Yoshiwara in Tokyo in addition to singing on street corners in other major cities. Like many other singers, he also traveled around the country following routes that adhered to a calendar of local festival and shrine days. Some of these itinerant singers worked this circuit alongside the operators of night stalls (*tekiya*) who sold cheap goods at improvised booths, staged simple plays, and ran gambling games.

Before the appearance of sound recordings, radio, and the emergence of the highly capitalized music industry, singing and selling songbooks appeared an easy way to earn a living. The income may not have been steady, but for someone like Azembō, with little in the way of formal education or special skills, the allure - and at times, the reality - of easy money was always there. The *enka* producer and historian Nishizawa Sō estimates that it required less than half a *sen* (100 *sen* = 1 yen) to produce a songbook that the singer sold directly to members of the audience for two *sen*.[17] Based on this estimate of costs and assumption of direct sales, he calculates that a moderately successful *enka* singer at the turn of the century might make 40 yen a month, or approximately five times the amount earned by a carpenter, policeman, or junior civil servant.[18] Azembō, who was more than moderately successful during his peak years, enjoyed dressing in Western-style clothes and frequenting entertainment districts as customer instead of performer. Despite his later slide into poverty, sales of thousands of song booklets created brief but prosperous periods for him and his family.

These flush times depended on the fickleness of what was becoming a mass entertainment market. The public's demand for novelty and the need to produce songs in a timely way meant that the songwriter, who was often the singer as well, was constantly under the gun to produce topical tunes and catchy melodies as quickly as possible. As copyrights meant little to singers of Azembō's generation, there was also a good deal of borrowing. Melodies might be refitted with new lyrics and the versions of the substituted song (*kaeuta*) continued to circulate for years. Although individual performers might have enjoyed prosperous periods, there is little doubt that *enka* singing was a risky business made riskier still by competitors who appropriated moneymaking tunes.

The demand for variety led to a proliferation of *enka* themes. The common subjects of student songs (*shōsei bushi*) - the loneliness of the big city, regret at a dissipated life, and unrequited love - did not lead directly to the syrupy romantic songs typical of many *enka* today. The student song was but an interim form, followed by other subgenres, such as the military songs or marches (*gunka*). These songs enthusiastically belted out support for war against the Chinese and Russians from 1888 and became wildly popular during the first modern conflicts on the continent.[19]

The war songs overlapped with the emergence of yet other categories, such as those dedicated to promoting social and political reforms and expressing support of the poor against the rich. The trend was not entirely new, but built on a social flattening evident in the waning years of the Tokugawa if not earlier. Pre-restoration songs mocked politically impotent samurai unable to put down popular uprisings. After 1868, officials continued to be abused in ditties that observed the new Western-style hirsuteness of government bureaucrats:

If growing whiskers makes an official
Then rats and cats, one and all, officials be[20]

Later socialist songs emerged from such early critiques of officialdom. These *enka* differed from the Liberty and Popular Rights *sōshi bushi* in that the singers, usually unallied with established political parties, delivered a broader social critique. Their lyrics lambasted equally party politicians, government ministers, and capitalists along with the modern servants of the new Japanese state, careerist bureaucrats and accommodating educators. The music reflected the disappointment and anger of performers such as Azembō who appeared to have expected something more politically and economically egalitarian than the machine politics that came with constitutional rule. Azembō particularly disdained types such as Hoshi Tōru, the flamboyant party politician who, until his assassination by an outraged former samurai, was known for being both utterly corrupt and thoroughly successful in insinuating his political party into national politics. Singers condemned these politicos as operators whose parties had become legal, but in the process had lost moral legitimacy by shamelessly politicking for personal or factional profit. As *A Life Adrift* makes clear, Azembō saw such politicians as no different from 'whores.' The party men reciprocated the singers' dislike. As established party leaders, now a part of the predictable system of rule of law, and increasingly involved in established bureaucratic offices, they no longer needed singing shock troops.

While *enka* singers, Azembō included, continued to write and sing songs with a political edge, they took on larger targets. From satires that lampooned party corruption, they moved to satirizing bureaucratic scandals and gave voice to the public's complaints about poor sewers, lousy train service, high rice prices, and the government's slow response to outbreaks of cholera. From social concerns, they broadened their repertoire to appeal to contemporary tastes that demanded ever greater variety. By the late 1890s, they produced happy songs, silly songs, songs broadly humorous and full of puns and sexual innuendo. They commented musically on celebrated events such as a soldier's solo horseback crossing of Siberia and wrote faddish ditties extolling the miracle of railway travel or teasingly complaining about mannish women so bold as to work as telephone operators. During the first two decades of the new century, they also captured and spread slang considered fashionable by a new generation. One of these was *ma ga iin*, which meant something like personal flair or 'coolness' and later mutated into the expression *kakko ii*.

Official oppression and changing musical fashions account for the fading popularity of protest *enka*.[21] Meiji state officials, like officials in most places, failed to appreciate the principle of legitimate political opposition, loyal or otherwise. They routinely created laws to smother dissent and other forms of political protest, including restrictions on meetings by nascent political parties and sale of antigovernment publications. Repression became more severe with the 1910 Great Treason Incident in which police responded to an alleged plot to assassinate the Meiji Emperor by summarily rounding up socialists, including the leading anarchist writer Kōtoku Shūsui. The investigation that started in late May 1910 ended in death sentences for two dozen conspirators on January 18, 1911. Despite appeals for mercy from political groups outside Japan, Kōtoku and eleven other alleged confederates were executed by hanging before the month was out. The remaining defendants received reduced sentences of life in prison as a show of official mercy. From flourishing a mailed fist, the state moved to using it to crush opponents. The lesson was not lost on anyone, least of all those involved in socialist politics, including *enka* singers.

Repression continued after the Great Treason Incident in 1910 through new laws and extralegal actions, many of them prompted by official fears over Bolshevism abroad and an incipient leftist movement at home. The state's legal authorities permitted cracking down on labor protests, used martial law and deadly force against rice rioters in 1918, and took a forgiving attitude toward 'spontaneous' police attacks and murders of anarchists. The most of famous of these assaults resulted in the liquidation of the anarchist Ōsugi Sakae, who was strangled by a policeman in a jail cell in the aftermath of the 1923 Kantō Earthquake. His murder, an ideological cleansing, took place alongside the ethnic cleansings that saw mobs lynch thousands of resident Koreans, Chinese, and other outcasts.

The passage of the Peace Preservation Law in 1925 legally codified a new national policy that outlawed communism and any attempt to alter Japan's unique Emperor-lead national structure (*kokutai*). Now it no longer required an extraordinary act such as plotting the death of a prince or emperor to bring about severe legal sanctions. New provisions made it possible to punish even 'dangerous thoughts,' a euphemism for another euphemism, 'red ideas,' with the death penalty. Under the Peace Preservation Law, the already illegal Japan Communist Party underwent unrestrained and repeated secret police suppression in the late 1920s.

Such unambiguous suppression prompted *enka* singers to compose songs with apolitical themes. Yet it was not simply the heavy hand of the authorities that caused a new generation of singers to avoid songs of social and political criticism. Changing fashions and technological advances also caused older *enka* forms to fade in popularity. Entertainment choices had become richer with the introduction of movies, new musical instruments, record players, and the advent of radio broadcasting. The music business also became big business. In 1926, Columbia Records bought a controlling interest in Nichikku, the domestic gramophone company, and through it introduced

Japan to the Jazz Age. The stylistic innovation imported from the US soon flourished in dance halls, cafes, and Japanese language versions of American tunes.[22]

To younger audiences with more modern tastes, Azembō and his generation of *enka* singers appeared increasingly old-fashioned. For his part, Azembō, who usually worked as a lone musical craftsman, was unfamiliar with the ways of music as a modern industry in which corporations and the state had direct and controlling roles. His comments in *A Life Adrift* about the 'industry' indicate his awareness of changing trends and need to find a way to maintain control over his intellectual property. To this end he attempted several times to organize an *enka* association. But the lack of copyright laws to protect lyricists left him and fellow singer-songwriters vulnerable. Many *enka* performers also found it difficult to adapt new technologies and what some disparaged as 'mechanized music.'[23] A few singers were able to make the transition to the new world of radio broadcasting and movie musicals. But many more resembled Azembō, who found the use of a microphone something simply unbearable.

Capricious public taste, new technologies that enabled the creation of a more homogeneous and market-driven mass media, and government controls on broadcasting and mass entertainment, curtailed the diverse forms of early *enka* and ultimately led to the dominance of the romantic *enka* audiences appreciate today. Azembō and others like him did not entirely disappear. In fact, Azembō continued to be a fixture in the Asakusa amusement quarter into the early 1940s, albeit as a retired *enka* artist and active essayist. But by this time, conditions were ripe for the sophisticated in-studio creations of musical products by Koga Masao (of 'Koga Melodies' fame), Watanabe Hamako ('China Nights'), and others. That *enka* could still carry a sharp political edge was evident in the work of Ishida Ichimatsu, a self-styled Azembō disciple, who was jailed for his satirical songs during the 1930s.[24] But Ishida and others like him were exceptional. Far more numerous and mainstream were the producers of melodies of love and longing that became models for the postwar singers such as Misora Hibari, Kitajima Saburō, and Itsuki Hiroshi.

The shift toward the apolitical may have been inevitable and, as some critics have noted, was not entirely regrettable. Although many prewar songs were steeped in politics, detractors have noted that the music lacked gravity and was rife with incongruous stands on various social and political issues. Although clever and subtly poetic at times, the *enka* songs were also musically and lyrically repetitive. As might be expected of a popular genre, catchy melodies were recycled for uses completely at odds with earlier versions (one cannot say original versions because authorship was often impossible to ascertain and songs, whether approved by the original lyricist or not, enjoyed multiple reincarnations). Lyrics were also inconsistent, at times lascivious and at others sternly moralistic, just as their messages could be both politically informative and wildly misleading.[25] Although critics seeking consistency condemn the musical and thematic irregularities in *enka*, the form might be better understood and appreciated as evoking the dynamic, gritty, and all to human inconsistency of life in prewar Japan.

Enka, perhaps because its thematic variableness and musical rough edges, has become a lasting part of popular memory. The music critic and historian Takahashi Shin'ichi maintains that one reason for this is that these songs supplied a history absent from a malnourished official past. Prewar education effectively propagated nationalistic myths based on tales of founding deities and legendary emperors. But it was weak on what might be called felt history. Azembō's songs, catchy tunes associated with memories of wars, trains and streetcars, strikes, earthquakes, sensational murders, sex scandals, inflation, and economic depression, carried the evocative immediacy of events actually experienced.[26]

Azembō: Text and Context

Memoirs are historically valuable but also treacherous. The value is in the immediacy of an inside perspective. Who can speak more authoritatively than the very subject of the study? The treachery is in the writer's temptation to prettify the image in the narrative mirror, settle scores, edit, and editorialize. All of these complications are evident in Azembō's memoir and are magnified by his need to placate wartime censors. The pattern of additions and omissions in *A Life Adrift* starts with the prefatory poem, 'Advance! New Order, Advance!' It reads in part:

New Order, New Order
Hatching from your shell, a New Order born
We believe in you, we adore you
...

Expand to your heart's content
Robustly flourish New Order
...
Become a single living being
And then
Dance as you crack the stinging whip of reform
...
Our nation and all our citizens exert their will
To smash to bits all obstacles at home and abroad
To realize Imperial Rule that weighty duty to achieve
...
A hundred million with a single heart
...
Go! Advance naked!
And let us destroy the self and serve the greater good.

While this paean to the defense state, so forgettable that is often omitted from studies of Azembō's career, enjoys pride of place at the very start of *A Life Adrift*, more famous and representative songs are missing or truncated in the memoir. Azembō's scathing lyrics from 'Bugle Song' ('Rappa bushi') written more than three decades before the New Order poem, for example, are omitted:

From that hairpin adorning the locks of the nobleman's
mistress
What so brilliantly shines?
Perhaps diamonds?
No, no
Just the greasy sweat from a darling peasant's head
...
Among those worldly gentleman who love their liquor
What so brilliantly sparkles?
Perhaps champagne?
No, no
Just the bloody tears from the darling factory girl's eyes
...
And decorating the jutting breasts of state ministers and
generals
What so brightly glitters?
Maybe the Medal of the Golden Pheasant?

No, no
Just the whitened skulls of our darling soldier boys[27]

The contradiction between what is present and what is missing in Azembō's memoir leaves one wondering which voice to believe. But the problem is less one of voices in absolute opposition, than that of a single voice modulated to suit changing times and different audiences while still in harmony with Azembō's basic values. The strained poetry of 'Advance! New Order, Advance!' illustrates the point. It may have been written in fear of censors, but its nationalistic theme can also be traced back to songs Azembō wrote earlier in his career. Even when attacking bureaucrats and political bosses, he never expressed his nationalism as anything less than a profound love of Japan and an aggressive dislike for the nation's enemies, real or suspected. His love of country did not prevent him from exposing the injustices inherent in the state's modernization project, yet neither did it prompt him to suggest abandoning that great undertaking.

His seeming contradictions represent views widely held throughout prewar Japanese society, a fact that helps account for Azembō's tremendous popularity. His ability to represent and thereby shape popular attitudes is reminiscent of Gramsci's description of the organic intellectual, whose ideas, usually formed outside established educational institutions, become widely propagated and at times challenge the dominant social and political order.[28] The strength of the critique might vary from the mildly irritating to the revolutionary. What continues constant is the role of organic intellectuals in creating and disseminating alternate visions of how society should run.

Azembō, the self-taught *enka* singer, filled a Gramscian role in becoming one of the first stars of a new national mass culture in modern Japan.[29] His songs, distributed throughout Japan through sales of song sheets that sometimes sold in the hundreds of thousands, were sung by tenant farmers in rural hinterlands and factory hands in Tokyo and Osaka. At his career's peak, his lyrics became so well known that a single verse might serve as shorthand expressing popular attitudes about political corruption, sex scandals, spiraling prices, war, or love of motherland. As these categories attest, he embedded in his songs contemporary views on class conflict, gender relations, and racial attitudes toward international rivals.

Ordinary people valued Azembō's music because it was of them and for them. At times, the identity was so close that they adjusted lyrics to reflect local feelings, substituting the name of their own factory for the ones satirized in Azembō's songs.[30] They also appreciated the music for being distinctively modern *and* homegrown, qualities rare among the cultural innovations that flooded into Japan from the mid-nineteenth century. Although musicologists now trace *enka's* origins to pre-Meiji forms and Korean musical styles, Azembō's audience embraced his music as Japan's own. As Azembō's memoir makes clear, he shared much with his contemporary public. As a Tokyoite, he observed politics at the central level. He also lived through the 1918 rice riots, 1923 earthquake, and Japan's economic depression of the 1930s. He watched Tokyo grow into a burgeoning metropolis and collapse in fiery rubble around him, and wrote critically of what he perceived emerging from the ashes. His songs also vented popular outrage through lyrics that were bitingly satirical yet also fatalistic.

Azembō's views also overlapped with those held by many of Japan's extraordinary leaders in the arts, politics, and social reforms. During his lifetime, that period encompassing Japan's emergence as Asia's only modern, industrialized, constitutional monarchy, it was not unusual to consider home and abroad as two different realms. Other Japanese intellectuals, artists, and activists - individuals as varied Uchimura Kanzō, Takamura Kōtarō, Ichikawa Fusae - followed a path similar to Azembō's. They often spoke of humanity but meant a smaller group and in times of crisis embraced the Japanese state.

Although Azembō held views that often coincided with cultural and political elites, he was also of what he sang: a genuine denizen of society's lower depths. But did his music influence his commoner audience? This question is difficult to answer conclusively. On one level, Azembō's songs obviously spread an awareness of the unfairness of life in an industrializing modern state. Through graphic imagery, clever puns, and poetic commentary based on incidents from the news - bribery scandals, market cornering to boost food prices, worker abuse - his lyrics informed people throughout Japan of the tricks being played on them by their putative betters and political leaders. But did the public provide a confirming echo to his message? Or, to put it slightly differently, Azembō's song sheets sold in the thousands and unauthorized pirating spread his critique of the modern even further, but did popular awareness of Azembō's messages contribute to popular social activism?

Evidence that might answer such questions is indirect and inconclusive. Although it is clear that Azembō's lyrics created or at least contributed to the stream of a new political discourse that had clear ideological implications, less certain is how this language translated into collective action or political mobilization. What is clear is that both the forces for reform and forces of order equally appreciated Azembō in their own particular ways. Sakai Toshihiko, the first Chairman of the Japan Communist Party, for example, enlisted Azembō to write music for the socialist cause. Meanwhile, the Tokyo Metropolitan Police considered the singer-songwriter so potentially dangerous as to have him tailed throughout most of his adult life. That the authorities banned some of his songs also indicates that they considered him the bearer of 'dangerous thoughts' capable of influencing others.[31] At one point in his life, Azembō attempted to exert that influence by taking part in speaking tours and holding formal office as a member of the Executive Council of the Nihon Shakai-tō.[32]

There is no doubt that Azembō was appreciated for his *potential* to move the masses. Nevertheless, the danger this popular singer posed was less in the realm of 'dangerous thoughts' than in his life as impassioned example. He had no academic credentials, but his songs sang of his life as a resilient ideology expressed through persistent struggle and willingness to sing louder than the authorities that attempted, through direct and indirect repression, to silence him. For Azembō to continue to speak out at all expressed a ringing eloquence that carried far. He persisted after losing his wife to overwork and poverty, after being forced to see his son passed about as minimally important baggage, and after giving away his unaffordable second child as if she were a kitten from an overly large litter. During his descent into poverty he continued to speak out against social inequality and the superficiality of contemporary life, albeit always with a soft spot for the goodness of the Japanese people and the importance of the nation.

Yet, despite the socialists' attempts to enlist Azembō in their cause and the police efforts to keep the popular singer out of politics, the degree of direct response by ordinary people to Azembō's litany of complaints and antigovernment screeds is difficult to measure.[33] Nishizawa Sō, an unforgiving critic of Azembō's version of *enka* history, argues that the singer did not so much change the age as reflect it. Nishizawa's interpretation of *enka*, particularly the way that they were written for an emerging mass market, argues that the music was but a by-product of the times. In short, Nishizawa sees the entire *enka* movement as merely echoing the widespread emancipation in the lives and thought of Japanese people who had lived for nearly three centuries under the constraints of the old Tokugawa hegemonic order. According to this critic, Azembō and fellow 'song peddlers' (*enka-ya*) did not create the age but were molded by it; they did not sell enlightenment or emancipation, but song sheets and nothing more.[34]

Nishizawa dismissal of the *enka* movement as historically insignificant is too categorical. Nevertheless, his argument calls attention to the ambiguous and sometimes contradictory worldview expressed in Azembō's lyrics. As calls to activism, the songs themselves are mixed messages. Many are clearly Allen Ginsberg-like howls of protest. Yet, they offer no specific agenda, no suggestion of how to change things in any concrete way. This reluctance to prescribe results in two quite different messages. The first is that the system satirized is tolerable and the songs are really just entertainment; the second is that the songs are serious, but that nothing short of total revolution can be done to change the evils depicted in his darkest lyrics. The message (or messages), advocating both defiance and detachment, is as much resigned as it is radical. This mixed quality calls to mind Linda Hutcheon's observations on the politics of parody, particularly where she observes that parody contests human assumptions, but can also legitimate what it mocks.[35]

Azembō might have readily accepted this judgment. He did, after all, both love Japan in the abstract and disdain its leaders in the concrete. The unqualified affection for blood and soil, nation and ethnicity, captured in his sense of 'Japan' tended to blunt the edge of his parody. And the need to continue to produce commercially viable *enka*, or at least accounts of the life in the *enka* world, dulled it even more. As Azembō reminds us repeatedly in his tale of life adrift in modern Japan, he was always more the working performer than the political activist.

Late in life, Azembō preferred to dress in the robes of a Buddhist ascetic. Before taking on the external trappings of quietism, he early on wove his Buddhist beliefs into his lyrics. The perspective is evident in lyrics and poems that are critical, playful, and funny but also accepting of the world as it is. These suggest a spiritual detachment and recognition that any hope for fundamental improvement in humanity's bad behavior borders on self-delusion. Yet, neither the ideas nor the upbeat rhythms of his songs are completely dark. In fact, the music expresses faith in the resilience of common people and an abiding appreciation of the sensual joy of simply being alive. The message is more a protest of the human condition than a program for realistic change. And in this sense, his Gramscian role as an organic intellectual works both to prod the social and political hegemony to change while bolstering its existence by arguing that fundamental change may be futile.

Notes

[1] Soeda Azembō's birth name was Soeda Heikichi. He used a variety of pen names over the years and, as is the convention when referring to artists in Japan, is now better known by the adopted first name, Azembō, than by his surname.

[2] Another interpretation of the name Azembō is that Soeda himself was not the 'mute cicada,' but because the threat of summary imprisonment prevented him from openly singing his views it was as if he had a cicada stuck in his throat. In other words, he was internally muzzled.

[3] Azembō's career in many ways confirms Jasper Johns's observation that 'Artists are the elite of the servant class.'

[4] Azembō and his son, Tomomichi, together wrote over three-hundred poems and songs. Unfortunately, many of the original songbooks were lost in the 1923 Kantō Earthquake. Kanagawa Bungaku Shinkō Kai, eds., *Soeda Azembō, Tomomichi bunko mokuroku*, Yokohama: Kanagawa Bungaku Shinkō Kai, 1994, p. 1.

[5] Soeda Azembō and Soeda Tomomichi, *Asakusa teiryūki*, Tokyo: Tōsui Shobō, 1982 (reprint, originally published in 1930).

[6] Christine R. Yano, *Tears of Longing: Nostalgia and the Nation in Japanese Popular Song*, Cambridge, Massachusetts: Harvard University Asia Center, 2002.

[7] For Edo forerunners of the *enka* form see Gerald Groemer, 'Singing the News: Yomiuri in Japan during the Edo and Meiji Periods,' *Harvard Journal of Asiatic Studies*, 54, 1 (June 1994), 233-61. Page 260 discusses the transition of some *yomiuri* into *enka-shi*.

[8] One early *sōshi* lyric reproduced in the *Tochigi Shinbun* on 28 July 1882 called for 'revolution' (*kakumei*) and the overthrow of the cabinet if Itō succeeded in promulgating a German-style constitution that created a Prussian instead of a British-style parliamentary system. The songs were somewhat indiscriminate in selecting targets for criticism. According to Kurata Yoshihiro, lyrics 'put on the chopping block' not only state ministers but even attacked the new phenomenon of women students. Kurata Yoshihiro, '*Haryari uta*' *no kokogaku: Kaikoku kara sengo fukko made*, Tokyo: Bungei shunjū, 2001, p. 81. On the range of subjects see p. 126.

[9] Itagaki Taisuke endorsed songs such as '*Dynamite bushi*' (1886) as a means to stir up popular anger and politicize public discourse. Around the same time, the various parties he led used '*Yoshiya bushi*' and '*Minken kazoe uta*' as campaign battle hymns. The second, a 'people's rights counting song' was in twenty verses, the first sang, 'One: there is no person above another because rights don't change ...', which echoed Fukuzawa Yukichi's 1872 comment in *An Encouragement to Learning* that proclaimed heaven made no person higher than another. The songs were among the 'souvenirs' that activists brought back with them from political conventions. Fukuzawa and others wrote commentary on their widespread popularity. In the early 1880s, songs about the American Revolution were also used as accompaniment to Bon Festival dancing. Kurata, '*Hayari uta*,' pp. 69-75.

[10] There were other song and dances that were not political but simply racy songs and performances. Nude dancing became the rage in some bars in the early 1890s and films of such performances as the 'naked dancing geisha' became famous Japanese exports to Europe and the US in the mid-1920s. The exports prompted the central government to create new laws to censor films and music. In the entertainment districts, songs to accompany the nude performances and sex games (versions of strip poker and other entertainments) were called '*ha uta*' during the Taishō and Shōwa years. Kurata, '*Hayari uta*,' pp. 96-7 and, for films, p. 127.

[11] Nishizawa Sō stands out as one authority on *enka* who firmly and unambiguously claims that most *enka* singers had nothing significant to do with the Liberty and Popular Rights movement (*c.* 1874-89) and were basically street entertainers of the lowest order. He argues that Azembō and others like him were moved only by money. Later claims to fame as artists concerned with social conditions and politics, Nishizawa contends, were self-servingly creations of personae that never existed. In Nishizawa's massive study, more a comprehensive collection of essays and copies of memorabilia (songbook covers, photos, newspaper articles, and other items) than an integrated study, Azembō and his son, Tomomichi, are the chief villains. Nishizawa maintains that their first-hand accounts of the *enka* singer's life are largely advertisements for themselves and historical distortions. For a summary of Nishizawa's views see Nishizawa Sō, *Nihon kindai kayōshi, I*, Tokyo: Ōfūsha, 1990, pp. 1500-05.

[12] The *sōshi* street-corner gatherings were explicitly banned by police order in 1892. See *Tokyo Asahi Shinbun*, March 11, 1892.

[13] *Sōshi* singers also took side jobs to promote products, advertise businesses, and collect debts owed loan sharks. Politics sloshed around with petty commerce. Kurata, *Haryari uta*, p. 134.

[14] Soeda Michio suggests that the 'evolution' of *enka* might also be marked by the changing use of musical instruments and the audience appreciation for complicated forms. He suggests that in the beginning, the original singers relied only on their unaccompanied voices. By the end of Meiji and during the Taishō years, *enka* songs became identified with the violin, and evolved into songs that relied on the accordion and guitar during Shōwa. See Soeda Michio, *Ryūkō uta gojyū nen: Azembō utau*. Toyko: Asahi Shinbun Sha, 1955, pp. 5-7.

[15] In many cases, 'student' singers were only students in a loose sense of the word. They were also known for crimes, petty and more serious, committed as they wandered the streets. Their roaming gave opportunities to enter houses when the owners were away, strike up romances with womenfolk left at home, and arrange to take unwanted children into their professions and allied callings. Kurata, *Hayari uta*, p. 136

[16] Soeda Michio describes the lantern-lit stalls erected in front of shrine fences where *enka* singers performed during festivals in Ningyo-chō, Fukagawa, Nihonbashi, and Kudanzaka during the Meiji years and thereafter according to a schedule of festival cycles. See Soeda, *Uta gojyū nen*, p. 6.

[17] At the beginning of the twentieth century, 100 *sen* equaled 1 yen and 1 yen was worth approximately 50 cents US.

[18] Nishizawa, *Kayōshi I*, p. 15.

[19] Newspapers noted a change in children's song to military themes in 1887. One theory is that the children learned the songs by ear after hearing them as they were sung by columns of marching soldiers. Of course, ballads of samurai bravery existed before the appearance of Western-style marches intended to rouse the troops' fighting spirit. Kurata, *Haryari uta*, pp. 102-3.

[20] Takahashi Shin'ichi, *Ryūkōka de tsuzuru Nihon gendaishi*, Tokyo, Ayumi Shuppan, 1985, p. 25.

[21] Protest *enka* never entirely disappeared. Ishida Ichimatsu's career provides one example

of *enka*'s continuing connections with politics, activism, and social satire. See Mizuno Takashi, *Tatakatta 'Nonki bushi': tarento gi'in dai'ichigo, enka shi, Ishida Ichimatsu*, Tokyo: Bungeisha, 2002.

[22] Takahashi, *Ryūkōka*, pp. 80-1. On Japan and jazz see E. Taylor Atkins. *Blue Nippon: Authenticating Jazz in Japan*, Durham, NC: Duke University Press, 2001.

[23] See note 14 above.

[24] Mizuno, *Ishida Ichimatsu*, pps. 180-1.

[25] Takahashi points out that the tune for the socialist 'Rappa bushi' enjoyed a revival with new lyrics as the patriotic battle song 'Shanghai dayori' during the China conflict of the 1930s. Takahashi, *Ryūkōka*, p. 32.

[26] Takahashi, *Ryūkōka*, pps. 6-7.

[27] Unexpurgated copies of Azembō's lyrics and poetry are available in many postwar studies of *enka* history. Soeda Tomomichi, Azembō's son and an *enka* composer in his own right, authored several of the essential collections. For a representative sample see Soeda, *Uta no gojyū nen, passim.*

[28] *Enka* lyrics had multiple uses that went beyond opposing 'hegemony.' They also entertained, provided an escape, expressed joy, and soothed frustrations. They were undoubtedly popular because of they satisfied so many needs, chief among them excoriating officialdom and good society with satire and sarcasm.

[29] Itoh Akira sees this view expressed today in Japanese secondary school history textbooks in the presupposition of cultural homogeneity. He calls this contemporary form of blinkered humanism Japanese 'historical narcissism.' See 'Gramsci Study in Japan: Achievements and Problems,' http:www.italnet.nd.edu/gramsci/igsn/articles/a12_5.shtml p. 4.

[30] One such song, 'Song of the Four Seasons,' in which workers could insert the name of their own company told a rather black tale: 'The company bankrupt, the dormitories burned; the company president dead of cholera, wouldn't that be nice?' Soeda, *Uta no gojyū nen*, p. 46.

[31] Azembō's 'Socialist Rappa bushi' was banned the moment it was printed. Nishizawa Sō, pointing to the use of morals laws to ban Azembō's *enka*, argues that the authorities were more concerned with his songs' prurient content than their political message. For the socialist song see Soeda, *Uta no gojyū nen*, p. 41. For Nishizawa's counter-interpretation see Nishizawa, *Kayōshi I*, p. 34.

[32] Azembō obtained this post at the Japan Socialist Party second convention in February 1907 and participated as a speaker and reporter on tour representing the *Tokyo Shakai Shinbun* in 1908. His lyrics appeared in *Heimin Shinbun* on January 27, 1907. In 1908, he tried to publish them in Osaka but they were banned from May 4 on grounds that the lyrics were injurious to public peace and order. On August 25, Azembō was prosecuted for propagating socialist ideas, although the degree of punishment did not include an extended jail sentence. As for his ideology, he was close to Katayama Sen, but opposed the 'direct action' stands advocated by Kōtoku Shūsui. This is not to argue that Azembō was in any sense a theoretician. As Shimane Kiyoshi accurately notes, the *enka-shi's* socialism was an artist's socialism that was vague, diffuse, comprehensive, and imprecise. Yet, despite Azembō's later disdain for parties of any sort, he did support universal suffrage. Shimane Kiyoshi, ed., *Nihonjin no denki 23: Yokoi Kinkoku, Osaki Tatsugoro, Soeda Azembō*, Tokyo: Heibonsha, 1982, pp. 423-6.

[33] For instance, he sang bitter songs about the high cost of rice, market cornering, and the nasty taste of imported grain, but no one arrested for rioting in 1918 attributed their acts to Azembō's music. A connection between songs and direct action may still be found, if not in Azembō's work then in the songs associated with early protests, such as the 1885 Chichibu Uprising in response to harsh economic conditions following the Matsukata Deflation. Nevertheless, the

linking of song and popular action may be coincidental instead of causally connected. For the popular bitterness expressed in songs following the deflationary program see Kurata, '*Hayari uta,*' pp. 83-4.

[34] Nishizawa, *Kayōshi I*, pp. 33-45.

[35] Linda Hutcheon, *A Theory of Parody: The Teaching of Twentieth-Century Art Forms*, New York: Methuen, 1985, p. 23.

Prefatory Poem

Advance!
New Order, Advance!

New Order, New Order
Hatching from your shell, a New Order born
We believe in you, we adore you
New Order grow in good health
Expand to your heart's content
Robustly flourish New Order
We shall ever so carefully watch over your growth
And follow you wherever you go
March, march with dignity
Advance, advance bravely
Oh how confident your stride and air
At your core driven by the power of a new humanity
The integrity of the New Order's beginning
We show our respect for this epoch-making bold undertaking
We bid farewell
To the free economy and individualism
We thank you for your pains
But bid farewell
Advance New Order
No mere reaction to the past
Go forth to grasp a new overarching truth
Yes, this Order must be 'New'
Revitalize our people drained by impotent politics
Complete in one body go forth
As a living, moving creature
Become a single living being
And then
Dance as you crack the stinging whip of reform

Your complete unity surpasses the solitary nation and single party
How good, how good
Your necessary path made clear in the Imperial Edict
Our nation and all our citizens will exert their will
To smash to smithereens all obstacles at home and abroad
To realize Imperial Rule Assistance
Achieving that weighty duty
Rests on your shoulders
A hundred million with a single heart!
Intuitively understanding one another as if through radio waves
The exquisite performance of action carried out
To lead authoritatively is your mission
Go! Go bare-skinned and pure!
Destroy the self and serve the greater good
Be swift, truthful New Order
The dizzying shifts in the world situation
Cause pressing issues, domestic and foreign, to pile up
There's no time for argument, argument is specious
Specious argument is the work of the peripheral nerves
More words mean fewer deeds
Too many captains make for faulty sailing
Go straight ahead, in that fundamental direction
Advance with confidence
And with dignity, New Order

Be strong, New Order
You must first establish the basis of our national policy
You must use all of your powers to create a new economy
Devote yourself body and soul to this work
You must exert control, complete and consistent
You are distinguished and we leave the matter to your abilities
And we are not the only ones to do so
The time for planning is past: Act!
From brain work to resolute action
The slow hand spoils the fish's freshness
Dash forward, be bold
Rebuild the national economy on a pure foundation
Great acts undertaken in all directions
That is what we want
Be swift!

A day late means a thousand days lost
No, worse yet, the nation's millennium plan will be flawed
There is no easy way to realize a solution
Problems cannot be avoided
Stride forth and stride forth again
Push aside the many difficulties and carry forward
Pay no heed to the thorny path
Standing astride the people's will
Sharing their joys and sorrows
Powerful New Order
Passionate New Order
Advance now, advance with dignity
For the sake of carrying forward
The inevitable fact is that all must sacrifice
Everyone must be resigned
Lead with strength and righteousness
Demonstrate by example your living politics
Impart to the nation's people new life and stir their blood
Now rouse the nation to self-awareness of the need
We are exhausted waiting, waiting for your lead
Our nation's people at every level are resigned, resigned too fully
Braced to give first priority to the public good
Strike!
Iron is easily forged when hot
And what has made our nation's people align themselves in countless rows
Compliantly obedient to the reform?
The New Order of Imperial Rule Assistance![1]
You, of course!
You are the byword of meaningful reform
You are the foundation root of guiding policies
The eminent spirit of Japan
Our totalitarianism
Our New Order built on the fusion on all creation
Public service's passionate sincerity, its vitality
Endless energy, vitality giving birth to vitality
The manifestation of power at the highest level
Advance with dignity to create a Greater East Asia
The Triple Alliance
Brace yourself again

Once again, whip yourself to a higher level to dash forward
Herald of world restoration
The greatest endeavor since history began
Create!
The New Order is creativity's general mobilization
Advance now
New Order
'Resolution vanquishes even demons'
Ban empty talks and conferences
'Talk in place of action is the lot of the lazy warrior;
To see the nation's great work as a job for others, the place of the
fool.'
So declared a Meiji Restoration stalwart
Trample those who fail to understand this
Pay them no heed
Advance now, with dignity
Forward! New Order!

A thousand waves, ten thousand waves
The world's waves are tempestuous
The bold task is to make our course through this ever-threatening and
frenzied sea
There is conversion in the midst of the storm
The best time is the midst of autumn
Signs are auspicious
The New Order of this time of harvest

(Published in the *Rikugun gakuhō* or *Army Gazette,* November issue, Imperial Year
2600 or 1940)

Note

The government sponsored Imperial Rule Assistance Association (*Taisei Yokusankai* or IRAA) was
organized in 1940. Azembō's poem appeared in the Army Gazette shortly thereafter to commemorate
the event. As the key organization to spearhead the New Order, the IRAA rules mandated that political
parties dissolve themselves voluntarily and join with a host of civic, military, and other organizations
to advance the aim of 'fulfilling the way of the subject in assisting imperial rule.' The Prime Minister
was *ex officio* head of the organization that aimed at integrating national and local rule. The disparate
interests of the organizations that made up the Association prevented its effectively realizing this aim. In
endnotes here and in following chapters, basic information about the Meiji, Taishō, and Shōwa periods
is based on the following sources unless otherwise noted: Nihon Rekishi Gakkai, ed., *Meiji ishin jinmei
jiten*, Tokyo: Yoshikawa Kōbunkan, 1981; Kōdansha, ed., *Kōdansha Encyclopedia of Japan*, 9 Volumes,
Tokyo, Kōdansha, 1983; and Janet E. Hunter, *Concise Dictionary of Modern Japanese History*, Berkeley,
University of California Press, 1984.

Chapter One

My Early Years

At the Ragman's Warehouse

Greetings

I live in one of the rooms in one corner of the second floor of this warehouse now. It's small, just four-and-a half *tatami* mats. I can best describe it as a mouse's nest. But it is cozy and bright with two glass-paned windows, one each on the east and south sides. Opening the southern window, I can see the Takagi steel factory. I am used to the noise of the factory's motors. I prefer the racket to lousy music.

My address is Honjo Kikugawa-chō, 2-chome. On the roof a sign reads 'Used and Discarded Goods Yard.' Mr. Takahashi Shōsaku, the establishment's owner, is the Chief Director of the Greater Japan Discard and Reuse Wholesale Commercial Association and the Sub-director of the Greater Japan Discard and Reclamation Wholesalers Federation. Even without these exalted ranks, Takahashi Shōsaku is known as a powerful man among junk dealers. Indeed, long before the New Order's proclamation, his campaign for union reform had already made his name known to 13,000 dealers in the more than seventy branch Discard and Resale Dealer Associations in Tokyo, Nagoya, and Osaka. His reputation for chivalry echoes far and wide. It reaches even to far-off Manchuria and North China. No less than the stalwart Toyama Mitsuru lauded him as possessing 'a warrior's soul and an entrepreneur's genius.'[1] The accolade says it all. He truly is a grand old man.

I am a clerk in this establishment, but in name only. In fact, my existence is much like human rubbish. The real employees are a chief bookkeeper, assistant bookkeeper, settlements clerk, invoice clerk, sorter, packer, and tool man. All battle valiantly at their respective jobs. I loiter about among them and grin bitterly when I overhear the children who baby-sit the toddlers say, 'That man is the boss of the wholesale yard.' Children seem to think that anyone who idles away the time must be called 'boss.' Of late, during the air raids and fire drills, the neighbors and the neighbors' neighbors, the employees, their wives and children all rush together into this junkyard to form one big group. The sense of a powerful, enveloping embrace is tremendous.

In the old days ragmen were despised. But now their skills at actually reviving 'paper raw materials,' 'rags for export,' and all manner of other discarded goods give them a new standing as 'production workers' whose existence is quite important. This is especially true at this time of material shortages born of a state of national emergency. In the aftermath of international incidents new national policies have increased the ragman's stature many times over. Certainly everyone knows about the campaign to reuse discards. This is part of the policy of developing Asia and serving the nation whereby once a month every household donates a little in the way of scrap goods so that within a year the total contribution to public coffers reaches more than 500,000 yen. Yes, everybody already knows about this so there is no need to discuss it again now. Of course, there are other fascinating topics I could take up. But here I must turn to 'The Tale of the Ragman's Rubbish.'

My assignment is to tell my own story. Azembō tells Azembō's own story. The tale is not what the world calls an autobiography. Neither is it a proper story of a self-made man or a tale of inspiring magnificence. It is the story of a remaindered item in life's marketplace, of goods discounted by a decimal point. It is no more than the stupid story of a stupid man. I think it best not to raise any expectations and to tell you this at the outset.

The Monster Train

I go back some fifty-five years before now to a time when Japan did not have much in the way of a railroad. There was no Tōkaidō line; only the short run between Tokyo and Yokohama was open to traffic. I was born the second son of a farmer in Ōiso, along the old Tōkaidō road. In the springtime when I was fourteen, my father took me to stay with my uncle who lived in Fukagawa in Tokyo.[2] On our way to Tokyo, I saw a monster running to our right over a hillside near Aokidai in Kanagawa. To my eyes it looked like a monster, but my father said, 'That's what's called a train. We'll board it for the ride to Tokyo.'

Before that first glance from a mile or so distant, I had never seen that monster called a train. I had heard stories about steam engines and how people wanted to ride in them. Now I beheld the real thing first-hand. That train was like a living being, blowing smoke and running about. I obeyed my father without saying a word and followed him to Kanagawa Station. I remember we got on the train, but I was so overwhelmed that I cannot recall anything else. It was like an illusion after which nothing remains and no memory can be recalled.

Even after arriving at my uncle's I continued to act like a farm boy who tended to woolgather. My father and uncle intently talked over something but I really did not grasp the subject. I simply could not clearly differentiate my own situation from what was swirling around me or get a hold of what was significant. I recall overhearing that, although I was intended to go into the naval school and be taken to Yokosuka, I was too young, not yet fully fifteen years old, to qualify for service. I heard these things but recall them only dimly. I do remember my uncle gazing into my eyes saying, 'You're going to become a naval officer and sail on a battleship.' I still have the impression that he laughed as he said this. I had never seen a battleship and it was all dreamlike at the time. As for me, I just wanted to see the sights of Tokyo and satisfy a strong desire to fool around. Drinking miso soup in Tokyo was like drinking sweet rice wine. I only clearly remember eating sweet white beans, sweet boiled herrings, and sweet kelp rolls. Everything was sweet. After two or three days, my father left me to return to the countryside.

3

My First Look at Tokyo

I fooled around for a time. I took the one-*sen* steamer from the Sumida River and visited Kannon Shrine at Asakusa. I tried out the one-*sen*-for-two-districts horse-drawn tramcar. The fashion prevailing at the time in Asakusa is reflected well in the song 'Sendai-bushi:'

> Walking along the bricks of Asakusa
> There's a toy store, a photo studio, a fancy goods shop
> There's the splendidly soaring five-storied pagoda
> Beyond the mountain gate is Asakusa Temple
> Behind the temple in the heart of Okuyama
> A white fox is lost in her pining for love
> Come, come everyone to the fields

At the time, the twelve-storied tower had not yet been built and the five-storied pagoda was Asakusa's tallest building. Beyond Okuyama, the rice paddies now called 'Senzoku Tanbo' were then known as 'Uratanbo.' As to the meaning of 'white fox,' nobody really knew. Okuyama featured various shows. There was swordplay by Nagai Heisuke. But the most popular show was the 'Herculean Women.' In this show women wrestled and demonstrated feats of strength. One woman lay on her back and rested a small boat across her belly. She then allowed onlookers to get on board. The audience would applaud by shouting '*Ittcha, ittcha, ittcha na,*' a line from a song.[3] This song itself is a folk ditty from the Bōshū coast. The troupes of women performers of amazing feats of strength were almost all from Bōshū and the song gradually became well known.

> Burdock root, cooked burdock root *mata*
> Oh boatman *nae*
> Oh you with the dark complexion *zuirasano*
> The taste is so good *nae*
> *Ittcha, ittcha, ittcha na*

People who went to see the women performers would come away humming this song and it eventually became popular. Later, whenever visiting the Bōshū coast, it could be heard everywhere.

A professional reciter's theater stood at the back of the pond. There were several rows of seats in front of the stage and a wooden fish was struck now and again to accompany the chanting of *chongare,* a satire of current topics sung to a familiar melody.[4] The performance became something like a parody of a sutra recitation. As the chanting approached its climax, someone would pass a bamboo basket among the rows of seats to collect money. Of course, fans of recitation would throw in a little change, but when other spectators saw the basket approaching, they quickly got up and slipped away. After watching to see that the collection was over, many people once again quietly slipped back to resume their seats. The money collectors never forced their bamboo baskets on children like us.

Akiba-no-hara was the liveliest part of the quarter. There were professional reciters and booths for shows of all stripes. There was a '*charine*' show at which a baker would show up grinding his hand organ and calling '*charine* buns, *charine* buns.' These bean jam buns sold for five *rin* apiece. On the far side of Saemon Bridge, there was a theater called the 'Candlemaker' that featured farcical *kyōgen* plays. Actors by the names of Icchō and Genchō enjoyed good reputations. While performing a scene in which a burglar came tearing through a drawing of a wall, they would yell out 'crash bang!' to ridiculously mimic the sound of breaking through. Then one of them, with loot slung over one shoulder, would announce, 'I have attained my heart's desire. Before the authorities arrive let us flee! At once!' They would then bustle down the *hanamichi* runway while behind them a voice would yell, 'Wait, villain!' (*kusemono*). At which one of the burglars would punningly retort, 'Who dares touch a smelly man (*kuseemono*)!' causing the audience to burst out laughing.

Among the stage names of the Candlemaker's actors, Nanchō was the father and Icchō, Genchō, and Sanchō were his children. We generally called this kind of farcical *kyōgen* 'Candlemaker's drama.' Sometime later, Tsuruya Danjurō among others performed ballad drama with greater artistic refinement. Still, we tended to find the 'Candlemaker's drama' far more fascinating.

Satakeppara was another spot for having fun. The old jail district in Kodenma-chō called the 'Prison Fields' was also an entertainment area. All of these places had balladeer halls that rang '*deroren, deroren*' with the striking of the wooden fish.[5] These were the amusement quarters available to us and we knew of no others and as entertainment districts they ranked second only to the Ryōgoku district.[6] At the time, a meal came cheap in the neighborhood. One could buy a belly-filling portion of red bean soup for

5

two *sen*. The covered rice dishes were huge, too. They came with two *mochi* sticky rice cakes stuck inside. That was big enough, but later it was called 'cut *mochi*' and the servings became even larger.

The Cholera Epidemic

My uncle was an on-board steamship engineer and tended to be away from home for long periods. My aunt was a woman of little education. She was a cold person and for some reason or other, we did not get along. Just after my cousin Hana-chan was born her mother took up singing lullabies to coax the baby to sleep. She sang in a low voice while lying down with the child. The melody was really marvelous, the rhythm truly wonderful. But the lyrics! Singing a lovely nursery melody over and over again she repeated the lines, 'Sleep now, sleep now, on a cat's behind up crawled a crab, and when at last it scratched it off, once again up crawled a crab.' I felt that even her childish mind could come up with something better than this. But she was, after all, a countrywoman, the kind of person who when asked to recall her fondest memory of life bucolic could only say, 'In the grain fields it was great fun to quarrel while we reaped the wheat.'

My uncle's job as a ship's engineer meant that he was always bringing friends over for a good time. I got to know several of his crewmates and they all made me their pet. Among them was Mr. Ishii who took us to a horsemeat restaurant as we returned home after visiting the night stalls along Takahashi Street. As Mr. Ishii drank his sake he offered me a portion of the meal saying, 'This is horsemeat. Eat, eat!' That was the first time I had ever tasted horsemeat. I remember seeing the sign plastered on the wall with writing that said, 'Horsemeat Stew, two *sen* per serving.' (The other day the three of us, my son Tomomichi, Furukawa Miki, and I found the same restaurant and had horsemeat. There is no doubt that the place has changed hands, but the appearance of the storefront and interior was just the same. So much so that I was soon deep in memories of the past.)

The neighbor next door to my uncle was Mr. Manabe and, as might be expected, he too was a crewman and my uncle's friend. He was a man who was often away from home. His wife was young and beautiful and had an innocent air. Every day five or six thirteen-year-old girls came to play. I went to play, too. We enjoyed all sorts of games. As I was bored with my aunt, I often went to the neighbors to have fun. The wife next door joined in our games, covering our eyes and playing hide and go seek, and giving us sweets. At that time the young wife sang, 'Let Us Go,' strummed the samisen, and often laughed.[7]

Let Us Go

A raven on a moonlit night, so I have said
But this clock that can tell no lies
Zuitokya I don't care even if no one goes
But let us go, go
Well, let us go, go

Summer came. It was the summer of 1886, the nineteenth year of Meiji. Cholera spread and scores of coffins were carried from our neighborhood. Here three coffins, there five, until the number grew alarmingly large. The epidemic engulfed other towns, too. Coffins from all over had to be carried to the crematory at Suna Village (now Suna Town). As the roads there ran both in front and back of our neighborhood, we often witnessed the processions. 'Nothing but coffins! It's horrible!' Although this was the common lament, people still counted, 'Three more, five more!' They reported the numbers to each other and made a to-do. My aunt told me, 'Don't watch that, stay inside.' But, after all, people were making a commotion and I wanted to go see what was happening. During a single evening, I saw seven or eight coffins go by in a row. When children sang 'Let Us Go,' and they did this all the time, the adults, especially the old women, grimaced and whispered to no one in particular, 'No, no, we don't want to go, we certainly don't want to go.'

I also vaguely remember the earlier great cholera epidemic of 1882. In my village the authorities placed a twenty-gallon barrel filled with carbolic acid smack on the village border. This was to be used for disinfecting by villagers on both sides of the divide. They also placed a bamboo dipper for pouring. Shaking with fear, we ladled up the disinfectant into a bamboo container and ran home without glancing back. I think the latter epidemic was even worse than that of 1882.

My uncle was a hard worker. He went to night school to augment his insufficient education and obtain a higher ranking mechanics license than the one he held. One evening after returning home he told of how a policeman had grilled him after mistaking him for a Liberty and Popular Rights activist.

At the time, I did not know what the Liberal Party was and did not realize the significance of what had happened. After conversations with the ship's crew about engines and machinery, I gradually desired to become an engineer. I thought I could become an even better engineer than my uncle.

Going to Sea

In the end, my uncle and I fell out, and I left his home to become a sailor. My first job was cabin boy. To become an engineer, one had to start out as a coal shoveler and move up to boiler attendant, and then to oil man. After on-the-job training, one then had to take an examination. I was still too young for the test so there was no hope of moving up. I first signed on as a crewman on the Asano Steamship Company's *Tsuru-maru* and later moved to the *Hōzui-maru*, another of the company's ships. Then I joined the crew of the Yūsen Company on board a regularly scheduled boat out of Kobe whose senior officers were all foreigners.

At night off Enshunada, I was on duty in charge of caring for the lower-class passengers (that is, the third-class passengers). I went up the metal stairs to the bridge with a tap, tap, tap to make my night watch report to the chief mate at the helm. I said, 'Boy calling watch.' And the man at the wheel replied, 'Alright.' I made the report every hour on the hour. You really could not sleep while on this duty. Aside from the chief mate's hourly 'Alright,' I could hear only the noise of the engines and the sound of the ship as it cut through the waves. I tasted the loneliness of night at sea. It was while aboard ship that I heard that the Constitution had been promulgated.[8]

Sometimes we would get hit by major storms and I would grow pale and suffer terribly. Mr. Shimizu, a second mate engineer, took pains to look after me, but finally said, 'Face it. It just looks like you aren't going to get used to a life at sea.' In short, he meant that I lacked something and that deficiency made me simply constitutionally unsuited to be a sailor. I came to think the same thing and decided to give up the seafaring life. After two more trips and upon docking at Yokohama, I left the ship. I visited Fujitaka, one of my friends who worked as a crewman on the *Nagoya-maru*. When we weren't playing around together in Yokohama, I enjoyed myself on my own. Meanwhile, I made a temporary home by sharing quarters on my friend's boat.

One day I returned from town to find that the ship was nowhere to be seen in the harbor. I gradually learned that because of the cholera epidemic the *Nagoya-maru* had been suddenly placed under quarantine and dispatched to anchor off the Yokosuka coast. It had already completely departed from Yokohama. Furthermore, I understood that, come what may, its current itinerary meant that the ship would not double back and return to its last port. I had been talking over what I should do with my close friend and before anything had been settled things had come to this. I was at wit's end. I had to follow him; I had to meet him once more no matter what.

That evening, I climbed up to the precincts of the big shrine in Noge and watched the lights of the ships in the port. I stretched out on the bench of a tea house on the shrine grounds. Just as a dog was licking the soles of my feet and I was drifting into a doze, a Shinto priest came around to wake me up. I was questioned about my circumstances and allowed to make a fine bed in the shrine office. The next morning, I was awakened by the banging of a drum to call the priests to their duties. I saw that the sun had risen and was soon treated to a hot breakfast. The priest's kindness impressed me deeply.

The Laborers' Lodging

I began to walk towards Yokosuka. Somehow or other I felt I simply had to meet Fujitaka once more. There were not any high mountains, but I walked over many hills before going through the Jusantoge Pass. My memory is hazy, but I do recall sitting down on the enormous root of a big pine tree to take a rest. I was worn out and hungry. Just then, a man looking like a day laborer came along, sat down next to me, and began to talk. I told him about the quarantined ship. Then I asked him about places where I might catch a barge. At that the man replied, 'Barge my foot. Even if there were one they wouldn't allow just any old guy to come aboard. After all, Yokosuka is a military port, you know.'

I was disappointed and felt completely stuck. The man said, 'Look, it's no use going to the ship if you can't get aboard to see your friend. Better than that, why don't you come with me to my boss's place?' After that he told me all about the easy-going life of a day laborer, how much fun it was, the delicious food they ate, and all manner of other things. 'Somebody like you can keep an account book. It's easy as pie.' He was so eager and had a good

9

face so I didn't take him to be a bad person. I decided to go along with him. At that moment, I felt something would somehow work out.

Our destination was a place called Katsuriki, a rocky point, near one of Yokosuka's inlets close to the settlement of Kusugaura. The job, army subcontracting work, required cutting stone from a boulder strewn hillside and hauling it to sites where, on military orders, the first and second coastal battery installations were being built offshore between Kannonzaki and the Kazuza Futtsunosu sandbanks. The main contractor was the Taguchi Group. We worked for the subcontractor, Rokkenbori Denkichi, as members of our boss's work crew. The worker who lured me into taking the job was one of Rokkenbori's relatives. Many months earlier he had flown the coop, which made showing up again more than a little awkward. He had brought me along to lighten the shame of his return. In effect, I was like a souvenir present that he offered up upon returning from his travels. From Cape Katsuriki and hills nearby, I could see the *Nagoya-maru* laying off the Yokosuka shore. I could see it but could not do anything. I gazed at the ship on which my friend sailed and while vainly watching, I worked.

Of the people in that work crew, the ones that appear before my eyes now are the boss, Denkichi, his wife Iwa-san from Nijima, Sada-san, a guy called Oiran Sei who bore a tattoo reading 'Oiran.' In the other lodge was Kane-san and dozens of others whose faces I can no longer recall individually. The two most popular people in the *hanba* worker's bunkhouse were stupid Ōmori, a dull fellow about forty years old, and me. People called out to the good natured Ōmori's by shouting, 'Hey, Ōmori, look here.' It was a way to get his attention that both threatened and mocked. I was called, 'Hey, kid' and was alternatively prized and treated like a fool. We worked and worked.

At the time the wage for an experienced laborer was 25 *sen*; green workers received 8 *sen*. Of course, this did not include the cost of our meals. We ate more than ordinary men. In addition to the regular meals, we ate at ten in the morning and three in the afternoon, making a total of five meals a day. The work was hard and it was easy to get hungry. We opened holes in the rocks using chisels and blasting caps. We prepared for the explosion, lit the fuse, and ran away. Sometimes we used picks to break up rocks and place the shards in straw baskets. Anyone able to shoulder a carrying pole with two or three baskets was considered a full-fledged worker. I could do that and earned praise for the effort. Rice was amply provided and I think I ate a half-gallon at a sitting.

10

I remember someone saying, 'Ōmori eats a regular share of rice, but outside of shouldering the carrying pole he has no skills whatsoever.' I recall that Ōmori often complained to me, 'It's payday but up to now I have never received a single *sen*.' While rubbing his shoulder he would grumble, 'The heat of that pole has got my shoulder so swollen.' As for me, I was given five or ten *sen* in wages every two weeks. Every payday the boss told me that next payday he would pay me in full. It was odd. I could read his face so knew the truth, but for some reason I was not at all angry with him. We worked happily along, singing:

> To redeem myself
> The ransom to be paid
> Is here on the tip of this blasting cap
> At the end of this cold chisel[9]

Even worse than being forced to watch my friend's ship in vain was not even being permitted to go into town. Of course, I could have physically made the trip over the hill on my own, but a watchman was posted to prevent anyone from leaving. I couldn't continue to live like this; I had to do something. I began to worry that the time was drawing near for my draft physical. I somehow had to find a way to escape from here and regain my freedom. I meticulously prepared an escape plan that overlooked nothing. At last the time came. I got my bag and umbrella from the lodge where it had been left in Ken-san's care. I suppose the tale of my escape edges into novelistic territory. Given my present circumstances it is too bothersome to go into so will skip retelling it here.

A Flophouse

Having made a complete escape from Katsuriki, I threw away the workman's coat with its work crew logo and straw sandals on the beach at Kusugaura. From my bag I took out the cotton unlined clothes, waistband, and wooden clogs and re-dressed myself. The things I no longer needed I threw into the sea. I flipped open my Western-style umbrella and felt wonderfully relieved. I set my sights on Yokohama and began to walk in that direction feeling marvelously carefree and content. From the front of the naval factory I passed through the shipyard to the Marine base at Itsumi and from there headed for the entrance to the incline going to Jusantoge Pass.

11

It was already after three in the afternoon. I didn't think anyone was about, but looking down the slope I saw the thin but kindly face of a snake catcher who dealt in *mamushi* vipers.[10] The man, who appeared to be in his sixties, asked me, 'Where are you going?' and I told him I was bound for Yokohama. He warned me saying, 'That's ridiculous. The sun will be down soon.' While I considered this he said, 'Better to spend the night in Itsumi and set out again early tomorrow morning' and kindly told me where to find lodging.

At that time Itsumi had two flophouses, the Izu-ya and the Kōshū-ya, which stood side-by-side.[11] He confided that, 'I have been staying at the Kōshū-ya for a long time, but you should go next door to the Izu-ya. The Izu-ya is a better place.' I followed his suggestion by immediately heading off to spend the night at the Izu-ya. The room charge was four *sen*. I ate at a cheap restaurant and then slept. The young lady of the establishment, a girl called Oei-san, told me that it was not economical to eat at a restaurant and that I should cook in my lodging to save money. It was the first time in my life that I stayed in a flophouse.

I had thought that I would depart early next morning. At daybreak I heard someone shouting toward the upstairs rooms, 'Anyone looking for work?' It was a work gang foreman. Already five or six fellows who looked liked his regulars had quickly responded to the call and were ready to go. While I absent-mindedly took in the scene, he turned to me and asked, 'Hey you, aren't you coming, too? It's work that anybody can do.' I thought for a moment. I had no money so if I made some here I would have cash for the road. So I decided to go along.

The work that day was basic preparation for laying the foundation for a building in the marine corps compound. It meant helping pull a heavy hawser across the ground as we chanted the heave-ho cadence of '*enya, koriya.*' The job was done in half a day. The day wage was 25 *sen* so were each handed 12.5 *sen*. While working in the *hanba* before this job I had existed for a long time without ever seeing any real wages. When the cash for my half-day of work was placed in my hand, I felt happy.

In a flophouse in those days one could manage to get by on twelve or thirteen *sen* a day. Even now I remember that when the price of a half-gallon *shō* measure of rice shot up to eight or ten *sen*, everybody would say it was too much, too much, and raise a commotion. Thin, long-grain Chinese rice was imported. That Nanjing rice sold for four or six *sen* a *shō*. I don't remember exactly how much it was. But I do recall sailors walking about town in groups of threes and fives singing:

Rice costs ten *sen*
Yakima ya no ya
And that Chinese rice stinks
Noochosan

That was a popular song at the time. It seems that foreign rice had been imported for the first time. Although there was record of it having already come into the country during the Tokugawa period, it was our first encounter with the rice with that long, thin face.

Fate is a strange thing. I had left Yokosuka, thinking that I was making my farewell departure, and now I seemed once again to be sinking roots there. It was not easy to pull together money for the road so I gradually drifted into becoming a day laborer. I worked as a hand on a warship, a coal loader, and a shipyard collier. Along the way, I made a friend there and lived in shared lodgings. I also gained the trust of a new labor boss, Uejima Kame, and joined his work gang. In this way, Yokosuka became my second hometown. And it was at this stage when I came to be thrown together with the political activist *enka* singers. If I had not met that snake catcher when I did, what might have become of someone like me? I only spoke to him along the way. He only told me the way to the flophouse. But the face of that old snake catcher even now appears as if right before my eyes.

Notes

[1] Toyama Mitsuru (1855-1944), a former samurai, worked for the Liberty and Popular Rights movement in the 1880s and later went on to become an ardent pan-Asianist, albeit one who advocated Japanese leadership of the region. He is widely recognized as the godfather of leading right-wing nationalist groups in prewar Japan.

[2] Standard biographical chronologies usually state that Azembō was thirteen years old when he went to Tokyo. The discrepancy probably arises from the practice of counting a child as one year old at the time birth. One account of Azembō's removal from his home village to Japan's largest city explains it as caused by the boy's need to leave after he had caused a dangerous brush fire while playing with matches. The author suggests that being made an outcast is a key reason for Azembō's bohemian attitudes and his life adrift. Soeda, *Uta gojyū nen*, p. 8.

[3] Repetitive words such as "*Ittcha, ittcha, ittcha na*" are melodic refrains that have no literal meaning but are nonetheless an integral part of the song. They fulfill a function akin to humming or sound phrases that increase the rhythmic tempo of the music. Compare the 'na, na, na, nanana, nanana' refrain in the Beatles' song 'Hey Jude' or 'Tra la la boom di-ay' in the children's song that begins with this nonsensical lyric. In this text, these musical expressions appear in italics in lyrics and poems.

[4] The 'wooden fish' mentioned here is a percussion instrument that is struck with a single short dowel-shaped rod and is more commonly used in Buddhist chanting as a way to keep time when sutras are read. 'Wooden fish' is a literal translation of *mokugyo*, a name derived from the carved drum's form that resembles as a wide-mouthed fish or frog.

[5] '*Deroren, deroren*' is one of the many onomatopoetic expressions used in Japanese that mimic the sound being described. Here it is the echoing sound of the carved wooden drum being struck to give an echoing sound.

[6] Ryōgoku, one of Azembō's favorite haunts is located on the eastern edge of Tokyo in Sumida ward and today is known more as Japan's center for sumo wrestling than the raunchy entertainments that made it famous during the Meiji era.

[7] The song appears to be 'Sa, Iko Don,' a ballad popular in the 1880s that told of a bountiful harvest.

[8] This is the 1889 Meiji Constitution that made Japan's national government the first in Asia to be based on a system of written laws applicable throughout the state.

[9] The song refers to the fact that workers in the labor gangs typically borrowed from the crew boss in advance of receiving wages and thereby became indebted to the point of becoming hostages whose redemption could only be won by working ever harder.

[10] Common name: Japanese *mamushi*; scientific name: *Gloydius blomhoffii*.

[11] The suffix '-ya' indicates an inn or lodging in this context. It is also used to designate other businesses.

Chapter Two
The Period of Sōshi Politics and Political Songs

Asia's Prospect

After settling down in Yokosuka, I found what entertainment I could in occasionally going out to listen to *naniwabushi* recitals, tales narrated to the accompaniment of the *shamisen*. I also took in performances at the storyteller's hall. One evening I thought I would take in a recital and set out along the road to Ōtaki-machi. Along the way, I ran into three oddly dressed men screaming out something at the top of their lungs. I pushed my way into the middle of the large crowd that had closed in around them.

The young men wore braided hats pushed back to the rear of their heads and white *obi* bands wrapped around and around their waists. They passed a thick stick from hand to hand, one to another, as they alternated between chatter and song. They went through this routine for some time before it seemed like things were really going to get started. Then one fellow in a vigorous voice well suited for speechmaking, hit a high note and was immediately followed by the next performer who proclaimed, 'Now, listen to this song!' after which the three harmonized their voices and began to sing out. They bellowed, 'Resentfully, indignantly, we observe Asia's prospect.' The words surprised me and I began to listen carefully.

How hateful to consider Asia's prospect
Civilization spreads steadily month after month
Yet even Japan blessed by the bountiful fortunes of war
Cannot rid itself of the foreigners' laws
Cannot restore control of its own taxes
The red-bearded louts rudely rampage
And one step away, Korea
Time after time, the people there bow down childlike
Terrified before the powerful birds of prey
Day by day, states decline
If China is a sleeping elephant
When it awakes one morning
It will become a formidable enemy
But now cajoled by the blue-eyed foreigners
Confucius's descendants foolishly rejoice
Wisdom still has yet to reach them fully
Within China civil warfare without end
Afghanistan, Persia-stan
Annam, Burma, India
Beyond these, countless small countries
All the colonies of England and France
In the end, it is the East
Trampled beneath the power of the West
And of those crushed
Not one has gained equality
Resentment and indignation fill our breasts
To be the England of East Asia
This is the duty our country has accepted
You young men, full of life and promise
Hone and sharpen your arts, both civil and military
Polish those twin tools, the sword and the pen
England, France, Germany, and Russia
Defeat them and don't be choosy about picking a foe
The flag of the Rising Sun shall shine forth
Our nation's flag from the summit of the Himalayas
Flying high, oh what great joy!
What bliss, what bliss!
(Tonoe Suikyō)[1]   16

The three men sang and in the bargain presented an eloquent argument about the situation in Asia. My surprise changed to excitement and then became a deep interest. The men also sold printed materials. These were called '*sōshi bushi*' or activists' songs. The songs continued. This one is called 'Lament.'

Ten men and ten different views
Ah yes, the world is full of difference
To each his own and no accounting for taste
Japan from ancient times, a beautiful country
In this world, an exceptional place
Is there something lacking?
I think not
But now, recklessly, it's all the West, the West!
Would you throw out your own sushi
To eat your neighbor's gruel?
In the world, we call this stupidity
Westerners are just the same old people
Imported goods are just the same old goods
Don't fear the foreigners
Don't cherish the imports
We might use both
But don't be enslaved by either
Meeting in mutual respect is fine
But if the foreigners should act high-handedly
Better not bother with them at all
The so-called civilization of those civilized nations is a veneer
Their real nature is cunning
While the left hand makes a show of kindness
The right will take you for everything right down to your nose hairs
Be firm in your resolve
Do what must be done

It's a Lamentable World

Everyone, one and all, face the demons before your very eyes!
Be prepared, keep a clear head
From ancient times our Japan

A country overflowing with heroism
When stirred to bravery, even weaklings forgot their timidity
When roused by our common sense of righteousness
Even heartless beasts
In droves were transformed into men robustly brave
Yet today is the age of degeneration
Tin-plated and deep-fried
'-Isms' run through society
Fawning on the strong, feverish, lost
People's hearts are afloat in frivolity
And you know what's really amazing?
It's those girl students, their hair piled high
Light, white, spotlessly adorned
Scandalous tales about them pour forth day after day without break
The lady pulled by the rickshaw driver is all propriety
Adorned like a proper matron
But her friends are actors and clowns
And though called a geisha, she's a whore
Likewise the young misses, although we call them that
Are mere streetwalkers
Companies started up by swindlers
In gentleman's society, the fops mix and play cards
Oh so many modern monsters, one can't count them all!
Dirty deeds done with a self-satisfied look
To take pride in this civilization and enlightenment
Is horrifying, is cause for lament
It is a sad world, isn't it.
 (Kiseki Gakujin)

I was a person who started out knowing little about the world, but had begun to learn a little of life's real circumstances through heartfelt experiences. My education came from working among seamen, joining a labor gang, and becoming a coolie. And it was just as I had begun to make my way that I heard such songs by these eccentric-looking singers. I bought the printed song sheets and completely forgot about going to see *naniwabushi*. Even after returning home, it took a while before I could sleep. These words were written on the back of the sheets: 'We are recruiting like-minded compatriots from throughout Japan. We want only fellows of sound body, learning, and patriotic feeling.'

18

The Youth Club (Seinen Kurabu)

What had the singer activists, these *sōshi*, dragged me into? Where would they drag me hereafter? Their songs suddenly and fundamentally transformed my childish view of life. I completely memorized the ones I had bought. I mastered the melodies and my voice sounded pretty good, too. Two or three of my friends praised me, saying my singing was the best. From that point, it wasn't long before I sent for a songbook collection from the Youth Club and found myself strolling the lanes and byways of Yokosuka singing *sōshi* ballads.

At the time, the wholesale cost of the song sheets was four-tenths of a *sen* but the *sōshi* sold them at a markup of a *sen* and a half. I sold them for two *sen* each. The fear I first felt when performing on a street corner at last gave way to a deep absorption. It felt all the more wonderful when sales were brisk. After several days, I resolved to throw my lot in with the *sōshi* singers.

At this time, I returned to my hometown after a long absence to take the military induction physical. My mother and older sister prepared fine clothes for me and awaited the return of this unfilial prodigal son. Just as soon as I arrived, my sister told me to try on the new clothes and helped me into them. My mother smiled and said, 'As they say, clothes make the man.' Her words made me happy.

I received an unsuitable 'B' rating in the physical and returned to Yokosuka, where I continued to mimic the life of the *sōshi* singer. While making Yokosuka my base, I wandered to Misaki, the Miura Peninsula, and tried to cover as far as the Bōshū Peninsula. One time after I sang a *sōshi* song in Bōshū, the owner of a large store came out and told me, 'That was wonderful! It was a truly soul-stirring performance. Here is a little something just to show I share your feelings.' With that, he handed me a one-yen note!

During my willful wandering I became famous in the Youth Club despite the fact I had as yet never seen the inside of the place. 'Hey, there's this guy called Soeda who's really on the move over in Yokosuka. What's he up to anyway? He ordered several hundred more music books today.' I later learned that this kind of comment circulated around the club's headquarters.

19

A year passed. Acting on my own desires but also because I had been encouraged by club headquarters, I went to Tokyo and became a formal member of the Youth Club. I received a warm welcome, a reception that was genial and not overly ceremonial. I was surrounded by the bearded faces of rough *sōshi* who laughed and said, 'Well, well, here you are.' Yet, in that gruff greeting there seemed to overflow something like the affection shared among colleagues. An atmosphere magnanimous and free enveloped me and I felt deeply moved. I was happy.

'You? Aren't you Soeda?' So asked the older lady who smiled as she welcomed me. She was a big and burly woman, the wife of Itō Yasu'ichi, the club's housemaster. Mrs. Itō was the one who always took care of sending the printed copies to me. All the *sōshi* adored her and called her their 'aunt.' These *sōshi*, young men who were usually ferocious as tigers when confronted by outsiders, became child-like, even gentler than kittens, in the presence of this 160-pound housemother.

In those days the club was located at Kyōbashi, Shin Tomi-chō, 1-9 banchi. There were about thirty members, including the composer, Kiseki Gakujin (Hisada Saichirō), and Suikyō Gakujin (Tonoe Hiroshi).[2] Other members included Suzuki Ichirō, a certain Shirai, Sō, Tomihari, Eguchi Genjirō, Shioda Takatsugu, Miyairi Kiyomasa, Mashio Kensaburō, Nonoda, Hamaji, and many others. Besides these people, there were *sōshi* who regularly dropped in and out of the club's headquarters. Although many of the regulars sang *enka*, most devoted the largest share of their time to political activities. Politicians of real mettle, the likes of Tanaka Shōzō, also visited the club.[3]

At that time, aside from performing political *enka* and selling sheet music, the *sōshi* also engaged in violent election campaigns. Whenever there was an election, many club members mobilized for action. *Sōshi* support was considered so important to the success of a campaign that candidates doled out huge sums to throw into the club's political action fund. *Sōshi* worked for Seki Shinnosuke, Morikubo Sakuzō, and Itakura Chū. They also campaigned on behalf of Hoshi Tōru. As these names suggest, they mostly acted on behalf of the *Jiyūtō* Liberal Party. The majority of Youth Club members usually spent their time on the streets singing *enka*. At election time, virtually all of them turned out but few did any singing.

When I became one of the group, Eguchi Genjūrō from Niigata Prefecture, was counted among the first-rank singers. I joined with him on the street corners and enjoyed great success. Both of us liked the song 'Hopeful Youth' and sang it often. It was a kind of *yukai bushi* (song of delight).

Hopeful Youth

Hoary with age, the virtue of pines and oaks so pure
In turbulent times a loyal subject
Is a rarity seldom seen in east or west
But read the annals of history
And you shall find the duties of young men must be fulfilled
The burden is heavy, heavy
All the more when the nation is weak
But it is indeed these very times of adversity
That we must rouse ourselves
Behold the United States of America
When bound by Britain
They fought back
And established the foundation for independence
How were things then?
When under England's thumb the suffering grew heavier day by day
The extremes of cruelty and tyranny unceasing
The clouds of grief filling the four directions
The gale blew, the storm raged
Washington and his famous generals
At their summons
Volunteer soldiers immediately gathered
They fought fiercely never tiring
At last routing the enemy
The flag of their independent country
Now streamed in the morning wind in thirteen states
Pride now polished by adversity
In the midst of weakness and countless hardships
Their song of victory so valiant

In those days, these rough ballads actually sounded like real songs if sung with a good voice. In fact, when I was in particularly good form I found myself occasionally taken with the sound of my own singing voice. But other songs, like the 'Yattsukero bushi' ('Beat 'em Song') or 'Muchakucha bushi,'

('Song of Absurdity'), sounded like nothing other than angry quarreling. There wasn't much in the way of melody. Such *enka* were just shouted and roared out tunelessly. The issues of treaty revision, the abolition of licensed prostitution, and election interference were all subjects roared about in the *sōshi bushi*.

Treaty Revision
Part 1

The Tokugawa shogun prevailed for more than three centuries
Accustomed to peace undisturbed
Society drifted into effeminacy
High and low incessantly ever softer
Morale reduced to nothing
Then in that sleepy year of 1853
Suddenly the sound of cannon fire
Roared out in Sōshū Uraga
We awoke astonished from our springtime dreams
The entire country boiled like a seething cauldron
Men of valor ran to the east, rushed to the west
Alongside the call to close the ports and oust the barbarians
Other doctrines called for imperial restoration and overthrowing the shogun
In the midst of turmoil unceasing
Without a moment's rest or time to catch your breath
The shogun's officials, their vision like a frog's in a well
Concluded a treaty
With the American Consul Harris
And created a major setback for our country
From extraterritoriality
To the loss of our right to control tariffs
These were stolen from us
Today the harm remains as does the regret
Yet, considering the times
An age during which they knew not the real situation
There was no way to say which policy was bad, which good
Today we live in Meiji's brilliant reign
Day by day, month by month, civilization advances

Its brightness shining forth
But despite today's constitutional rule
Old notions exist as ever
More than twenty years have gone by
Over this long period our nation's people
How can we calculate
Their cares and worries?
With love of country in their blood
Across the cheeks of the brave sons of Japan
The tears of indignation and anger
Course down like rain
So why comrades do you hesitate?
Bravely march forth
Press for the enactment of equal treaties
Let us blow away the red-whiskered louts like so many bubbles
Let us clear our hearts of years of angry frustration
Truly, this is our great urgent mission
Ah, happiness, happiness

Part 2

Treaty revision is our greatest, our most urgent duty
Look at our diplomacy!
A history of more than thirty years spent
Countless changes and turnovers in people
Numberless attempts at revision
If we can't achieve revision now
There can only be one reason
One cause:
That our hearts are not united
Would that we resolve our nation's woes
But pursuing personal fame and private ambition
Pushes that goal beyond our grasp
The nation's people, one and all, unified
We must sweep away personal feelings that divide us
Expend every particle of your sincere patriotic spirit
Face the problem giving your entire heart and soul
If we do so, is there anything we cannot achieve?
The disputes of political parties and isms

Are but for the sake of self-interest and greed
Men pursuing these
Must fail at creating a clear-sighted plan for the next century
And by failing must become traitors to their country
The time is long past for treaty revision
The deadline long ago gone by
If there is but someone to throw off the old unequal bonds
It is now, now that the time is overripe!
If we shall conclude a new treaty
Let us with calm confidence
Decry the existing treaty
As worthy of only contempt
To end extraterritoriality and return our right to tax ourselves
Can this be achieved
With shallowness, petty tricks and deceptions?
High and low, let us put our hearts in accord
Upright and proud, let us march together
Never relenting, never retreating, to the very end
Let us give all for this our Imperial Nation
Truly, this is our great and urgent duty
Ah happiness, happiness.

Part 3

Leap into action, you men of sincere patriotism!
What in the world is civilization and enlightenment?
What is humanism?
From their mouths they chant freedom,
In their treaties they write inequality
The worthlessness of words without practice
That is the value of empty theory
At the center of the Settlement Concession System
You will find the touchstone of their ism.
Evading our laws
Parasites eating into the weak
Gambling, whoring, swindling, defrauding endlessly
Without a glance toward morality or ethics

Such a gathering of villainous monsters
Are found in the Settlement Concession
And more!
Bestiality in Nagasaki
That riot of ill repute[4]
Extraterritoriality is the cause
Considering it leaves one mortified and filled with regret
Our passionate hot-blooded compatriots
Bestir yourselves for the sake of the country!
Polish the principle of power!
Raise high the flag of public opinion
And below it lift our Japanese sword!
With its single blow cut to shreds
The existing treaties and throw them away
For the independence of the sacred lands of the East
Raise high in the Eastern heavens the august virtue of the Emperor
A glorious new treaty
Concluding this should be our great urgent task
Ah happiness, happiness!
 (Kiseki Gakujin)

Beat 'Em Song

So, what's with the treaty revision talks?
It's probably stupid even to mention them now
That old monkey of an Earl's haggling
Almost - almost - came to something
But all the frog's hippity hopping could not bring him to the top of the well
His vision from the bottom can only be narrow
So all he can to do now is woo them with toady-ism
Maybe they just didn't like the cut of his beard
To save things from head-to-toe calamity
The bear strolled nonchalantly out from his cave
 To negotiate with each country in full public glare
One way or another, he thought he would declare
Victory!
But just then

25

KABLOOM!
Kurushima's bomb exploded astonishing all
In the clouds enveloping Kasumigaseki
The bear's replacement emerged but to no avail
Breathing out a blue mist
Maybe his wife is German, who can say
Anyway, this guy, too
Knows only kowtow-ism
Like the rest, he is ill-suited for any great undertaking
So our call is to you
You high-spirited Sons of Edo
All of you straightforward as a straight razor
This is the place for you to step forward
I implore you don't retreat another step
If things don't go well, then that's the time
To take the sword of Japan
Even to the distant corners of the world abroad
Resolve to die *korasa nosa*
Somehow or other, shouldn't we all be willing to go?
Expending the utmost of the utmost for our country's sake
Giving our all
Let's beat them silly!
  (Hisada Kiseki)

In this song, all the animal figures are unsuccessful foreign ministers represented by puns on their names or events tied to their public image. The 'old monkey of an Earl' is Fukushima Taneomi and the frog in the well, Inoue Kaoru. The bear in the cave represents Ōkuma Shigenobu, who on October 18, 1889, lost his right leg to a bomb thrown by Kurushima Tsuneki. Mr. Blue Breath represents Aoki Shūzō, who in fact had a German wife. The 'spirited Sons of Edo' refers to the Tokyoite's temperament and the mention of a 'straight razor' alludes to Mr. Enomoto Buyo, also called the razor minister. Mutsu Munemitsu became the Minister of Foreign Affairs in the second Itō cabinet in August 1892. Overall, the song mentions each foreign minister from 1885 to 1892 and satirizes the weak diplomacy of the period.

On one hand, the public tended to lump all foreign countries together in their anger over the treaty revision issue while at the same time fearing that the powers could not be denied. Their resentment led them to create all

26

sorts of insulting expressions for foreigners such as 'red chops,' 'red beard,' 'pointy nose,' 'blue eyes,' and 'hairy foreigner.' Of these 'hairy foreigner' did not carry such a strongly negative meaning. On the contrary, it was a kind of humorous expression. Everyone referred to all foreigners as hairy foreigners. We also referred to Japanese people who did not know how things stood by saying, 'What the hell, that guy's a hairy foreigner.' In other words, it was used to describe someone unfamiliar with things in general or who proved a puzzlement to ordinary people. For the Japanese, there was always something characteristically incomprehensible about foreigners.

The Kingdom of the Student

In those days, young men talked national politics until spittle would form in the corners of their mouths. Most loved to argue. They argued passionately, but also with a good deal of imprecision. They thoughtlessly brandished the names of Napoleon and Bismarck. Although their youthfully high aspirations cannot be denied, they also tended to be impractical and heedless. If one simply looked like a student then wherever he went he was called with great deference, 'Mr. Student, Mr. Student.' It was the kingdom of the student. Yet, for all their airs and affectations, on balance most of them were sincere.

At the time, the *nouveau riche* had yet to make their appearance. There was no socialism, no labor problem, no cafés. No coffee for that matter. Accordingly, there were no café waitresses, either. We had no movies or baseball, no women office workers, no actresses, no women professionals. Later there was a girl *gidayu* singer, who chanted to the accompaniment of the *shamisen* and became popular, but she was a rarity. Eventually, the 'Oh, what to do?' group emerged. But the time of which I write was before the fall, predating both female students and the birth of the Maroon Club.[5] Consequently, there were not yet large numbers of failed young scholars, only loads of hooligans who passed themselves off as students. These students lacked anything that properly could be called recreation. The books you could borrow from the penny lending library were limited to things like Tokai Sanshi's *A Beauty by Chance Encountered (Kaijin no kigu)*, Suehiro Tettcho's *Snow Plum (Settchūbai)*, and Yano Ryūkei's *Edifying Tales of Statesmanship (Keikoku-bidan)*. It was only long after this that Rōka's *The Cuckoo (Hototogisu)*, and other works by Gensai, Namiroku, Rōhan, and Ichiyō became available.

What came first for the students was eating, followed closely in second place by, well, eating. They had a great appetite for *shiruko*, a sweet bean soup, which sold for two *sen* a serving (nowadays the classier version of this is called *gozenjiruko*). *Daijiruko* (what we today call country *shiruko*) sold for one *sen* a bowl. Students, who could not afford the real *yōkan* bars made of sweet bean paste, called sweet potatoes their '*yōkan*,' and this was their favorite snack. When the season turned to winter, everyone ate roasted sweet potatoes. For one *sen* you could buy eight big slices of potato. For someone to put away two-*sen* worth was considered nothing short of heroic. At the time, one *enka* sang, 'All for half a *sen*! Roasted sweet potatoes, at once my pocket heater and a meal.' There was a story about a former student who, his school expenses cut off, was driven out of his boarding house and came to live in the Youth Club. He was never known to take a meal at the eating shops but simply subsisted on sweet potatoes for half a month. In the end, he came down with diarrhea and other ailments.

The students were truly larger than life when it came to their eating habits. They took a similar big-hearted attitude toward the world around them. One story from that time tells of repeated bouts of gluttony at the Manhachi-rō restaurant. To begin with, competitors would eat five or six bowls full of a rice dish called '*gorohachijawan*.' This was just to qualify for the main event. The next heat might require gobbling down a hundred *monaka* bean-jam wafers or sixty pieces of sushi or a hundred *senbei* rice crackers or, depending on the event, fifty, eighty, or a hundred *manju* bean-jam buns. There was keen competition to break old records and it is said that in this absurd competition to be the champion glutton, not a few laid down their lives.

I don't exactly remember which Matsui Gensui it was, the first or the second, but do recall that he drank a huge amount of soy sauce to win one of the competitions. He suffered from it badly afterwards. According to the version I heard, he writhed in agony throughout the night and just before dying imparted his secret method for top spinning to his followers. I also recall hearing that a certain Kanayama, before the Meiji Restoration a *hatamoto*-rank warrior and one of the former shogun's direct retainers, swallowed a few pints of salt and instantly died. 'Ah, thinking nothing of spending a thousand *ryō* of gold in the pleasure quarters, the noble Kanayana trades his thousand *koku* stipend for three measures of salt' - these are lyrics from a song left over from the incident.[6] Snatches of this tune were sometimes tossed around at the gluttony contests. Deaths aside, many, many competitors became sick.

The venerable Toyama Mitsuru was also famous for his gluttony. His trick was to vomit after eating, but glutinous *mochi* rice cakes caused a problem with that strategy. They came up in the shape of stiff bars so it was very tough going. Inukai Tsuyoshi contrasted with Toyama. He was a light eater. It was often said, 'Toyama is a big eater but Mokudō (Inukai's nickname) eats like a bird.'[7] I find it fascinating: regardless of gluttony or moderation in eating, both make for health and long life (of course, Mokudō's case is a bit exceptional because he was murdered). Anyway, in those days, general society, human nature, and customs, differed greatly from today in many respects. Students were especially rough, uncouth, and vigorous. They were also innocently simple.

Even more so were the *sōshi* political bullyboys. They were bohemian in looks and blunt in manners. They strolled about occasionally brandishing the thick stick that usually rested on their squared shoulders. They wore black cotton homespun kimono embossed with a family crest and tied with a long and wide, white cotton *obi* that they wound around and around the waist. They also wore long scarf-like cloths around their necks with the bigger ones displaying as many as five crests. Some scarves were short and some long. The shorter could be a couple of yards and the longer one perhaps four or five yards, all of which they wound about their necks. Both students and *sōshi* wore Satsuma-style wooden clogs. They were proud of the broad white heavy *kokura* clog straps that distinguished this footwear.

When in Yokosuka, I already owned a *haori* half-coat that I tied with a white *hitohiro* cord. At the time no one else dressed like this in Yokosuka and I drew stares and enjoyed a lot of attention. A girl I came to know who worked as a nursemaid used to call me 'Mr. Hitohiro.' The name stuck and everybody began to refer to me that way. It was a funny name, 'Mr. Hitohiro.'

In those days Tokyo students were known as people with 'unkempt hair, grimy faces, and clothes both shabby and too short' recognized by the small dirty towel they wore hanging from their waists. The *sōshi* activists dressed somewhat more stylishly than the students. Nevertheless, one can say without fear of contradiction that, by and large, the difference was not all that great. Both groups alike loudly bellowed forth their songs.

Students, student, oh don't you despise them
Cabinet Ministers and Councilors they, too, were once students
Yosakoi, yosakoi

29

These were the lyrics they shouted as they strutted down the main boulevards.

The Peace Regulations

After three or four years in the Youth Club, it was clear to me that most of my friends were not just uncouth but actually more than a little wild and completely unromantic. Whenever they opened their mouths they talked about the direction of the political movement and about attacking the 'clique government' for its electoral interference across every prefecture in the country. Nobody referred to the central government as 'the government,' but everyone always called it the 'the clique, the clique.' If they got to drinking sake, someone would pull out a sword, dance about, and sing:

> Exiled from the center by at least three miles
> Under watch by the police
> It's not so bad
> Sometime or another in some prefecture somewhere
> Jail will be my home
> I am resigned to this

Every one of them had become one of the realm's self-styled patriots.

The Peace Regulations were promulgated at the time of the first Itō Cabinet in 1887. The law made possible the exile of several hundred patriots to at least three miles from the city's border. The first people to be caught up in the law's regulations were Hoshi Tōru and more than thirty of his followers. This was the government's first step leading to a severe policy of restraining dissent and it set public opinion boiling. Political activists finally grew immeasurably angry and clashed with government officials in incidents that verged on riot. The rough and tough *sōshi* soon poured into the fray and it was not long before our club became a very lively place indeed.

Before this, resistance had arisen to the Governor of Fukushima Prefecture, Mishima Michitsune, and his tyrannical rule curtailing free speech. Kōno Banshi (Hironaka) of the Mumeikan (the Liberal Party's political society) was sentenced to eight years for his involvement in the 'Fukushima Affair' and was imprisoned in Miyagi Prefecture.[8] When word of this spread, Liberal Party supporters throughout the country rose up as one. Their blood seethed at the ruling clique's oppression. They convened a general meeting of the party in Tokyo to find some way to resist the government's actions. Freedom to speak and write underwent extreme suppression. In the end nothing could be done.

This Fukushima Incident spanned 1882 and 1883. In 1884, the Kabayama Incident occurred and thereafter the Chichibu Incident and a whole string of new disturbances, everything from city riots to farmers' uprisings, broke out one after another.[9] Despite the furor, the Constitution was promulgated and the National Assembly opened. Meanwhile, elites from the pre-Restoration domains of Satsuma and Chōshū continued their despotic control of central politics. Violent episodes of electoral interference broke out in voting districts in every prefecture across the nation. Both the popular party and the government party took part in the pyrotechnics, neither giving the other any quarter in the struggle. The entire situation was simply dreadful.

If we call what occurred then an election campaign, people today will find it truly hard to grasp how things really stood at the time. Recall that these contests took place before the reform of election laws and the so called campaign was more like warfare and riot than anything else. At candidates' rallies pistols were drawn and shots fired as people risked their lives to participate in the movement. Many campaign workers were cut down, stabbed to death, wounded, and thrown into jail, imprisoned for more than mere property crimes.[10]

I joined in on several occasions. Of course, I always took the side of the Liberal Party, the party of the people. In fact, the *enka*, 'Song of Absurdity' ('Muchakucha-bushi') captures well just how absurd conditions were at the time:

> Confusion, violence, I don't understand
> Interference, insufferable
> Look! Look at the February '92 general election!
> Kumamoto, Ishikawa, Saga, Kochi
> And besides those other voting districts
> The two parties, one for the people and one for the government, compete
> Bloodthirstiness rising to the heavens
> A Shinagawa gale so strong
> A gang of rogues

Brandishing their weapons in broad daylight
They tread the voting station underfoot
Destroying people's homes and spilling blood
Outrageous wrongs unchecked
Their faces carry an expression that pretends nothings amiss
Worse yet, they set about actually instigating attacks
Afflicting righteous patriots with suffering
Bedeviling innocent good people
Upsetting society's order
The evil of such savage abuses sullies
An enlightened reign
Whose prestige rests on constitutional rule
And what will you do?
Can you bear to see trampled
Today's freedom of speech?
Interference cannot be borne
If it can, then politics is beheaded
How can that be?
I just don't understand
(Hisada Kiseki)

'Shinagawa-style' refers to the election interference of 1892 and pokes fun at the acts perpetrated by Home Minister Shinagawa Yajirō. 'Politics is beheaded' or 'politics of the freshly severed head' was an expression popular at the time. This also mocked Shinagawa Yajirō and his habit of saying, 'I will stake my life on it!' when testifying before the Diet on one thing or another. This was merely his habitual turn of phrase and the exaggeration just highlighted his hypocrisy.

I recall something else about the commotion during the election campaigns. I had almost forgotten that among the *sōshi* there was the old veteran activist, Ōba Kikujirō. (He had frequented the club for a long time and was well versed in all kinds of subjects. It seemed that the older he got, the more vigorous he became. He often told me stories of his past.) This was the time when a certain candidate, who shall here go unnamed, won election. While Hisada Kiseki and Ōba, just the two of them, were looking after the campaign office, a large number of *sōshi* from the competing party laid siege to the place. The office was within a hair's breadth of being ransacked and all within were endangered. Ōba pushed aside Hisada to stand alone in front of the entryway where he took up a large lance and yelled out, 'Come on! Come on and I will run you through first to last!' He slammed one end of the lance into the floor and went into a dramatic stance. The sharpness of his glinting eyes terrified the enemy into beating a retreat. Nothing came of the incident. His form was truly remarkable. Hisada liked to repeat the story from time to time.

There were many other courageous men who I have heretofore left out of my tale. There was Tsuda Kanjirō (nicknamed the Blowhard) who owned the fencing gym in Kanda and Tsujimura (a friend who once established the Rickshaw World Party, a title that sounded exactly like Shakai-tō, Socialist Party). There were many others besides these. Anyway, in those days, the election fracas was not like the recent cases of 'sly and sneaky electoral infractions.' No, it was something completely different from such uninspired incidents. It was deadly serious. In outlying regions, it was common for members of the government and opposition parties to put on headbands, tie back their kimono sleeves, and with swords drawn carry out pitched battles along mountain paths and in country fields. Yes, their spirit was different from that of people today.

During the run-up to the elections, every club member went out to work on the campaign. Despite the mobilization, there were never enough people to meet the demand. When we became shorthanded, recruitment calls went out from the scattered *sōshi* political groups. In some instances, an activist band from one place would approach members of another to get them to jump ship. Given such conditions, it is no wonder that selling *enka* music tended to be postponed during political campaigns.

Around this time, a woman *sōshi* activist (who also admitted to being a prostitute) visited our club upon her return from Vladivostok, Russia. She taught us the '*Vladivostok-bushi*' that was being sung by all the Japanese women she encountered there. She caused us to think about the problems faced by women on the continent. The idea immediately found expression in the lines of an *enka*:

> Our parents in Japan
> Are you awake, are you sleeping?
> Do you remember us?
> Have you forgotten?

There are many poetic expressions meaning that mothers and parents care for their children, the mother pheasant in the wild yearns for her chicks and the night crane dreams of her children, these sorts of things. But the children's sentimental yearning for their parents is by no means any less strong. In once sense, the feeling of parents for their children was akin to the feeling they held for their country. '*Vladivostok-bushi*' was not a dirge of intense grief or unrelenting sorrow. Nor was it a womanish song of homesickness and longing. In part, it contained a strong, masculine sense of patriotism. The doleful *enka*-singing woman was, on the contrary, a model of feminine bravery, a heroine. She carried her frail body into the severe cold and into the deep distant regions of still undeveloped northern Manchuria and Siberia. She withstood meeting customers in darkness and the sorrow of bidding these sojourners farewell at morning's light. And to what end?

> Russia is fearsome, everything stinks
> Spirited Japanese, they are penniless

I often sang the song of the Vladivostok women and usually added something by way of explanation. I would narrate that their purpose was to earn money, but many were duped into going from the very first. Still, they managed to turn around this ill fortune and make some good of it. This was something that took spirit and bravery. The ranks of cowardly no-accounts who wander about looking for geese that lay golden eggs, who lose the object of their quest and then beg others for help, could never match the spirit possessed by these women.

This next episode, the prostitution abolition movement, took place before I entered the club and I have only seen printed accounts of it. Shimada Saburō and a fellow Christian who served with him in the Diet's Lower House at the time, Nakajima Nobuyuki, headed up the abolition campaign.[11] The Santama area *sōshi* were mobilized to assist in the effort. 'Beat 'em Song' ('*Yattsukero-bushi*') was rearranged to narrate a story something like this:

> Many believe that prostitution should be abolished. Just in the capital and surrounding thirteen prefectures, more than 2,000 *sōshi* have been mobilized. Nakajima and I believe in Christianity. If we loosen the braid holding her Shimada coiffure, if we remove the long red outer gown of her kimono, what shall we make of this wrongful behavior? Human nature yearns for novelty, but once we accept that prostitution should be abolished there will be no regrets. If you disagree you'll face our fists!

Although the debate to end or continue licensed prostitution appeared all of a sudden and just as suddenly disappeared, much like a firework sparkler, it in fact was more like a lit fuse that would lead to reconsidering this problem in later years. A commercial publishing company also put out a volume titled 'A Full Account of the Great Debate over Continuing or Abolishing Prostitution.' This work (a small eight-page octavo) received wide circulation.[12]

Sōshi and Sales

As I noted previously, there were two factions among the members of the Youth Club. The first included young men who pushed the political movement to the exclusion of most everything else. The second faction included people who stood on the streets selling songs. I gradually decided to join the song sellers. Even during election campaigns, I sided with the minority group that favored sales and tended to confine myself to the club's quarters. In the midst of all that buzzing activity, I sensed that I had at last found the true life of *enka*.

Tonoe Suikyō was a songwriter and boss of the *sōshi* activists. When there were no election campaigns money dried up. Occasionally a visitor would drop in and buy us drinks. We called these guys 'ducks,' which means they were our pigeons ready to be duped. Tonoe noted in his diary, 'Today's catch wasn't too good. From sundown, we drank "*hakuba*" or "white horse" thanks to Soeda's strenuous efforts. Once that was gone, we came home.' I recall the incident from time to time. Tonoe could really drink. 'White horse' referred to the cheap unrefined milky-colored rice wine or *doboroku*.

In later years, Tonoe was invited to become managing editor of the newspaper, *Jōshū shinpō*. He lived in Maebashi City and was awarded the Dentsū communications award after twenty-five years of service. He worked for ten more years after that. He died the year before last and his post went to his eldest son.

Without notice, the world changes around us. We made up entertaining songs, got outraged over this and that, and rather heedlessly (because we could do little else) lived our lives. And while we carried on, the mainstream became weirdly muddled.

The *sōshi* cried, 'Allowing the Satsuma-Chōshū military clique to remain in place will be an ugly stain that will remain forever!' Yet, while admonishing one another, squaring their shoulders, and generally acting puffed up and arrogant, there emerged among the activists some who sold out their principles and began to dress themselves in garb of a different cut. At times, someone among the Cabinet ministers would take the post of 'handler of Diet members' or there would be uproarious incidents such as a 'Diet members' power struggle.' Cases of 'bribery of Diet representatives' became rife. Gradually, the rot at the top of the political world spread to its base, reaching the *sōshi* and their compatriots. People called the incidents and their perpetrators 'corrupt elements.' Despite the jeers, corruption piled on corruption and time after time disgrace followed disgrace. Made to watch these developments, I became disaffected with politics to my very core.

Tonoe said, 'Diet members and prostitutes are now on equal footing. One group sells their bodies, the other sells its integrity. Both do it quite shamelessly.' But fortunately or unfortunately, members of the Youth Club had backbone. They turned to social reformism and continued their stand in favor of independence and liberty. In addition to singing *enka* on the streets, they sponsored political speech rallies on such subjects as 'Putting Down the Profiteers!' and 'The Reasons for Society's Corruption.' At these they appealed for political ethics and reform of society as they attempted to whip up the public's morale. Audience members paid five *sen*, ostensibly for checking their shoes and sandals, so we came to call the rallies 'footwear speeches.'

In our songs we satirized the political world with lyrics such as 'Corrupt politicians, buy 'em by the dozen or by the head, you pick the price!' We also lampooned fakes in the corporate world and the foibles of so-called gentlemen's society. In bringing out the flaws in society, we entered the golden age of the *enka* singer.

At this time, Lieutenant Colonel Fukushima (later General Fukushima) also stirred up the stagnant political atmosphere by making an earthshaking expedition alone on horseback from Germany, across Eurasia and Siberia, to Japan. About the same time another soldier, a lieutenant senior grade, made a solo voyage in a single boat that was almost as startling. In the club, Hisada Kiseki immediately set about composing songs to commemorate these exploits. Hitherto he had written *yukai-bushi*, cheery albeit satirical songs, and these he sang with a voice refined by experience. Just as soon as we memorized the lyrics we took to the streets. Even if we had not mastered them completely we could make out the words on the song sheets by standing beneath the streetlights. It was really quite easy.

Although Ogawa Kuniomi was not officially a club member, he sang along with us at Hongō Akamon, reading the lyrics by the light of the outdoor street lamp. His singing soon attracted a huge crowd. A funny story from that period told of a severely stage-frightened Ogawa who became so panicked at the sudden appearance of the audience that he simply dropped everything and ran back to the club. The aim was to make customers buy song sheets. To do this we first had to get a crowd to gather, which meant that it was essential to make them listen carefully to the song and cause them to be moved by what they heard. Although the '*nagashi*' style of the strolling musician was also then in use, if you were going to stand in one place and sing it was first necessary to roust out a large crowd. Everyone laughed because, 'Ogawa ran away terrified by the good fortune of suddenly being surrounded by so many people.' The story lingered for a long, long time after the incident. At the time, Ogawa was thirty-seven or thirty-eight years old and sported a lovely moustache on both sides above his upper lip. He always wore a crisply neat '*hakama*' kimono and had the air of a gentleman of style. He could sing expertly. Unfortunately, in the end, he was not truly successful in the song business.

Kojima, a fellow from Chiba prefecture, joined the club bringing with him a little money and immediately set about putting to memory the melody and lyrics for Lieutenant Colonel Fukushima. After mastering the material, he went out every night selling his wares. He soon began taking out more songbooks than any of us and returning with fewer of them than anyone else. He also came back earlier for five or six days running. Everyone thought this was mysterious. Some members exclaimed that a genius had appeared in our midst, someone who could sell more while spending less time! But one night, as one of our number crossed the Manse Bridge, he glanced down to see a man throwing papers that scattered as they fluttered into the river. In passing, the onlooker caught a casual glimpse at the profile of none other than Kojima. This was soon bandied about the club. In no time at all, he was strapped for cash. Later he joined a group of *sōshi* activists at their place in Shiba ward. I saw him a couple of times thereafter but don't know what became of him since. It was not just enough to like *enka* or go about the business absentmindedly. It was no good unless you seriously threw yourself into the enterprise.

Sales of the song about the Lieutenant went extremely well. '*Returning at Dawn*' sold even better. At the time, many so-called *enka* singers attempted to jump on the bandwagon of the success of these tunes by dressing similarly to successful singers and copying their routines. These would-be performers did not necessarily come off as the genuine article. As ever, my partner at this time was Eguchi. He loved drinking sake and people called him 'Embee,' a term of endearment they created by combining the 'e' of Eguchi's name with '*nombe*,' or 'heavy drinker.'

As copies of 'Lieutenant Colonel Fukushima' sold well we were tremendously pleased with ourselves. Whenever we returned from performing *enka* we always stopped by an eating and drinking place for a late meal. It became customary for Eguchi to do nothing but drink, never bothering to eat a thing. Even after I had finished eating, he wouldn't let go of the sake bottle. Instead, his head bobbing like a doll, he just made repeated bows while staring into my face saying 'Sorry, sorry' over and over again. At the time, I didn't drink a drop.

Speaking of students in those days, there was the Keio school in Mita, law students at the law institute in Kanda, and medical students at the Saisei-gakusha in Hongō. Three student dropouts from Saisei joined our club. Their life of dissipation resulted in a cut-off of their funds for study, which started a descent that led to them to be kicked out of their boarding house and finally to wind up in our group. One of them, Mr. Kondō, and I teamed up. I heard he eventually opened a clinic near some station on the Tōkaidō Line and became a rather successful medical doctor. As far as *enka* singing went, I was his superior and took the role of directing him. But he was by far the master when it came to debauchery. It was Kondō who led me into the byways of the pleasure quarters and from whom I learned the ins and outs of that world. He was the second son of a wealthy family in Mie Prefecture and had earned a certificate from his first term at the Saisei medical school. He had money sent to him for the second part of the course, the one that would complete his certification and enable him to become a practicing physician. He instead carried his stipend off to the Yoshiwara district and its special study hall for debauchery. His parents gave up on him. His singing was good enough to make him a top performer and his story can go on endlessly, but let me stop here. Anyway, at this time, those club members engaged exclusively in selling *enka* prospered and flourished.

Lieutenant Colonel Fukushima and Lieutenant Senior Grade Gunji

Fukushima Yasumasa's lone expedition on a single pony was tremendously popular among most people. It became the rage just as soon as it appeared in *enka* lyrics. The opening line to the song, the refrain 'Behold! Behold! That magnificent feat of heroism! Hail Lieutenant Colonel Fukushima!', was soon on everyone's lips. Adults, children, women, chief clerks at the shops, one and all repeated the phrase almost as if it had become an unconscious habit of speech.[13]

The song about Lieutenant Senior Grade Gunji did not become as popular, perhaps because it was outdistanced by the spiritedness of Fukushima's accomplishment or maybe because Gunji's achievement was less flashy.[14] We can see a difference in considering their two very different send-offs. One departed surrounded by throngs bearing paper lanterns emblazoned with glorious painted slogans. Such fanfare attested to Fukushima's having captured the crowd's fascination at its high point. Yet Gunji, after arriving in the Kuriles and thereafter not sending out any news for the longest time, seemed to have left quietly and consequently been utterly forgotten. Nevertheless, while being awed by Fukushima, we indeed must never forget Lieutenant Senior Grade Gunji's iron determination and passion.

The Expedition of a Lone Horseman

Behold! Behold! That magnificent feat of heroism!
Hail Lieutenant Colonel Fukushima!
The military men of the Empire of Japan
Their prestige in all its weight rests upon him alone
He bore it on his own shoulders, our Yasumasa
To go to wilds yet untrammeled, a place yet without footsteps
To that vast Eurasian continent
Only he alone on this exploration
Astride his brave steed
His majestic form brilliant for all to see
Having rocked Berlin to its foundations
He departed Germany and entered Russia
Traversed Mongolia and on to Siberia

In the far distance gathering bands of dark clouds
Despite the Russian Czar's warm reception and care
Despite the rich hospitality of military officers and their ladies
Thinking of the long road ahead and its many perils
His breast leapt with a flood of feelings
A pledge once given
The determination of a Son of Japan
Is like a mulberry bow capable of shooting arrows that will pierce stone
Should his dead body be left exposed in the wild
How could he even then yield, how bend?
Against the wind, enwrapped in blowing sand
Blowing snow so fine that it chilled to the bone
The bitter cold he gave no heed
The smoke from a homesteader's fire was rare
The track gave out
Beasts roared in the valleys
And surrounded by such sounds he traveled through the night
Breaking through, across summits and deserts
From astride his horse at the peak of the Urals
His steely gaze took in the three continents of Eurasia
Alone achieving such a height left him proud
His courage and fearlessness akin to Ursa Major
In this troubled world, meritorious achievements
Can be cited with examples manifold
Yet in a great reign unmoved even by crashing waves
Comes gallantry surpassing even that of the past
He was praised throughout the world
Drenched in the glowing rays of our nation's flag
His fragrant name spread abroad
His brilliant achievement
Shall endure unchanged eternally!
Oh joy, oh joy!
(Hisada Kiseki).

On February 11, 1892, the Lieutenant Colonel left Berlin riding his beloved horse 'Gaisen' ('Triumphant Return'). From there he crossed into Russia, and then into the open wilds of Siberia, which he proceeded to traverse. On his return trek, Gaisen died in the village of Borjino. He bought a new horse he named 'Urals' and resumed his trip. The crowds awaiting his return to Japan gave him an enthusiastic welcome, one that bordered on frenzy.

> Now having distinguished himself draped around both shoulders
> He wears garlands of his glory
> Waiting to welcome our returning Lieutenant Colonel
> At Nagasaki, Kobe, Yokohama
> On the boulevards of Tokyo
> His compatriots forty million strong
> With cheers and applause they welcome him
> At banquets overflowing with sincerity
> A crown for fame so elevated
> The sound of fireworks lifted high into the sky
> The glory shines unto the five continents!

As the lines suggest, the enthusiasm for Fukushima edged into mania. Attesting to just how popular the song became, the Asahi Shinbun used the song's clout and its familiar melody in a campaign to expand its circulation. Their revised version went:

> Behold! Behold! That magnificent feat of erudition!
> Hail the Asahi Shinbun!
> The newspaper of the Empire of Japan
> A heavy burden upon our company's shoulders
> Yet our staff and workers bear it with pride
> Our reporting gets the jump on all those other papers.

After rearranging the words as puns on the song's lyrics and printing up sheets of the Asahi version, the company organized a team of twelve or thirteen employees, probably newspaper vendors and delivery boys, in jackets bearing the company's logo. The unit leader conducting the group wore a coat and hat, both adorned with shining gold brocade. Thus arrayed, the group stood on street corners in a single row and as they faced passers-by they sang this song and handed out flyers. At the time, I thought that this was a churlish thing to do, but considering it in today's light makes it appear to be a brilliant business stratagem by the newspaper's management.

41

Murayama Ryūhei bought for a song the Osaka site of the old Uwajima domains mansion and storehouses and started his newspaper business there.[15] Now it has become a resplendent and central location in this key business district. From 1884 or 1886, he dispatched and maintained special correspondents in Tokyo. In 1888, he purchased the newspaper *Mezamashi Shinbun* and renamed it the *Tokyo Asahi Shinbun*. He then began managing both the *Tokyo Asahi* and *Osaka Asahi*. The first day that the *Tokyo Asahi* went on sale, the company chartered the city's horse-drawn trolleys, at the time Tokyo's only form of public transportation, and allowed people to ride free courtesy of the Asahi Company. This was tremendously popular and it goes without saying that it was a public relations coup (although the word at the time was not 'public relations' but 'advertisement'). With this, the eighteen existing Kantō region newspapers banded together to obstruct the *Tokyo Asahi* advance into their territory. Vendors were told that anyone selling the Asahi would not be given other papers to sell. There was lots of trouble among the wholesale vendors in the Kantō as the dispute lingered on. I think that the fight settled down just about the time the refrain, 'Behold! Behold!,' made the rounds. At the time, the Asahi had not yet taken the form of a joint stock company. Or maybe it had. My understanding of corporate business practices at that time simply did not exist. Even now I am impressed with the various methods at the disposal of our entrepreneurs.

Song of a Boat Expedition

If you seek a soldier who gives all for country, a model of glory
Begin with Lieutenant Senior Grade Gunji
A member of the meritorious legion
Ambitions renewed by blessings bestowed
His courage pushed to yet a higher notch
To the distant Kuriles he goes to secure and hold new lands
His grand plan unchanging
And crowds of cheering well wishers along both banks
Gathered without break
To send him off wishing for safe passage free and clear
On the long embankment stretching ten miles down the Sumida
Crowds upon crowds, mountains of people
Across the wide stretch of the river's surface their cheers echoed
Sounds of applause, shouts of 'banzai'

Voices chanting words of celebration
A scene as if the heavens had opened
At Yokosuka, Uraga, Tateyama
At every harbor and port where the ship called
Hurried preparations
Volunteers expended their all in warm receptions
Easily shouldering honor's heavy dictates
In the four directions morning fog obscuring
Such impenetrable blackness, east and west unfathomable
Wild waves and roaring seas
The sea-tossed boat like a leaf on the water
Yet holding fast the tiller
Ever forward our Takeo and in his heart
Therein a plan enfolded
One that at last brings him to the Kuriles
Trading gun and sword
For unfamiliar plow and hoe
Giving no heed to the changeable climate
Opening up the barren mountains and fields
The lock at the northern gate is sturdy
But the will of our Lieutenant Senior Grade
Is truly like the bulwark of the Japanese empire
Our forty million compatriots
Take the Lieutenant Senior Grade's courage for your model
If you give your all for our nation
The power of our Japan
Will surpass that of Europe and America
Delightful, how delightful!
(Hisada Kiseki)

A Sudden Change Back Home in Ōiso

Heat cools and the popular goes out of fashion. And so it went with the incredibly popular song about Lieutenant Colonel Fukushima. The fire died down. Our inability to sell songs meant hard times for *enka* singers. We had *genki-bushi* and *tenrai-bushi* and other such ditties. But those lacked what typically went into *enka*. What genuine songs we did have used lyrics the likes of 'The Sino-Japanese negotiations collapse, Shinagawa mobilizes the

43

battleship Azuma' or the one about Ōi Kentarō and his treason incident.[16] We also resorted to *sōshi* plays, songs to accompany sword dances, and drinking party performances. But what we truly needed at any cost were new *yukai-bushi* and *kinmai-bushi enka* songs.

After reaching a highpoint, the fever for political activism also steadily cooled, but noisy debates continued to maintain the form if not the substance of political engagement. Over time, one after another, important political problems, changes in cabinet line-ups, issues in the Diet, and the like became raw material suitable for *enka*. But the new subjects did not cause business to thrive. Meanwhile abroad, Kim Ok-kyun was murdered in Shanghai and the Tonghak Rebellion broke out in Korea.[17] The drumbeat signaling the Sino-Japanese War grew steadily louder and louder.

I had planned to travel to the Hokuriku region but just before departing I received a letter from home saying that an urgent matter required the family to gather and that I should return immediately. While wondering what in the world could be wrong, I straightaway headed home.

I had tended to forget about my hometown of Ōiso. I found that it had changed so much as to be almost unrecognizable. I had departed a country village on foot, but this time I returned by way of Yokohama by train. Although it was still a one-track railroad, the Tōkaidō line had already been put through. I had heard that some of my fellow villagers had followed the line's expansion by joining the ranks of track-laying workers. Many among them lived transient lives, simply moving apace with construction work to finally wind up who knows where.

Soon after the 1868 Restoration, Ōiso's local swimming beaches underwent development as summer villas became popular and were built in large numbers. The sky was the limit as far as the prospects for new construction was concerned. Atogayama, the hill that we used to climb on our way to school, had been half excavated away and Atago Shrine had been dismantled and removed to a place down the slope. The villa of Yasuda Zenjirō now stood on the shrine's old location.[18] Foreigners' villas also dotted the landscape. Ōiso had been completely colonized by the villas. In the middle of a pine grove in east Koiso, close to the border of west Koiso, was Sōrōkaku, the home of the then Prime Minister and Count (later Marquis), Itō Hirobumi. It became a place where politicians came and went with great frequency. We felt utterly estranged from these people.

What my father and elder brother wanted to talk over was providing business start-up money to my immediate younger brother. He wanted to quit the position he currently held in a clothiers in Odawara to go independent and open his own clothing store. We had gathered to decide if it would be possible to pay out the needed capital. The entire family met in a kind of family conference along the sides of the square, open fireplace in the middle of the kitchen.

My natal family was one of middling farmers. It took all our effort to make a living and as is typical of farmers we always needed money. In normal times we had little ready cash. Now, as a new age dawned, our circumstances were tighter than ever. My younger brother argued that he could easily multiply his profits and easily repay any capital that we might advance him now. He would be sure to repay us, absolutely sure. To his entreaties, my older brother responded with worry while my father assumed a neutral air.

My younger brother was clever and, on top of that, a merchant skilled when it came to persuading others. It was easier than taking candy from a baby for him to convince his father. The old man already overflowed with love for him. And our eldest brother was too easy-going and honest to stand in the way of allowing him to do whatever he wanted. I gradually came to realize that the foundation work for the arrangement had already gone forward and the situation was pretty much a done deal by the time I was consulted. Still, I did manage to put forward one suggestion and made sure that all were doubly clear about it by saying, 'I agree on giving him the money. That said, it should be done as if we were dividing up our inheritance and with the understanding that there will be none left for him hereafter. If at some time down the road business sours or in the event he goes under, there won't be anything added to what he has already received.' Everyone agreed and the meeting disbanded cordially.

An entrepreneur's luck tends to shift. Not surprisingly, after sixteen or seventeen years of tempest-tossed changes, the ability to control the business situation slipped from my younger brother's hands. During this time, my father died and the original family's members had dispersed. The situation turned inexpressibly bad, bad beyond description. Of course, much to my regret, the terms I demanded at the family conference were not followed, leaving me with troubles that I could not forget.

We called the family home 'the home to the south of Hongō.' It had been handed down from one generation to the next many times. Fine old trees surrounded the main house and outlying wings. Chinquapin, chestnut, birdlime, and camellia all stood in the large garden surrounding our home. A deep canal ran from the side of the house and toward the rear. Nearby there was a bamboo grove where shoots regularly sprouted. I yearned for those childhood years when we enjoyed the fruits that came with the changing seasons. Now the land had been sold off to others, cleared, and all of it transformed into empty fields. Long-resident local people often remarked, 'Hongō's face has changed completely.' Every time my elder brother heard these words he felt utterly mortified.

My family supplemented loans already extended to my younger brother from other sources. They mortgaged the fields and then the hills and finally enlarged the debt to include the house itself. Instead of having to suffer with one single financial burden the quick and dirty story is that my younger brother simply sucked the place dry to the point where he finally gulped down his own family's ancestral home. After returning to Tokyo, I left to travel in Hokuriku.

The Sino-Japanese War

Traveling alone in Hokuriku presented many hardships. (I could regale you with lots of stories about encounters on the road, but cannot take the time here.) Business thrived in Arai and Takeda in the Echigo region so I decided to take a break and try my luck there. Around the time I reached Fukui Prefecture in Echizen, the clouds portending war between Japan and Qing China had grown thicker. People everywhere reviled the Chinese with abandon. They called them the 'pig-tailed chinee,' 'chan-chan boys,' and 'slant heads.'

After settling in at a lodge where I would stay the night, I chose a good spot downtown and began singing *enka*. Soon I was surrounded by a crowd. I sang a variety of songs including one I was particularly good at, '*The Bulwark*' by Hisada Kiseki.

The Bulwark

The golden bird banks toward the west
Evening clouds enclose the fortress

Throughout the post the signals
Resound solemnly from the bugle
Resolve echoing
Born of military discipline, rules rightly followed
And the warriors gathered hereunder
Winter blasted
Made to weep by the snow
Summer beaten
Tormented by their own sweat
Their parents in the homeland
How do they fare?
With no wings to fly
These are caged birds
With no fins to swim
These are netted fish
A precious photo in the moonlit haze
Wait, pledge to wait
For now the work is for the country's sake
For our great emperor's sake
To throw away one's life for such a cause is priceless
A Japanese sword and Murata rifle
Drilled and drilled again this man of five feet
Standing in front with the regiment's flag
Dancing around the bullets that rain down
Cutting down the Chinese troops
Marching through four hundred counties
Heroic exploits in the midst of cannon smoke
Soldiers astride Arabian ponies
The Medal of the Golden Owl hanging from one's chest
With uplifted spirits overflowing they are welcomed home
They return to applause
The brocade banners fly gloriously in their hometowns
Dance of joy! Dance of joy! Dance of Joy!
Such happiness! Such happiness!
(Hisada Kiseki)

It was always the custom to give a preface before singing the song and a concluding comment after it was over. When I tried to give the explanation at the start of the *enka* someone among the crowd yelled out, 'The chinks are weak. One Japanese can send ten of their kind flying.' I countered saying, 'Don't be afraid of a powerful enemy, but neither make light of a weak one. It's no good to underestimate the weak.' Immediately, someone shouted that I should not side with the Chinese and accused me of being a spy for the enemy. All of a sudden, the audience began to turn into a dangerous mob. The commotion brought still others who pushed in from the rear to find out what the excitement was about and the mood grew threatening. Just when it looked as if I were going to be given a thorough beating, a patrolman broke through the crowd to attempt to quiet the situation. When that did not work he ended up bustling me off to the police station, which resulted in the crowd simply following along in large numbers. After about an hour, the crowd finally began to thin out. Yet, as the situation was still considered dangerous, I was escorted home in the protective custody of a policeman.

I thought I had truly come to the land of the blockheads. But upon reconsidering I concluded that the situation was that they were all just highly agitated about the China problem and were simply demonstrating their national identity as Japanese. In any case, I straightaway got out of Fukui.

War broke out shortly after my return to Tokyo. The clash in the waters off Toyoshima, the Battle of the Yellow Sea, the fighting to ford the Anjō River - battle after battle brought victory after victory with something like an air of inevitability. Papers sold like crazy and extra editions soared. Business boomed at the ringing of the vendors' bells. Women working the pleasure quarters even gave tips to the newspaper delivery boys. The bugler Shirakami Genjirō, Lieutenant Senior Grade Matsuzaki, and Captain Sakamoto of the warship *Akagi* became famous overnight.[19]

War's Outbreak

Our empire rich in benevolence and chivalry
To guide neighboring Korea
Toward the honor of becoming an independent nation
Totally and for all time
Maintaining the peace of Asia
And doing the complete opposite: China
Arrogant, disrespectful of Korea
Ranting about Chosen's place as a tributary

48

And in the darkness secretly plotting an evil course
Resorting to violence in breaking ties with neighbors
To punish this, war is declared
By great imperial mandate
In indignation we clench our fists, grind our teeth
Withstanding such mortification our people
Our fighting spirit whipped to a highpoint
Like dry grass whipped by a powerful wind.
(Hisada Kiseki)

After this, numerous songs were written and sung one after another. There was 'Manterei,' 'The Great Victory at Heijō' ('Heijō Taishō'), 'The Great Victory of the Yellow Sea' ('Kōkai Taishō,'), 'Kurenjō,' 'Rikoshō,' 'Ikaiei,' 'Lieutenant Senior Grade Matsuzaki,' 'Captain Shima,' 'Harada Jūkichi,' 'Boku Eikō,' ' Tei Joshō,' and 'The Flowers of Shanghai.' In addition, there was the 'Three Heroes,' a ballad of the three soldiers - Kanezaki, Yamazaki, and Fujizaki - who had been taken prisoner and executed. To list all of these songs would provide a close description of the situation during the Sino-Japanese War, but there are too many to enumerate here.

But let's do take up one, 'Harada Jūkichi,' to serve as an example. In later years, the three braves and their bomb and similar heroes left their names in history's annals. But the courageous feats of Harada Jūkichi at Pyongyang have a quintessential Meiji coloring to them. His acts also became the subject of a contemporary lithograph print, copies of which inundated shops during the war. It was also presented in Hakubunkan publishing company's *Record of the Sino-Japanese War.*

Harada Jūkichi

As the fight at Pyongyang dragged on
The Motoyama and Sakunei squads
With strength irresistible carried all before them
Marching forward to take Bōtandai
From this highland they looked down upon

That strategic fortress of Pyongyang
Unable to tarry the brave soldiers charged
But in vain only to become targets for enemy bullets
The bodies of the slain piled in heaps
Yet, no thought of retreat
At a critical stall in the advance
Suddenly from the midst of his comrades
Comes leaping one brave soldier
Bullets showering down thicker than rainfall
And from the base of the ramparts
As agile as a monkey he darts to the top
This man who nimbly plunges over
Is our Harada Jūkichi
Squad leader Mimura follows
With a death-defying fighting spirit
The enemy soldiers beaten to desperate straits
Find their legs wobbly and in that instant
The fortress gate is pushed open
Our troops are beckoned in
And thanks to them Pyongyang falls
Past and present nothing can compare to such a feat
Truly worthy of his nickname, the bulwark
His honor, a warrior's paragon
Worthy of being handed down to the generations
Dance of joy, joy, joy
Oh happiness, happiness!
(Hisada Kiseki)

I tucked these songs under my arm and went to Yokosuka. It goes without saying that the war transformed this military port into a bustling place. For me, it was also filled with memories. It was there that I first heard the activist's songs as I stood on Ōtaki-machi, that busy, unforgettable street. And it was there that I sang. The crowd responded with roaring applause. The song sheets sold so quickly they seemed to fly from my hands.

At the same time, a couple sang Nagoya *jinku*, tunes with the 'yo-ho-hoi' refrain. (They were the Tatekawas, the originators of the method of selling their Nagoya *jinku*. Later they became bosses of their own group in Asakusa.) They stood a bit away from my spot but kept singing 'yo-ho-hoi,' in a way that gradually attracted notice by becoming louder and louder and drawing the crowd's attention away from me. This presented a situation that I inevitably had to find some way to counter. There was no reason for 'yo-ho-hoi' singing to be particularly popular, but at the time it was rare to be accompanied by a woman when engaging in street-corner singing. When the couple saw my popularity, something evident from crowd surrounding me, they perhaps felt the need to resist. I, of course, never intended just to go singing and singing upon starting a song. Yet, when I noticed what that couple was up to, I felt I simply could not be the one to stop first. We kept at it until at last the clock showed it was past midnight. They finally stopped and went home so I quickly packed it in, too. At the time, the sale price for the song sheets was one for two *sen* and I remember on that single occasion I earned more than fourteen yen. Later my apprentice, Takahashi Sumao, became one of Tatekawa's followers in Asakusa. The bonds connecting us were certainly curious. Aside from *enka*, there were many other popular songs about the war. Most of them were simply rewriten based on songs that already existed.

Gone to Pieces

Minister Ōtori must be an extraordinarily great man[20]
Saying he will give his all for his country
The Chinese minister is a mess
Chacha raka chan dewa chacha raka chan
Those Chinese gun placements must be poorly built
Not a single round hits its mark
And all their defenses a mess
Chacha raka chan dewa chacha raka chan

A succession of battles and a string of enemy defeats left their army debilitated. In February 1895 China appointed the German legal scholar Detring as an advisor to assist the two Chinese envoys, Zhang Yinhuan and Shao Youlian, who led the delegation assigned to sue for peace. As Detring's and their credentials were found to be unacceptable for serving as diplomatic officials, they were all sent packing from Kobe. Thereafter, Li Hung-chang set out for Japan as their replacement.[21] Koyama Rokunosuke shot him at Shimonseki. This incident impeded negotiations for a time, but in the end, the negotiations won for Japan a 200-million-tael indemnity, Taiwan, the Pescadores, and the Liaotung Peninsula. But the three countries of Russia, Germany, and France put forward their so-called joint recommendation whereby they interfered and Japan could not avoid returning the Liaotung Peninsula to China.

The Vastness

The flag of the rising sun shines forth from Himalayan peaks
England, Russia, Germany, and France from behind the cloudy vastness
Issued forth their common goodly advice
When we recall the return of Liaotung
The cloudy vastness seems to close down over us
Japanese swords and Murata rifles
Marching and charging across the five continents
In a dream I saw all utterly destroyed
And then a crash of thunder shook me from my dreams
Behind those vast clouds a pale moon glowing
(Hisada Kiseki)

'Peace Talks,' 'Koyama Rokunosuke,' 'Taiwan,' 'Savages Uprising,' and the 'Sakurai Transport Corps' were among the *yukai-bushi* and *kinmai-bushi* we sang. The 'Charging Warrior,' 'Sound of the Wind,' and 'Reform Vigor' - all were popular. We also wrote the song 'Postwar Rule.'

On April 13, His Imperial Highness Kitashirakawa no Miya departed for the field after his appointment as Governor General, charged with pacifying Taiwan. In the midst of a spring rain, the *Ikai-maru* weighed anchor in Ujina. By October, Taiwan was all but conquered, but the Governor General and Imperial Prince Kitashirakawa, alas, passed away at the site of this last appointment.[22]

The Sound of the Wind

The unrest in East Asia is happily ended
Pachu tenrai yan
Hoisted in Taiwan, the flag of the rising sun
Menmetoee sutorin tan
Tenkeshutton choito yukepoi
Undo that elegant coif
Pull your hair back Western style
Pachu tenrai yan
Become a nurse for our nation's sake
Menmetoee sutorin tan
Tenkeshutton choito yukepoi
(Fuwa Sannin)[23]

The Charging Warrior

Japanese men for our nation's sake
Stand! Rise up! Army of righteousness!
Through the break in the distant clouds
See the pig-tailed chinks in wait where tigers once lurked
Let us go, embark on our battleships
Sail forth, through wave peak and trough
The enemy routed at Asan, at the Daidō River
They deserted that stronghold, barely escaping with their lives
Trembling at even the wind-stirred pampas grass
Those terrified pig-tailed chinks
With no strength to defend those fortresses
They desert and flee for Mukden
At last at the walls of Beijing, here the pig-tailed chinks begin to weep
Ahh! Charge! Charge!
(Fuwa Sannin)

Song of Vigor

Look carefully at the Eastern situation
We cannot, truly cannot, let slip our guard
Wear straw sandals but step firmly
Rove over Europe and Asia
And tremendous deeds achieve
Truly this is joy
Truly this is stirring
Truly yes, this is a man's way
(Ukiyo Saburō)

Postwar Corruption

During wartime, the political world tightened up a bit, but with peace the politicians once again relaxed and corruption reached a new zenith. The people were exhausted. Profiteers maneuvered in the darkness. Frauds and entire companies intent on swindles arose one after another. We were outraged that

53

society fell into such a state. Yokoe started composing a song with lyrics that went, 'Anyway, now all it takes is ready cash, ready cash.' Even though he stopped in the middle without finishing it, the expression 'ready cash, ready cash' became popular throughout society.

Elder Statesman

The victor over China in war
Not Enomoto but Japan's Hinomoto Rising Sun
Valor lifted our hearts with joy
Rising taxes on sake and tobacco
Heavy burdens for the nation's people
Yet we bore these lightly
From two decades past, that stone wall Itagaki
Has stood a bulwark shielding people and officialdom
Now Itagaki and the state have cut a deal
With hearts mutually entwined, a gulf no more
From what I've heard
Even that famous sharp sword, Watanabe
Cannot sever the unseverable ties that bind party and state
Of course, now it's the postwar system that has been administered flawlessly
And politics has been just fine, too
Resolute rule based on corruption à la Takashima
Or on everlasting unshakeable swindlers like Ōyama
Who can tell lies from truth?
Saionji has enjoyed sixteen return matches
Saigō was fated just one lucky roll
Eye-catchingly smooth
Trading places is that Ōkuma
And he after a desperately rough ride
Got aboard with fellow riders on the Shinagawa stagecoach
People with their different -isms
Now march forward together
The government's failed policies
Matsukata's debacle and the like all around
But the parties spend days in-fighting savoring their personal grudges
Meanwhile the nation's great work is forgotten
Truly, it is enough to make you gnash your teeth in anger
Dance of joy, of joy, of joy

Sweet delight, delight![24]
(Tonoe Suikyō)

Swept along by contemporary trends, the political activists in the Youth Club also softened. Instead of their past practices of spilling blood at polling stations or firing pistol shots at speech rallies, they now worked just for the money. Whether for the government party or the opposition, they campaigned for cash. Now during election contests the two parties, the Party of the People and the Party of the Government, would emerge but from a single organization to take part in a sham battle akin to a farcical *kyōgen* comedy. There were times when all we could do was have a really good laugh at the goings-on. Yet, in time, Youth Club members lost interest in a political movement that lacked seriousness. Pure *enka sōshi*, in fact, tended toward social reformism. Speeches and song were the sources of their strength. They used these two strong arms to attack the market-cornering of the rice dealer Hamano Shigeru and attempted to put down that pyramid scheme. They also targeted the so-called two-*sen* savings club swindle and cases of fraud and loan sharking that had become rampant everywhere. In November, one of the most famous scandals, the Iron Pipe Incident, occurred in Tokyo.

The Iron Pipe Incident

Poison is poured
Into the waterworks, that lifeline of a million people
They caught Maruhashi Chūya[25]
For plotting to murder the people of Edo castle
And just like foam on the water
The plot came to naught
It's a tale from the past
But listen and I will tell you a more modern story
One from our clearly enlightened Meiji age
About that thoroughly impressive waterworks project
A poisonous company undertaking
Tokyo's citizens year after year
Waited with endless patience
But the water project's iron pipes
Were to come from a swindler's subcontracting company
A firm whose sullied name was infamous
Far and wide for fraud and speculation

55

Hamano Shigeru and Amenomiya[26]
Their company in decline, its fate at hand
They at their wit's end came up with a hateful trick
They used dubious materials of unacceptable quality
To hoodwink officials
Escaping blame for their evil deception by burying it underground
But some things will not stay down
They must be repaid for their works
A chosen few are selected
For the sake of our citizens
A select group is chosen for positions of honor to administer our city
Bribes blinded these people, the custodians of weighty responsibilities
Corruption and scandals ran rampant
Left to the law courts to right
A judge, fair and impartial, decided
They would wear red prison uniforms and manage on boiled barley rice
They may resent the guard's torments
Imprisonment at heavy labor is a heavenly retribution
But the time was ripe for their just desserts
Happiness, happiness!
(Suikyō Gakujin)

There was also a *kinmai-bushi* song that went something like 'a formula like rats multiplying.' It told of the *nezumiko* pyramid savings scheme whereby one bought a first-share premium for two *sen* and within a fixed period of time it would grow to come back as fifteen yen. The deal was supposed to go forward arithmetically but nearly everybody got cheated. In fact, I never heard of anyone getting paid the full return. Some greedy people set up dozens of these pyramid clubs. They got in on the ground floor and being paid first saw their two *sen* turn into a huge return. That's the way that Furuya appropriated the funds that enabled him to grow fat.[27]

Takashima-chō is noted in the song. This was a red light district in Kanagawa near Yokohama. Needless to say, the aforementioned houses, the Kamikaze-rō and Ganki-rō of Kiyu, were notorious places. Furuya came all the way from Yokosuka to have fun in Kanagawa. Of course, one reason for the long trip was to avoid playing around on one's home turf. But he also wanted to enjoy himself in the extravagant manner of foreigners and rich merchants.

When I went to Yokosuka with the songs 'Conquering the Two-*Sen* Pyramid' and 'The Iron Pipe Incident,' Tonoe and Nakanishi Sanchirō jumped on the bandwagon and started lecturing in two locations on the need to wipe out the pyramid schemes. Once at the speech meeting in Ōtaki-chō, Tonoe attacked that refined albeit extravagant pastime of elder statesmen and ministers, namely billiards. In fine fettle, he asked rhetorically, 'Is pool playing a tool to elevate our national prestige?', a remark that went over big with the crowd. At the time, a certain political activist, a *sōshi* who went by the name Onda or something like that, was living in Yokosuka, and he replied from the gallery, 'An excellent point!' and yelled similar words of encouragement. At the time, billiards was wildly popular among the higher classes. But then some sailors suddenly seemed to take something amiss in the words attacking the ministers of state and began shouting, 'Where do you think you are? This is a military port! A speech like that is an insult!' and began making a commotion. All at once, all the sailors were on their feet. Despite everything the speaker did to explain his comments and the hall proprietor's best efforts to calm the situation, the crowd refused to settle down and the scene continued in an uproar. The owner told Tonoe to give it up and come down from the platform, but he wanted to continue and endeavored to do just that. Then all of a sudden everything from cushions to braziers started flying through the air as all hell began to break loose.

At this point, a certain Mr. Mekane, one of the biggest bosses in the Kantō region, appeared on stage. He said, 'Now, now' and stretched out his arms in a gesture of putting down the uproar and things suddenly quieted. Tonoe left from the back, escaping unharmed. I came away impressed with the mysterious power of the local boss. Mekane was called one of the leading men of chivalry in the Kantō area. He was also called Azumaya-san because he owned a restaurant by the same name. When the elderly Mekane died the following year, the press announced his death along with an account of his career and mournful words about his passing. I did not know him well, but he was a man of great popularity. Nakanishi met his end late in life under unfortunate circumstances, but he was a man whose blood burned for righteousness. He had a son. Whatever became of him?

The Age of 'Oh, What to Do?'

After the two-*sen* saving club fuss died down, everything seemed in the midst of sinking into decline. Even the *tokkan-bushi* and *genki-bushi*, military songs so popular in wartime, went out of fashion. There was the song 'A Tour of the Northeast' ('Tōhoku man'yu') by Suikyō Gakujin, but it was not all that popular. The Japan Railway Tōhoku Line was completely opened in July 1893. This was before the beginning of the social reformist labor movement in Japan. Nevertheless, there had already been a strike during the line's construction. What was happening in Tōhoku just wasn't sufficient as material that might appeal to a more general audience. I guess you could say that the gloom in the northeast turned out to be more than just a local misfortune. We faced a real dearth of *enka* material. I asked Tonoe to compose songs. I told him if we did not publish a marketable song soon everybody would be hard up and it was his response to this request that he composed 'The Flower of the Japanese Empire' ('Kōkoku no hana').

At that time, Hisada Kiseki had been away for a while. His election campaign activities had gotten him thrown into the Urawa prison. When his family learned that he was making trouble for them, they called him back to his hometown. I think it was around the time of his electioneering. His parents found the life of a *sōshi* activist to be beyond their comprehension. His role as a groundbreaking activist *enka* singer proved insufficient to cut the emotional bonds that tied him to his family. After this episode, he changed course and went into education. He had had political ambitions and he might have seen them come to something. If only he could have persisted and remained in Tokyo at least until the time that the Itagaki-Ōkuma cabinet was formed. Later in life, he lamented that he had gotten off to such a start.

When Hisada Kiseki dropped into the Youth Club after a long absence, a new song, '*The Flower of the Japanese Empire*,' was selling great guns. Everyone was happy about the newfound prosperity. The song's various versions came out as *kinmai-bushi* and in other forms. Hisada used a low voice to narrate instead of sing the section of the song on 'punishing dissipation.' Eventually, this part, too, appeared as a verse to be sung.

The Flower of the Japanese Empire

As if in daylight in this nightless city
Bodhisattvas dance
Leaning against the *shoji* paper screens with their long pipes
Wreathed in clouds of tobacco smoke
Ishibe Kanekichi Kanekabuto

Despite his steady nature is now abstracted
And flying up the stairs
To take part in the grand drinking bout in the *tatami* room
Drinking in great good spirits
But more intoxicating than the sake
Her skillful words
Standing behind the screen that bore the image of paired mandarin ducks
Murmuring words of love
And over the world shone the moon on the last day of the month
Carried away by her words, all artifice and skill
Somehow unwilling to leave her
He gazes from behind, seeing her hair as she departs
Being pulled back, to return to another room
She whispers, 'Soon'
The sound of her words as she lightly tapped his back
Echoed to his marrow and he could not forget
He did not care what his parents thought
He was blind to the grief of his wife and children
Such considerations were as hopeless as chanting a sutra to a horse
As useless as nailing bean curd to a wall.

Hisada gave a bitter laugh, '"Swept away by a tap on the back" and the like – that doesn't sound much like the flower of the empire.' Hearing his comment, I thought that he had fallen behind the times.

We often exposed the tricks of the street stall barkers and peddlers who worked temple festivals and night fairs.[28] As comeuppance, the Youth Club was nicknamed 'The Fight Club.' It was around the time when the name stuck that our club also changed. At one time our members were content to carry thick sticks and roam about shouting in a gruff manner. But the completely rustic and rough *sōshi* disappeared and the *enka* singer that appeared now was no longer the master of the brawl. Before you knew it, the world and its customs had changed to just such a great extent.

Along with the transformation, Hisada's and Tonoe's literary styles also changed. Tonoe's pieces impressed the listener with a sense of breadth, a kind of capaciousness. Yokoe's songs, on the other hand, tended to overflow with warm emotion. Aside from songs that admonished dissipation, Tonoe also wrote airs about the dissolute student, the girl student, and the lecherous gentleman. Tesseki wrote cautionary ballads intended to warn the young as well as songs and airs for the *musume gidayu* women balladeers. These admonishing song styles make plain that the customs of the times had grown terribly dissipated. The 'Students, oh, what to do?' pieces were representative products of this era. The theme was even picked up in newspapers that featured articles, always in deploring terms that asserted 'In the trends in popular songs one can see just how corrupt society has become!' They even used song titles in their headlines to make the point.

An Air for a Girl Singer

Coquettishly hair done up in a *shimada* coif[29]
Heavy makeup over bare skin
Lips outlined in ravishing red
The soul of elegant innocence
The red backing on the shawl's underside
Is properly embossed with a golden crest
She leans on a rail and sweetly recites
As if a bird's voice from a vale
As if a nightingale singing
'Nozaki Village at Gotenba' and
'The Wine Dealer Umetada'
Laughing, crying, swept away
The listeners care nothing if all falls to dust
Completely transported
Most watch captivated
Lecherously, they pour their gaze over the young woman
Their amorous glances express a strange glint in their eyes
It is the men in this crowd, those making eyes at the woman
Who will become the catch of the day, fresh and live
In that upstairs room of assignation?
And therein most will have their fresh lifeblood sucked away
The sin is not with the temptress
But falls to the tempted philanderer
Family wealth, money, whatever there is
What will be left afterward won't fill a thimble
Sir, take heed and brace yourself
Better that you come to listen earnestly to *joruri* puppet recitals
Truly! Doing so will be a cause for celebration!

Dance of joy, dance of joy, dance of joy
Happiness, happiness
(Yokoe Tesseki)

Customary morality declined and indolence spread. As it did, students changed completely. Those who once wore the stiff, hand-made cotton clothes now cried, 'Clothes must be perfectly cut to fit collar and sleeve.' Many came to favor lustrous silks and wasted all of the money given them for school expenses in the pleasure quarters, in brothels, and running after the *musume-gidayu*. The 'Oh, what to do' crowd were all students. They went out as one to take in the performances of the *musume-gidayu* and when the curtain went up they cried out, 'I have waited, oh my goddess,' and blushed red. It was if they had been flipped by their sandal straps and at the climax of the act groaned, 'Yes, yes,' and 'What shall I do, oh what?' in a kind of heated frenzy. Following the performance, some of them trailed after the rickshaw that carried the performer homeward. We were the ones who named this group of students the 'Oh, what to do clan.' They should be compared to the later Taishō period *'Peragoro'* group or the fans of *Yasuki-bushi* and their 'Oh my, I'm gone group,' the *'Ara, ittchatta-ren'* because of their similarities. But the 'Oh, what to do clan' was really the forerunner of them all. Among the lyrics I wrote using the pen name Shirazu Sanjin is a lament that goes:

Holding the writing brush
He ground the ink stick his head cocked to one side deep in thought
How to put things in this long letter home
How to explain that the money he had cheated from his parents
To the very last *sen* was spent in his 'Oh, what to do' obsession?

Shirazu Sanjin and Ukiyo Saburō were pen names of mine in those days. (Later I also used Nomuki Sanjin, Oboro Sanjin, Bonjin, Azembō, as well as Master of Garyūkutsu, Master of Tenryūkyō, and Ryōkan.) Here is one of my songs of the four seasons. It was something I rewrote and which became quite popular in Kyoto's pleasure quarter:

Springtime Happiness

Two together lying beneath the cheery blossoms enjoying sake
The garden cheery tree and the misty moon
Rain and wind rile the blossoms
They scatter a few but cause others to open again

61

> The stale speech declaring faithfulness
> On his lips loyalty protested
> While he pillows his head in a beauty's lap
> In these tainted pleasures, he passes his days
> A trifle disloyal, this lustful old man
> Plum blossom viewing in the spring
> A gentleman's hand taken by that of a chaste beauty
> The wind blows wild with envy
> The wife wearing an *Azuma* coat
> Gathers her skirts a bit in a hurry
> (Shirazu Sanjin)

This song, of course, satirizes Itō Hirobumi, the master of the Sorokaku Villa in Ōiso in Kanagawa. Around this time, the '*Azuma* coat' was in fashion. One reason for its popularity was the often heard saying that 'the *Azuma* coat hides the rags beneath.' These were some of the *hōkai-bushi* songs that reflect something of the tenor of the times. Before I got into composing *hōkai-bushi*, Hisada and Tonoe had written the following:

> Considering my life as light as the morning dew
> That is scattered fragrantly across Shikishima
> The world of the Divine Law.
> If flowers, first the cherry blossoms
> If men, first warriors
> Loyal and brave, gallant and foreboding

Although the poem had a rough quality, it also expressed both splendor and composure. Furthermore, it differed completely from the run-of-the-mill world of *hōkai-ya* singing performed by balladeers who wandered around strumming old-style Chinese country guitars.[30] According to the political *sōshi*, that was another school of degenerates whose work was a kind of lewd heterodoxy that activists unreservedly despised. Somewhere I had read a ridiculous article about how the *enka* singers had descended from the *hōkai-ya*. Just for the record, let me completely deny that right here.

The Artillery Warrior

The taste of bitterness but in the end success born of adversity
As if blessed by the dew this rule of law

Blooming beautiful new nobility
A hundred flowers in glorious blossom
The bravery that subdued the Qing Empire
Has utterly vanished without notice
The shallowness of the makeshift and shameless
The way of the law
The fickleness of people's hearts
Deplorable, lamentable

The current of the times throws up a barbershop run by women
The self-styled dandy comes again and again
The way of the law
To have his nose hairs clipped
And business flourishes.
The traitorous merchant's habits
Irritated the native Tokyoites
He only called down upon himself his own destruction
The way of the law
Such barbarous rioting is the nation's disgrace

We must take care
Oyster shells and all of a sudden the hull of the ship was rotten
Under the sky during a long journey
The way of the law
The faded banner of the rising sun

Numberless regrets
With a flattering beauty they drank wine and brandy as if taking leave
of the world
Liqueurs and brandy
The way of the law
Beer it dribbles down their nose
And all go soft in the head.

The 'tasting of hardships' referred to the men who came through the Meiji
Restoration to emerge as successes, earning places in the peerage and emerging
as a 'new nobility.' 'Capturing the people's fancy' points to a barbershop in
Kanda, the first to be operated by a woman. She often left nicks all over the
men she shaved, but just a simple, 'Oh my dear, I am so very sorry' seemed
more than enough to wipe away their pain.

63

The Tokyoite reference refers to the 'Virgin Incident' in which the Murai Tobacco Company produced cigarettes named 'Sunrise,' 'Pinhead,' and 'Virgin.' In pushing sales of Virgin, the company offered prizes with its tobacco. Selling the product was soon banned because it resembled gambling, a turnabout that prompted the company to take out ads in the newspapers that again offered prizes in exchange for tobacco coupons, but the method of redeeming the goods, requiring some kind of little booklet, was ambiguous at best. This outraged short-tempered Tokyoites who tore apart the Murai Tobacco Company's store in Nihonbashi. Tobacco became a state-controlled commodity in July 1904.[31]

'Oyster shells' refer to an incident in which the government of Hawaii refused Japanese immigration to the islands. In retaliation, Foreign Minister Ōkuma dispatched a warship. Despite the gesture, the negotiations faltered. The ship, *Naniwa*, after many months of idleness moored in Honolulu harbor, became encrusted with oyster shells. The outcome made Ōkuma a national laughingstock.

Social Views

He lives in a great mansion of an architectural style
That exhausts all the marvelous skills to create beauty unsurpassed
His attire is of twilled brocade
And his coach is pulled robustly
By paired Arabian steeds
Sitting in his carriage the master of all arrogance
He lifts a Manila cigar to his lips
The aroma an indescribable fragrance
Wreathed in smoke he goes forward
To the Koyō-kan or the Kagetsu-rō
And lastly to the Kasuikai
Ponds of sake and forests of meat his pleasure
Under what lucky star are born
Such enviable men of wealth?
High officials, gentlemen, wealthy merchants
Drunk on your own prosperity
How do your eyes see
The winter rain in Asakusa?

And the autumn moon reflected in Hana-chō?
How do you perceive the images there?
Where that faint lantern hangs under the eaves
And from within the house a light but dimly glimmers
Tired out from a long day's work
But if the legs are stretched fully out
They will touch the skin of another
The body although large must be bent like a horizontal 'v'
For one night his roof rent
Provides only thinly padded bedding and an oak leaf-wrapped rice cake
Of course, his dreams are boldly ambitious
When hungry he goes to a tavern
Where instead of chairs there are soy sauce barrels
He has a bowl of rice and raw sake
Despite his stomach he can't afford sardines or cod
Times are too tough for that fine fare
Day after day work and beads of sweat
Bitterly, day in, day out
And if the rain falls and the wind blows
He must hold off spending for food
And can hardly afford to eat a sweet potato
One cannot hear the tale without tears falling
The competition in the struggle for existence
Day by day ever more severe
Looking out at the twentieth century and the future to come
What springs to mind is that foreign thing
A communist party, a socialist party
Such a reflection is not far away
When I quietly think about the social problem
And when I consider this
I am terrified
Goose bumps and chills settle over my body
(Yokoe Tesseki)

Admonition to Youth

A pheasant in a scorched field or a crane at night
The hearts of parents are all the same

Parents parting with their beloved children
So that the young may advance in the world still unknown
Although they conceal it, these parents weep inside
Bear the chill and don't catch cold
Don't skip meals and get sick
Taking such pains with thoughtful words
Such as deserve display as fine as embroidered brocade
We will be waiting here for the day you return
Kindness abiding deep in such words
Despite his brave high spirits
The youth's face at times bathed in a child's tears as if caught in the rain
Loath to part, to loosen that binding tie
The train whistle blows and there is no escape
The son's silhouette disappears behind the window glass
His parents there to see him off
The separation
Once unthinkable passes as if in the space of a dream
Suddenly five years have gone
The flowers have bloomed five times
The flowers have withered five times
His parents never missed sending him money for his studies
The morning flowers
The evening snow
And during midsummer
Especially during the scorching days of summer
When they heard of a noxious epidemic's spread
They worried about housing in the capital
They fretted that he lacked the money to buy things
They sent cash for medicine and many, many other things
They never doubted as they read each letter that arrived
What they were told he needed they sent and sent again
His father quit drinking the sake he so enjoyed
His mother gave no concern to her clothes
Morning and night they thought only of their son
How is he now, how is he faring?
Burned by the snow and bitten by bugs
They bear every hardship
And the son who intended to make a name for himself in one giant step

His heartstrings once so pure, so unsullied
Has become dyed in the delicate colors of the city
Bad company tempted him
Soft rounded forms and skin as white as snow
False friends bewitched his heart
The lure of the pleasure quarter, that land of warmth and softness
A small banquet on a spring evening
A sip of sake to greet the morning snow
Not knowing the power of his money
He was swept away
Believing himself appreciated as a connoisseur in refinement
The moon over Yanagi Bridge
Cherry blossoms drifting like snowflakes at Nakano-machi
Truly it was as if one hour was a thousands pieces of gold
Brilliant children adrift on their own, one hears that they feel this way
This sharply brilliant boy now alone
When silence reigns and he sits at his school window
He quietly recalls
The hardships faced by his parents
And a cold sweat trickles down his back

Defending the Nation

The haze settles from the cook stoves of a million people
Citizens of a state bountifully governed
Joyous celebration in the spring of the reign
'The people's wealth is our wealth,'
Expounds the emperor following the legend
On a freezing night he removed his cloak
To show he understood the people's pain and hardship
The emperor's tears the saddest of all
The depth of his sacred concern unfathomable
Somehow tears overflow
Even moving the realm's holiest sovereign
Everywhere hardships to be borne
And the duties of the ministers multiply
To rule the nation's business
The heavy burden of those people who

Must act with extreme care and caution
In planning for the nation's benefit
A respite for people's strength
Even a carriage pulled by a pair of Arabian steeds
Will tire the horses after they pull for a thousand miles
The ministers in their radiantly black Western cloths
Even if they shine brilliantly
No one will come
Should reverses visit the nation and the people
Become troubled by problems intractable
Our compatriots more than 60 million strong[32]
Cooperate as one, unbending
Thriftiness and a martial spirit
Cultivating these habits our Imperial Household
For countless generations imperishable will be protected still
And throughout the world our nation's prestige shall shine
Happiness, happiness!
(Hisada Kiseki)

My friends and I sang these kinds of songs while those in the higher ranks of the political world spent day after day in a struggle to put their clique in power. A tune such as '*Defending the Nation*' carried a general message similar to today's Imperial Rule Assistance Association, in short nothing other than celebrating our glorious imperial line and its continuous 2600-year existence. As a matter of course we put the Emperor's concerns before all else. Starting from scratch, we appealed to the public of that time through songs that called for a new spirit of leadership. It was just such a spirit that enabled people to protect the motherland to the depths of their loyalty and encouraged them toward unswerving determination.[33]

A half-century has passed since then. Now it is an ugly situation in which the *zaibatsu* and their ilk tenaciously twist words as they like, desperately cling to old approaches to maintain the status quo, and do all that they can to avoid any sacrifice of their own selfish interests. And they do so at the very time that the nation faces an unprecedented crisis! Comparing that time fifty years ago with today is like comparing heaven and earth or clouds and mud. It is enough to leave you utterly disgusted.

Around this time, Yokoe Tesseki composed the first verse of "A Train Journey". He gradually got around to publishing it and it was this song of train travel that preceded Ōwada Kenji's "Railroad Song" by fifty years. Hisada Kiseki also saw the song and exclaimed, 'This is really good. To be able to come up with something like this is really something.' Sometime before the song's appearance, Yokoe had formed the Blood and Iron Club, a group that was a kind of *enka* political *sōshi* association that composed pieces like this. But he soon grew irritated by the dullness and corruption of *enka* activists and returned to the fold of the Youth Club and writing pure *enka*.

The Train Journey

A hundred miles of mountains and rivers
Crossed in the space of a naptime dream
A trip by train
We have truly received the blessings of Occidental civilization!
No need for busy send-offs or welcome-backs
Enjoy the scenery from the window
With a whistle blast set out from Shinbashi
After that follow on to Shibahama
To the left the distant Bōsō Peninsula
In the offing boats at full and half-sail come and go
Wistfully behold the reddening sky
As on the right the famous Sengaku Temple comes into view
Consider the samurai retainers of old and their fortitude
And proceeding not much farther on you reach Goten'yama
Shinagawa Station can be seen by looking back
And then to Suzugamori where evildoers[34]
Their hate still unexpiated now sleep underground
Passing Ōmori the next destination
Rokugo River stained by streaks of flowing indigo
Crossing the river to Kawasaki
And in a twinkling past Tsurumi
Soon to Namamugi,
To the spot where the vigorous Satsuma warrior bravely
Cooled the blood
That once ran through the blue-eyed foreigner's heart[35]
Flying along soon reaching Kanagawa
Ships bustling, enter and leave port
Yokohama's prosperity

Can be seen from the bluffs on high
Where the Western buildings have taken over
Their expansive architecture and elegance
Causing one to gasp in a kind of admiration
On past Hodogaya, Totsuka, Fujisawa
And suddenly to Ōiso
Where elder statesmen wear brocade and feast on jade
These men of leisure in repose in their gardens of flowery paradise
While in the heavens clouds run quickly scudding against the sky
On to Odawara where a hegemony founded on the base of nine generations
At last fell to Hideyoshi's stratagem
But only barely, after repeated encircling
Fell Odawara Castle
Onward the traveler along sharp curves, up steep slopes
Detouring around Hakone
Through skillfully drilled tunnels
In more than ten places
Flashes of light and dark like day and night

The song goes on for seven verses and takes the listener down the Tōkaidō Line finally to arrive at Kobe. These original lyrics were welcomed widely and enabled *enka* singers to persevere in their calling for a good long time. They also provided material for later *enka* compositions. So, if at some time the then-popular song went cold we could scrape by performing the old standbys. If we did this, we could continue to sell our wares. Sometime around 1907, I added verses to the train song, updating it by including lyrics that mentioned newly built stations. I made it into a seven and five meter ditty, a kind of parody of the senior school song 'Ah! This Cup of Jade' ('Aa Gyoku-hai').

Notes

[1] Many of the songs included in *A Life Adrift* were written by authors other than Azembō. Tonoe Suikyō, one of Azembō's early colleagues in the *enka* world, stands out in this regard. Azembō himself used a variety of stage names at different times in his career or when he sought to make ambiguous the authorship of satirical lyrics, particularly those with a sharp political edge. He was born Soeda Heikichi, but also adopted a pen name when writing haiku poetry and a Buddhist name for his time as a pilgrim. The variants are mentioned in this chapter and elsewhere in the text.

[2] Azembō provides aliases in parenthesis for the performers and writers stage names and pen names.

[3] Tanaka Shōzō (1841-1913) became a member of the Diet's lower house in 1890, following a decade of activism in the Liberty and Popular Rights movement. He is best known for fighting the government on behalf of farmers and other residents who sought redress for massive pollution resulting from the Ashio Copper Mine.

[4] Rumors about the heterodox practices among Christian foreigners in Nagasaki and other cities included stories of bizarre sexual practices. Similar rumors circulated about the missionary community in China during a generally comparable period.

[5] The 'Maroon Club' refers to the color of *hakama* outer kimono coats of that distinctive color worn by Meiji schoolgirls. Melanie J. Czarnecki observes that '... The Meiji schoolgirl, adorned in her maroon (*ebicha*) *hakama* and arrow-feather patterned kimono, hair swept back at the sides and fastened with a ribbon moving freely in the breeze, rode to campus on her bicycle and it was all downhill from there. Unlike today, schoolgirl dress during the Meiji period was a code for class distinction. Only girls from the upper echelons of society were sent to higher schools. As such, the media, tracked the every move of these Meiji starlets fastidiously. They came to achieve something of a sex symbol status, rivaling the geisha. In fact, geisha would don schoolgirl attire in imitation of the new bad girls on the scene.' See http://www.aasianst.org/absts/2005abst/Japan/j-87.html.

[6] During the Tokugawa period (*c.* 1600-1868), the *ryō* became the standard gold coin issued by the shogunate. It was minted in a thin, oval shape. In 1858, it was valued at three-quarters of a US dollar for the purpose of international exchange. In 1871, it was renamed the *en* or, as more commonly Romanized, the yen.

[7] Inukai Tsuyoshi (1855-1932) was one the prewar period's foremost political liberals. He led movements to protect Japan's fledgling constitutional government and served in central government ministries. After becoming Prime Minister in 1931, in the midst of a lingering economic depression and during Japan's takeover of China's three northeastern provinces, he was assassinated by a band of dissatisfied military rightists in the May 15 Incident in 1932.

[8] The Fukushima Incident (1882) occurred when Mishima Michitsune, centrally appointed governor of Fukushima Prefecture, forced a road construction project on local residents that mandated higher taxes and corvee-like recruiting of local labor. Kōno Hironaka (1849-1923), a Liberty and Popular Rights activist, led popular opposition to the harsh building plan. Thousands of local residents protested Mishima's dictates by rallying in the streets and finally attacking a local police station. In suppressing the uprising, Tokyo ordered the arrest of several thousand Fukushima people and Liberal Party members, including Kōno, who was sentenced to several years in prison. Azembō tends to conflate the historical chronology. He begins talking about events of the early 1890s and then slips back to the early and mid-1880s. Although he does not say that he was directly involved in the earlier events, which makes sense

71

because he was only ten years old in 1882, some critics argue that he gives the false impression of being more involved than was actually the case. Azembō's harshest critic, Nishizawa Sō, goes as far as accusing him of being a total charlatan in fictionalizing a direct role in Liberal Party *sōshi* politics that Nishizawa contends were in any case irrelevant by the 1890s. See Nishizawa, *Kayōshi I*.

[9] For a basic description of these Liberty and Popular Rights incidents see Roger W. Bowen, *Rebellion and Democracy in Meiji Japan*, Berkeley: University of California Press, 1980.

[10] Azembō engages in a bit of the bad-old-days reminiscing in recalling electoral and post-election violence as history long past. In fact, political thuggery did not disappear. Instead, the *sōshi* evolved into *ingaidan*, a term often translated as 'political party pressure groups.' But 'lobbying' does not really capture the way *ingaidan* actually worked. The force wielded by these party auxiliaries, who worked for pay, typically relied more on physical attacks and intimidation than on persuasion or offers of monetary support. *Ingaidan* bullies associated with one party faction or another attempted to sway legislative policies extra legally into the 1930s and resumed their activities in the postwar years. I am grateful to Eiko Maruko Sinaiwer and her work on *ingaidan* for providing a sense of what some of the *sōshi* singers and their occupational descendants finally became, and how the *sōshi* tradition continued to influence politics long after singing stopped.

[11] The former samurai, Shimada Saburō (1852-1923), became a Liberty and Popular Rights activist, after which he embarked on a long career as a Lower House parliamentarian. He is famous for advocating a variety of causes on behalf of the still un-enfranchised citizens. In addition to leading the fight to eliminate prostitution, he also worked for relief of farmers injured by the Ashio pollution case and supported a campaign for universal suffrage. Nakajima Nobuyuki (1846-99) was also a Liberal Party activist after an earlier career in service to the new Meiji central government. He was among those activists expelled from Tokyo in 1887 under the provisions of the Peace Preservation Law. In 1890, he was victorious in the first election for Lower House and became its first Speaker. Later, he returned to the central government service, ending his career as an Imperial appointee to the House of Peers by Imperial command. His wife, Kishida Toshiko, was a leading activist for women's rights.

[12] In fact, Azembō opposed abolishing licensed prostitution. His view was that it would only throw the women into illegal work on the street and would do absolutely nothing to end prostitution.

[13] Lieutenant-Colonel Fukushima Yasumasa (1852-1919) made his seventeen-month horseback ride from Berlin to Vladivostok in 1892-93. His mission was not merely a publicity stunt, but also required that he observe the Russians and their work at constructing the Trans-Siberian Railway.

[14] Fleet Lieutenant Gunji Shigetada organized the Kuriles Service Society in 1892 to foster Japanese colonization of the islands. Although Azembō presents him as a lonely, forgotten figure even at the time of the expedition, Gunji in fact made his trip with forty confederates as well as an Asahi Shinbun reporter. The trip in open boats was clearly an adventure intended to generate popular attention to the northern territories. Gunji's campaign led to the founding of a small fishing and hunting outpost by the turn of the century and prosperity for the leader of the expedition.

[15] Murayama Ryōhei (1850-1933) took over the newspaper that eventually became the Asahi. He was a pioneer, albeit one widely imitated, in creating a popular press through sponsorship of baseball tournaments, mass advertising, and other events.

[16] Azembō refers here to the liberty and popular rights radical, Ōi Kentarō (1843-1922) and his involvement in the Ōsaka Incident in 1885. The incident aimed at overturning the government

of Korea and thereby necessitating the involvement of Japanese troops, which Ōi and his followers believed would lead to the destabilization of the Meiji government and a chance for their group to rule. Azembō is again jumping around a bit chronologically.

[17] Kim Ok-kyun (1851-94) early on advocated Korea's development along Western lines and to that end organized an independence party that attempted to overturn the Korean monarchy and seize political control in 1884. The coup, which enjoyed Japanese support, failed and Kim fled to Japan, only to be assassinated later by a Korean agent in Shanghai in 1894.

[18] Yasuda Zenjirō (1838-1921) created a financial empire based primarily on investments in banking and insurance, and early cooperation with the Meiji government economic reforms. As the head of one of Japan's four leading zaibatsu or financial conglomerates, Yasuda became the richest man in Japan by the time of his death.

[19] Shirakami Genjirō was a famous bugler who sounded the charge only to be immediately shot through the lungs. Although his fellow soldiers attempted to take the bugle away from him, he managed to belt out one last charge before falling down dead. The song telling of his heroism became a best-seller throughout Japan. Matsuzaki Naoomi was an officer who fought valiantly before being shot in the head. Sakamoto was a brave commander of the warship *Akagi* in the Battle of the Yalu.

[20] As a Ministerial representative of the Japanese Government dispatched to China in 1889, Ōtori Keisuke (1833-1911) set the stage for the Sino-Japanese War by his firm refusal to peacefully resolve key conflicts over Korea.

[21] Azembō's account is a bit at odds with the historical record. Gustav Detring (1842-1913) was, in fact, commissioner of customs at Tianjin, who enjoyed close ties with Li Hongzhang. He was sent to Hiroshima along with the journalist Alexander Michie to deliver a letter to Itō Hirobumi on Li's behalf. Itō snubbed the two representatives by refusing to acknowledge the validity of their credentials or to have any dealings with them. They soon left Japan. A few weeks later, Zhang and Shao, high-ranking officials with diplomatic experience, led a second delegation. See S.C.M. Paine, *The Sino-Japanese War of 1894-1895*, Cambridge: Cambridge University Press, 2003, pp. 250-2.

[22] The reference is to Prince Kitashirakawa Yoshihisa (also known as Kitashirakawa no miya Yoshihisa Shinnō; 1847-95).

[23] This is another of Azembō's pen names.

[24] This song's lyrics refer to a wide spectrum of corruption scandals and apparent sell-outs by opposition politicians, such as Itagaki Taisuke. 'Takashima' refers to the scandal surrounding the slave-like conditions endured by coal miners at the Takashima mines and 'Matsukata' to the deflationary economic policy that worsened economic conditions for farmers.

[25] Maruhashi (or Marubashi) Chūya was a masterless samurai who attempted to reverse Tokugawa reforms by overthrowing the Shogun's government in the 1650s. The plot failed and he was executed.

[26] In the early twentieth century, the railway entrepreneur Amenomiya Keijirō aggressively invested in steam locomotives and tramways leading to accusations of monopolistic gouging of the public.

[27] Azembō does not provide a first name, but is probably referring to the entrepreneur, Furuya Tokubee (1878-1936). This clothier expanded his family business into a chain of modern department stores, including a major store in the Ginza district.

[28] The reference is to *tekiya*, a kind of minor huckster, peddler, and grifter who worked festivals, open-air markets, and other public gatherings. Azembō has more to say about them in later chapters.

[29] The reference is to a traditional hairstyle worn by unmarried women, brides, and geisha.

[30] The *gekkin* Chinese-style guitar was widely used in Japan. It had a short neck and silken strings. It is also known as the 'moon guitar,' because of a circular body that is over a foot in diameter.

[31] The British-American Tobacco Company or BAT flooded the overseas markets, particularly Japan and China, not only with cigarettes but also with offices, factories, and salesmen. Instead of trying to compete with BAT, the Japanese tobacco firm Murai entered into a partnership with it. Their brands, featuring Western imagery, were popular among urban Japanese. Another company, Iwaya, played up Japanese traditions with such brands as Tengu, which was named for the red-faced goblin of Japanese mythology. In 1904 the Meiji government took over the tobacco industry to protect it from BAT's infiltration, using tariffs and distribution restrictions to effectively close the archipelago to imports. An additional reason for making tobacco a state monopoly was to increase tax revenues for carrying out the Russo-Japanese War.

[32] The population figures in earlier lyrics notes 40 million compatriots, which is a figure probably closer to the actual size of Japan's population at the time.

[33] Azembō's propagandistic comment supporting the Emperor and the preceding poem, not by him but by his associate, is another nod toward the wartime censors. Such pro-state commentary appears to offset complaints expressed elsewhere about selfish politicians and the 'social problem' mentioned earlier in this chapter.

[34] This was the site of the Edo Execution Ground near Shinagawa in Tokyo along the old Tōkaidō road.

[35] The reference is to the Namamugi Incident of 1862 in the village of the same name located just off the old Tōkaidō road in today's Tsurumi Ward. Charles Lenox Richardson, a British merchant visiting Yokohama from Shanghai, was on horseback headed for a sightseeing trip to the Kawasaki-Daishi temple with three British companions. At Namamugi, they encountered a procession of Shimazu Hisamitsu, Lord of Satsuma, but failed to dismount when so ordered. Their perhaps unintended disrespect angered the Lord's retainers, who cut down Richardson and seriously wounded his companions. The incident led to the Anglo-Satsuma War, in which British warships bombarded Kagoshima in 1863. The conflict further weakened the Tokugawa government and convinced its opponents among *daimyo* domains of the need for military self-strengthening along Western lines.

Chapter Three

The Eastern Moral Reform Group [1]

Crisis at the Parental Home: The Lace Factory

It was the spring of 1898. Hisada Kiseki came to convince club members to relocate with him to the Kansai region. I was invited, too, but at the time could not put off making a trip back to my family home. I was called to return because a major problem had arisen, one that upon returning home left me utterly amazed. My younger brother, the dry goods dealer, had stolen my father's registered seal. He then used it in mortgaging most of the family's mountain land and fields as well as the paddies in the Roppon-matsu district. He used the money as collateral to borrow from the Kōyō Bank and an Odawara-based usurer. All of this suddenly became known because the repayment period was looming and my younger brother had gone into hiding. My elder brother was beside himself. All my mother could do was to weep constantly as she teetered on the edge of a breakdown.

I met with my father to sort out what had really happened. It turned out that my father had made up the story of the theft of the seal. He had concocted the tale on the spot when confronted by my elder brother. In reality, my father had secretly used the seal to secure loans for his youngest son. My elder brother, true to form, was easily fooled by the deception. Father sighed and said to me, 'You warned us, but I just couldn't turn him down. So I agreed to the first loan. After that, your elder brother Tatsu felt that we could not sacrifice what we had already leant by refusing to help with payments the next time we were asked. In the end we wound up in this terrible mess.'

It was heartrending for my father and eldest brother to be deceived so utterly by my cunning younger brother, Yoshigorō. There was no getting around it; they had now been saddled with debts that would be hard for someone living in the countryside to repay. Even if they paid the accumulated interest and extended the loan period, they could not avoid mortgaging all the remaining land and buildings to secure the reorganized debt. The outcome of the family conference was a decision to sell outright the land best suited for villas, the 'five or six mountaintop fields.' The rest they would let go as needed. This was the only way out.

Under normal circumstances, such land could be sold at the normal market price. But that did not apply in this case. My elder brother sketched out the parcel descriptions on several sheets for us. By way of explanation, he said, 'These sections face the Sagami coast and to the right you can see Mount Fuji and the Izu Peninsula. To the left you can clearly see the Miura Peninsula and the smoke rising from Ōshima Island. The place is cool in the summer and warm in winter.' This brother really knew how to turn a phrase to make things sound good. Of late, whenever I see a real estate company's ads, I recall this incident. My eldest brother was the grand originator of this kind of advertisement. Ha, ha! I took those sketches and ran about Tokyo and Yokohama trying to sell the properties. In Yokohama, I stayed at the Matsushima-ya in Hisakata-chō, talked with many people, and visited many of the famous sites. On rare occasions I went out in the evening to sing *enka*, but at the time my heart really wasn't in it.

It was during this period that I realized to my core why land brokers are called '*senmitsuya*' or 'liars.' Although *senmitsuya* are not supposed to be direct partners in the transaction nor party to the property, they immediately insinuate themselves into the deal. I thought I could sell the land easily, but it proved harder than expected.

While staying at the Matsushima-ya, I became acquainted with a fellow lodger, a fortuneteller by the name of Nukushina. He told me he was mentioned in Tokutomi Soho's journal, *The People's Friend or Kokumin no tomo.* [2] As we talked about this and that, we hit upon the idea of establishing a sailors' relief society. It would be an organization to provide aid, communication, and ways to improve the lives of those who live on the sea. I drafted a prospectus for the group and left it in the care of my younger brother Zenjiro to have Asakura, a teacher at the Oiso elementary school, look it over. We were on the verge of having it printed up, but various matters made us put it off. Despite all that, the 'Sailors' Relief Society' ended up being established.

Having to accompany brokers and people who wanted to see the land we were trying to sell provided me many chances to visit my parents and the home in which I had grown up. Every time I returned, my parents talked about me getting married. As for selling the land, we came within a hair's breadth of success many times, but each time the talks would fall through. It was a tough business.

Ikeda Tomiji, my elder brother-in-law in Yokohama, sympathized with my parents' situation and my having to run about trying to unload the property. He did all he could to make things convenient for me. His own line of work was artistic handicrafts, such as drawn work and lace, or, to make what he did more easily understandable, it might be best to call him a 'handkerchief merchant.' Many such merchants became established in Yokohama early on. They did not actually sell their own handkerchiefs but bought materials from trading houses and processed the plain stock by darning and embroidering it. The finished goods would then be exported to America. My brother-in-law had been in this business for a long while. He enjoyed extensive trade ties and owned branch factories. Here is a song he often sang at that time:

> To those who know not Yokohama's famous places
> Let me tell about a few notable spots
> There's the British Wharf and the Park
> And from Noge Hill
> A temple bell strikes out the time, *bon, bon*

This was a tune from the popular '*meisho-bushi*' ('songs of noted places').

My brother-in-law did not drink sake and, truth be told, was rather exacting in the life he lived. But he did love the *gidayu* ballad drama. It became a household custom to gather his entire family, right down to the children, to gesture and sing as they did their needlework.

His business went very well and it was just when he was considering extending it that he took my elder brother into the enterprise. He asked him to manage his branch factory. I took on the task of finding an instructor to train factory girls at our parents' house in Ōiso. At that time, everything looked perfectly successful. My elder brother went independent and began to make his mark on his own. He was even able to expand his operation to twenty-five or twenty-six branch workshops. His reputation for producing goods of superior quality later helped spread his name widely in America. In specifying an order a US wholesaler would even say, 'This order must go to the Soeda factory in Ōiso for finishing. No other will do.' The day before payday my elder brother would return home from Yokohama with his bag packed full of money to pay the workers. The enterprise greatly benefited our own and neighboring villages. Everyone was satisfied. Thanks to this success, my brother handled the problem of the family debt casually, saying, 'Don't fret, as long as we send the interest payment we're okay.' No one seemed to suffer a bit from the indebtedness.

My elder brother-in-law also recommended that I get married; not only that, he convinced my elder brother and mother to agree to the plan. He himself repeatedly came directly to Tokyo to sell me on the idea. In the end, I took a wife and we set up house in Honjō Banba-chō. It was the first time I had a place of my own. At the wedding ceremony, my elder brother-in-law served as ceremonial go-between. Ikeda Tomiji, Takeuchi Yōsaku, and my elder brother also attended. They totally forgot about the problem of the family debt as they talked excitedly about the lace factory.

The Dissolution of the Liberal Party

Meanwhile, in the political world, our gang of senior statesmen spent their days treating government as if it were their personal property. Day in and day out, they scrambled to turn every little problem into an opportunity to hijack the cabinet or to hijack it back after it had been taken away. In August 1896, Kuroda Kiyotaka followed Itō Hirobumi as Prime Minister while holding a second cabinet post. In September, Matsukata Masayoshi became the Prime Minister, but early in 1897 the Kuroda Cabinet came back in. Then in January 1898, Ito Hirobumi was passed over for the Premiership as the Liberal Party and the Progressive Party cooperated to form the Ōkuma government. Before we had time to become accustomed to the shift, the Yamagata cabinet took over. In 1900, it was Itō again, but before this latest cabinet took shape, Itō became head of the Seiyūkai, his Society of Political Friends, in September. This group was a new incarnation of the Liberal Party. In the popular expression of the day, the Liberal Party had 'dissolved.' We could only look on and be flabbergasted by all these changes.

The New Political Party

Ask not what you can do for your country; ask what you can do for you
And so doing the political parties run toward self-interest
They make a grand appeal
Our aim: to reform constitutional government to perfection's point
And so the Marquis stands out in his aqua blue finery [3]
Ready now to face the harsh winds
And like clouds amassing
The political leaders gather all in a swarm
This is it!
This is the Seiyūkai, the Constitutional Society of Political Friends!
It holds a majority in the Lower House
A position of power unrivaled
It appears invincible
But seen from inside
What an infinite jumble of wheat and chaff
Of precious jade and worthless pebbles
You have the high-collar types and the entrepreneurs
You have the Satsuma faction, the Progressive faction, the Imperial faction
The malady is too far gone for remedy
And the Liberal Party faction
It is agreed that its man will lead
The struggle is as if over a prize piece of carrion
When the meat is in one mouth

79

Ever-present the fear
That others in the pack will nip one another in the frenzy to steal it
away
Illustrations of the evil are not far to seek
Consider the rise and fall of the Constitutional Party, our Kensei-tō
And the question arises: why should we go without our mouthful?
But he fears not, laments not
Our grand old man has dyed his side-locks
He is re-risen and with heart determined
The Marquis is ready to display his mighty skills
Dance of joy, dance of joy, dance of joy, delightful, delightful
(Yokoe Tesseki)

The World of Politics

The aristocracy is in high spirits
The Diet again and again ordered adjourned
That commotion in the Fifteenth Session
The Lower House despite its twenty-seven vote majority
Failed splendidly to maintain a vote of confidence
The resolution bill also failed to pass
A heavy load was lifted; done, done
The Marquis could stretch his legs and loosen his back muscles
Now, the stress is gone
He could now become giddy on brandy
Atop a lap dyed in *yūzen* scarlet
He could pillow his head and visit the land of sweet dreams
But before such repose
Foreign affairs bustled onto the stage
The Manchurian-Korean problem
The Russians and Qing Chinese and their secret pact like pesky
mosquitoes
Truly like swarming mayflies is the immense roar of the political
world
No, it is not easy to be a politician
One ought not cloud the nation's light
One ought not give up the nation's interests
He is truly a great Marquis

This holder of the Grand Order of the Chrysanthemum
Now his time has come
To brandish the skills
To slice through instantly that Gordian knot
Twelve new divisions for the Army
In a sweeping gesture make those 300,000 tons
Of new warships appear floating on the ocean
The people's flesh, the people's blood
Tax increase, tax increase, again tax increase
If for the sake of the nation, the increase should be a matter of course
Yet, do not betray such sincere loyalty
Heed the cries of the party of national unity
Hear the voice of the people
The nation is the nation of government
The sovereign's country is the country of the people
Our national prestige expands outward
Over the four directions throughout our islands
Do not make merry over spring blossoms
With all your heart consider our nation's benefit
Dance of joy, dance of joy, dance of joy, delightful, delightful
(Yokoe Tesseki)

The North China Incident brought forth a variety of *kinmai-bushi enka* such as 'The Fall of Taiko,' 'The Occupation of Tianjian,' and 'The Death Defying Messenger.' The 'Charging Warrior' was also popular as this new form of *enka*, the *tsūkai-bushi* or 'thrill song,' emerged. [4]

It was around this time, before and after the Salvation Army's campaign to emancipate prostitutes and eradicate that business, that the 'Strike Song' became popular. In Kumamoto, prostitutes at the Shinonome-rō brothel went on strike and the house's flowery name was borrowed to identify yet another style of *enka*, '*Shinonome-bushi*' or 'Shinonome songs.' (The year before last during my pilgrimage in Kyushu, I took a side trip to visit the Shinonome-rō. The story of the strike has become a kind of traditional tale and it is difficult to ferret out what really happened. [5] As the young Satsuki, my son, has done research on this, I will abbreviate mention of it here.) Here are a few lyrics that remain:

81

The Shinonome Song

On Gion Hill two trees can be seen
Now what's all this?
Money and the Nakajima house in hock
Shinonome Strike
Well, that's hard to say
But you did say something like that, didn't you?

Generally, the Shinonome songs took old ditties with representative refrains such as, 'Don't mope about life in the brothel. Look to the flowing stream and live your life like that.' I collaborated with Yokoe Tesseki in rearranging the words into a parody. The opening phrases caught on and were sung over and over again.

Prostitution emancipation
At this point freed from the brothel
But what happens now?
No place to go so become a rag picker
I don't get this strike
Now that's hard, isn't it?
But you did say something like that, didn't you?

The loan shark, too, if you have the money
But what's up with this now?
Rich politicians of wide repute
Strike, "I don't know" [6]
Now that's hard, isn't it?
But you did say something like that, didn't you?

Hoshi was stabbed but got his thousands
And what's with this?
His repute was trimmed a bit
Taking bribes, enjoying kickbacks

Now that's hard, isn't it?
But you did say something like that, didn't you?

Cooking the books on the public works

And what's with this?
Making a pillow of the geisha's lap
Taking bribes, enjoying kickbacks
Now that's hard, isn't it?
But you did say something like that, didn't you?
(Tesseki and Azembō)

The Thrill Song

Itō and company's twelve new army divisions are not just for show
And those 300,000 tons of new warships
Like Momotarō who carefully prepared his stores to defeat the ogres
We are now ready and can go as far as the islands of the goblins
Magnificent determination rids us of the Shinonome brothel
A strike in our new constitutional society
The spineless, the sea slugs and jellyfish
Sly badger dogs, entertainers, flatterers

Chasing pigs is forbidden
And don't drink too much or pick fights
Of course, that's the prerogative of Germany and Russia
But what a fuss they'll raise when we catch a pig of our own [7]

In this world where there are schools for geisha
We should be able to make schools for actors
And if we can make schools for whores
We can make reading nasal hairs a part of the higher school
curriculum
(Azembō)

Graft was everywhere. Hoshi Tōru had been exposed for taking bribes involving the Osaka Stock Exchange. He was the representative 'Rikken-ya' or on-the-make corrupt politician of the time, a term that played on the same 'Rikken' as in 'constitutional rights.' The next year, 1901, he was stabbed to death. Everything was money and after that, money. Constancy or principles counted for absolutely nothing. In general, this was the trend at the top and bottom of society. We had already lost even the slightest bit of interest in the direction that politics might take. With the exception of people who intended to become involved in *sōshi* drama, those who called themselves political activists were gradually moving toward extinction. Many '*enka*' players took to the road to travel about and live individually in rented rooms. Few were left living together as members of the Seinen Club and the group soon went into decline.

The Club's Extinction

Before the North China Incident, Tonoe Suikyō joined the *Jōshū Shinpō* newspaper and went off to Maebashi. On the day he departed, I saw him off at Ueno Station. He said, 'Hey, this is nothing. I'll be back before you know it. I will write songs and send them from Maebashi.' This is what he said, but the songs never arrived.

At that time, the student and *enka* singer Kitabayashi and I rented a room in Nishiki-chō. The main reason for the move is that I had come to hate the air of decline created by the vicious *sōshi*. Only a few members remained in the failing club, the malignantly violent activists and our group of *enka* singers. Of course, the two could not get along. As ever, the wicked attract the wicked and it got to the point that complete strangers were coming in and out of the place. After we left we seldom stopped by the club, but I heard that our old housemother came to complain that the only people who came in or hung about were '*goronbo*' ruffian types who caused nothing but trouble.

These bullyboy *sōshi* often would go to eating and drinking places and carry out '*kipparai*.' The term came from an expression used in the National Assembly when a 'bill' was proposed to cut the budget. It soon began to be used widely among the *sōshi* toughs. By doing '*kipparai*' they meant that they would pay only part of the bill for their entertainment, drinks, and food and would stiff the establishment for the rest. They would declare a *kipparai* 'assessment.' Of course, it did not end there. They sometimes refused to pay anything at all for their fun and fare. If you said you were strapped and couldn't go when invited to go drinking with friends, they would respond, 'No problem, just do a *kipparai*.'

The practice caused problems for the neighborhood, sparked drunken brawling, and in the end saw the police running off the *sōshi*. Although our housemother and her people at the Seinen Club were only nominally involved with these miscreants, they were the Club's registered responsible

84

parties and by this organizational tie found themselves pulled into difficulties. After a time, the Club became a forlorn place and was finally dissolved. That happened in 1901.

The years before and after the North China Incident make up a gloomy, disagreeable period for me. I think of Mrs. Itō and our long and close ties. Her husband, Yasu'ichi, went into the patent medicine business and had to peddle his wares in countryside provinces. There were all kinds of medicines. The only one that remains in my memory is Beltz Pills. The Itō family had sympathized with the spirit of the Club's political activists and had offered up their home only to see the bullies turn it into a hotbed of trouble. When I joined the Seinen Club, the Itōs' son, Gi'ichirō, was a student who commuted to an engineering school in Tsukiji. Around this time, a new electric railroad company was established in Kawasaki (one that ran a line to Daishi) and the son found a job with the firm and moved to Kawasaki. Oba-san and the other family members wound up going there, too. Of course, they were all taken in by their son. I should think it was a natural and happy outcome for them. Yet, many members of Club could not help thinking that they had been driven to ruin.

And what has happened to all the senior members of the club? Where have they gone? How have they fared? Hisada Kiseki went to Osaka with Eguchi, Katō and Suzuki. Not long after his move, he composed '*Naniwa-daika*,' 'Famous Flowers of Kobe and Hyogo,' ('Kobe Hyogo meishō no hana) a song about famous places in this part of the Kansai region) and sang *enka*. I have not had news about him since then. I did see him in Shimonoseki later after he had gone into educational work. Eguchi stayed on in Osaka and became a petty grifter. Later, Suzuki came back to Tokyo and became a boss of small-time swindlers. Akae Kinjurō and his elder brother Akae Kageaki tried to make something of themselves. They were always laughing and people liked them. I wonder what finally became of them.

From start to finish during his career in the Diet, Tanaka Shōzō took up the problem of mining pollution. He roared on about that for twenty years. During one of the legislative sessions he pointed to the Minister of Justice Yoshikawa and cried, 'What kind of beast is this!' He whipped up all manner of problems. I came across him as an old man who still wore the samurai-style topknot when I visited Kinoshita Naoe's home in Mikawashima. [8] At the time, the old gentleman talked about religious matters from the standpoint of a lay amateur. Naoe said it is precisely because he is an amateur that we

85

should listen to his views. About a year after that Tanaka was given a grand funeral in Yanaka village.

There were great men. There were drunks. And there were eccentrics. Yokota was a fellow, an expert at judo, who made his way from Osaka along the Tōkaidō by successfully challenging rivals to matches at various judo schools along the way. He was a giant of a man. He later joined the 'Oh what to do' or 'doo sure-ren' romantic singers. His preference for wearing nothing but silk kimono on that strongly built body made him look a little odd. He was reputed to have gotten into a showdown at Kudan with thirty rival members of that same '*doo sure ren*' group and to have returned home uninjured. He went out selling songs, but he was just terribly bad at *enka*. He had a special art of eating like a boa constrictor. When he had money, he ate everything in sight and then for two or three days thereafter would be content to refrain from feeding.

I recall an exchange that went like this:

'That guy Yokota, today's the third day and he hasn't had a thing to eat. What's with him?'

'Late last night after everybody was fast asleep he went down to the kitchen and filled himself up with water.'

Tomihari started the *Keihin Shinbun* newspaper in Yokohama. Sō went on to the school for railway workers and became a stationmaster somewhere. Itō Yūjiro kept one jump ahead of the law. From Korea and China he went to the South Seas. He stayed in the South Pacific for twenty years and is now a pioneer in the southward expansion movement. [9]

Ushioda Setsuji, using the name Tsukioka Kiyoshi, became a leader of a troop of new school actors that toured around performing in regional provinces. Katō, Yoshimura, Nakano Nobuchika, and Kuboto Rokumaru (the fellow called the 'bulwark') all moved from performing *sōshi* plays to become actors in '*shinpa*' new school theater. I have lost track of many of them.

Among them all, one who really makes me wonder is Yokoe Tesseki. Someone who had such talent, where did he go? What happened to him? He was a great drinker. If he had sake to drink, he had no other human desire. He was composed, even tempered, and on a par with Tonoe Suikyō. Perhaps he ruined his health with drink. That is entirely possible given his tastes. But I do not know and have not had any news about him.

Home and the *Nihachi Shinpō* Newspaper

My life, precarious and wandering, was clearly a source of suffering for my parents, siblings, and relatives. As making a living performing *enka* was not something that could reasonably be understood from the standpoint of 'commonsense,' I did not strain myself to make them understand. They nonetheless maintained that it was not good that I be left single. Thereupon, they determined that I should have a wife, impart some shape to my personal life, and settle down. [10] Yes, my family and people around me who loved to look after others, stirred by their sense of duty, set out to change me for the better. I had lived to be thirty years old. There is a saying, 'the thirties are the years to become established.' I thought that the expression made sense and agreed with it. I came to have a family. Well, perhaps rather than 'came to have,' I should say, 'was made to have.'

I put up several signs in front of the house in Kotō Banba-chō in Tokyo. One read '*Airyūsha*' or 'Love of Willows' and this was what I dubbed my house. Another read 'Home and Personal Belongings Covered by the Disaster and Fire Insurance Company Agency.' Only two houses, my uncle's and his friend's, were covered by the insurance, but the signboard remained anyway. Still another sign read, 'Publishing Office of the *Nihachi Shinpō*.' This was the industry newspaper for soba noodle shops and my friend Asai Kintarō and I jointly ran it.

The Asai family lived at 17 Asakusa, Fukutomi-chō in a turning just beyond the famous Momotarō Sweets shop where, once again, all kinds of signs were hoisted. His father was the *oyabun* boss of a group of noodle cooks, a kind of employment agency exclusively in that line that had started up in 1884. Originally, the old man was a famous policeman in the old Edo district of Hatchōbori.

The house was built with sturdy, thick latticework on the outside walls. On the second floor there were always twenty-seven or twenty-eight noodle cooks idling away the time. On the first floor toward the front, Asai and I made a drawing room to serve as the newspaper's editorial office.

87

Sometimes we would overhear conversations from across the counter that went: 'Alright, one cook for the something-something noodle shop' or 'Okay a delivery guy and cook to the Yabusoba noodle shop in Kuramae.' Cooks worked in the order that job requests came in. Some worked at a place for two or three days; others returned from a job even before a full day was out. Upon return, they just lolled about on the second floor *tatami* mats. That was what was usual for noodle cooks.

Indeed, they had many nasty habits that cried out for fixing. The correcting came to be our mission at the *Nihachi Shinpō*. I wrote encouraging articles about the cook who stayed employed at the same place continuously for six months and about the one who received an award or earned a citation of merit. Asai told me these kinds of occurrences were extremely rare.

Asai's friend, Ishimaru Motoji and Ishimaru's elderly mother moved into a back room of our house and we began sharing living quarters. Both Ishimaru and Asai were true children of Edo. Ishimaru was a leather bag artisan who got too deeply involved in debauchery and suffered repeated business failures. He tried to rebound by taking discarded leather bicycle saddles and fixing them by reworking the leather by hand. The business boomed and he became an instant success. He made a lot of money. Until Ishimaru originated the replacement cover, a saddle seat that developed a crack had to be totally discarded.

My wife hailed from Hishinuma in Kōza-gun. Her maiden name was Ōta, first name Takeko. She was a younger sister of Ōta Denjirō. Although she had a seamstress certificate she had never used it before coming to me as my bride. She was quite proper in deportment. Whenever I left for the day she saw me off at the entryway and politely said, 'Hurry ...', sweetly abbreviating the customary 'Hurry home soon.' She was a good wife.

One day, just when Masao, a young friend of the family, was playing the accordion, Suzuki Ichirō, a member of Seinen Club, stopped by for a visit. All of a sudden he said praisingly, 'My, what a wonderful family.' And looking again in Masao's direction added, 'Music is something refined. It calms the spirit.' Suzuki had a rough character, but that day he acted deferentially to my wife and didn't talk much. The only thing he said was that he had recently started going to the Unitarian Church. Shortly afterwards he went home. Our household was close and lively. Peace reigned supreme beneath our roof.

I had kept my distance from my uncle for years, but at last took my wife to meet him. His eldest daughter, Hana-chan, also came over to play at our place. When she suddenly stopped coming around, I thought things were a little odd. Later I found out the whole thing stemmed from my writing 'A Humorous Tale: The Hussy,' for the *Nihachi Shinpō*. The story line went like this: an uneducated mother creates a spoiled 'hussy' by devoting her daughter to the entertainment arts instead of giving her an education. It was an attempt to satirize what I saw as one of the evils of that time.

On being urged to 'Hurry up and get ready or you will be late for school,' Hana-chan would whiningly answer, 'Mom, let me miss school today.' And her mother would always respond, 'Oh, alright, but don't miss your dance practice.' In the newspaper story I recreated the give-and-take of the mother-daughter conversation with Hana-chan getting the worst of it. The real life Hana-chan reported the story to her uneducated mother telling her that there was no mistaking that I had intentionally written about her. I had not written the piece to offend her, but she took it in a completely wrong way.

My wife told me that Hana-chan had just willfully misunderstood and gotten angry and that there was no need for an apology from our side. She counseled me to just leave it be. I felt the same way. My wife was an exceptionally clear-headed woman.

A woman who came to be known as the 'the Hachioji Oba-san' frequented our house. She was a relative of an elder brother-in-law, Ogawa Kanekichi (a ship's smith) who lived in Yokohama. She took an old woman's job of accepting items on consignment from a dry goods wholesaler and peddling these from place to place. She said we could pay later and left rolls of cloth with us. In a snap, my wife accepted whatever the old woman recommended. She put my wardrobe in good order and my outward demeanor now looked as if I came from a wealthy family. The inside truth was that I was hard pressed. Neither my wife nor I were accustomed to running a household. Indeed, there was no reason to have expected that we would know anything about it.

It was around this time that I began experiencing chronically stiff shoulders. I often asked Masao to massage them for me. 'Masa-chan, how about patting my shoulders a little? I'll give you tobacco money.' He would answer that he did not need money for tobacco, but a little for a snack of roasted peas would be nice. He then massaged my shoulders. At the time, two *sen* would buy an overflowing bowl of the beans, enough for a day's allotment, and I bought that much every day. The snack was there for anyone who stretched out a hand, but Masao said, 'This won't do. Every time Nakamaru-san dips in his big paws the level of peas in the bowl dips to nothing.' A big man has big hands so Masao feared that all would be caught up in one dip into the bowl.

The end of the year grew near. My wife granted herself little time off from her sewing piecework. Even late New Year's Eve she called out to Ishimaru-san with whom she competed on the opposite side of a paper *shoji* screen. 'Aren't you getting sleepy?' 'No, still fine here.' And with this kind of repartee, they worked through the night. As darkness began to give way to dawn, I went with Ishimaru to the year-end fair at Ryōgoku to buy a decoration to celebrate the new year.

The *Shinpa* 'New School,' the Dim Rickshaw Man, and a Scattering of Snow

I recall something strange that happened just before the new year. My younger bother Zenjirō's school went on holiday and he returned to the countryside. When he went around to his relatives everybody gave him gifts. He received *mochi* rice cakes, sweet potatoes, *miso* bean paste, and the like. He got so many rice cakes one after another that they soon began to add up to quite a heavy and bulky load. In the end he had too many to easily carry so being a good and faithful lad he cut a live sapling to make a carrying pole. He was thus able to shoulder the load and set out on his return. When the stick broke along the way he simply changed it for a new one. I recall his sigh of relief on arriving back after putting down his load carried on a tree branch that he had stripped to make a carrying pole. In those days, regardless if one was commuting to school or somewhere else, no one used a vehicle. All the same, we were amazed when he returned, his step still light, after bearing a load as heavy as any that a farmer might carry home from the fields.

All was going well at home, with the exception of one of my fellow singers and housemate, Wakaba Torajirō. His nasty character made everyone dislike him. His *enka* singing was not too promising, either. I tended not to be overly picky, but in the end even I had to tell him he could no longer stay. On

90

leaving the house, he went directly to a police box to file a complaint. It was just like him to be such a sticky, unpleasant fellow.

Around this time, my young friend and apprentice singer Takahashi Sumao was taken with a new project directed by the chief of the Tokiwaza troupe of players, Mizuno Yoshime. Mizuno wrote and produced plays called '*Shōrei-kai*' in the style of *shinpa* new school drama. Lots of stars took parts. Okamoto Sadajirō played a villain and Kojima Bunei and Kawai Takeo were the male actors who played female roles. In addition, Nakano Nobuchika, Satō Saizō, Shibata Zentarō, Aoyagi Sutejirō, and Fukui Mōhei also had parts. Among them, Echigo Genjirō played a farcical role. He became overwhelmingly popular for his comedic talents and his chubby face that always looked like a pug trying to sneeze. His acting was very humorous, too. Takahashi was totally absorbed and wanted beyond all else to become just that kind of comedic actor. I asked Echigo to take him on and he began frequenting Echigo's place. Of course, Takahashi was not to receive any cash or other compensation. To make ends meet he earned money at night by roaming around singing *enka*. [12] He dressed in a hugely oversized splashed-pattern *haori* half-coat and wore the straw sandals favored by students. But where the students usually had footwear with white thongs his were bright red. He was quite satisfied with his get-up. My wife got a good laugh out of it, too.

Nakano Nobuchika had already achieved a degree of popularity. Among *sōshi* activists, he was renowned for pouring heart and soul into his plays. He treated drama as a tool for enlightening the masses. But once Nakano got into it, things apparently did not always go as expected. (*Sōshi* holdouts whispered among themselves that Nakano, after all, was going to become just another actor.) Using the name 'Tsukioka Kiyoshi' Ushioda Setsuji joined Nakano in becoming a *shinpa* actor. [12]

In the Seinen Club days, Ushioda and his group often went to watch the activists' plays. Sometimes the sense of fellowship based on shared *sōshi-bushi* and *sōshi* drama experiences enabled them to get into the performances for free. They drank sake and returned to the club through the nighttime snowfall. Swept up in the drama and the drink they would sometimes carry on for a while and not come indoors. They would pick lines from the play and say, 'And then he would appear like this,' and fool around replaying the play for a while.

From time to time I would also take in a performance at the Tokiwaza. One time I went out only to be immediately set upon and followed by a dimwitted rickshaw man. He rubbed his shoulder and said, 'Well Sir, let's go' as he tenaciously followed me everywhere I went. Ido Takuei was a Buddhist priest and Seinen Club member. Around that time he became a job broker. He had long hair and when followed relentlessly by a rickshaw puller he would wheel on his feet and scream 'Idiot!' That was his patented method for repulsing the rickshaw puller's attack.

On the other hand, there was Nakamaru Teizō, a sluggish giant known for his taciturn personality and constantly maintained air of moody silence. If accosted by a rickshaw puller's appeal of 'Boss, let's go!' he simply maintained his silence and kept walking. If the rickshaw man persisted in following and importuning, 'Let's go, Master,' he would haltingly answer, 'You are always free to go. So go.' And having made that simple statement would continue walking.

Shortly after the dawning of the new year, news broke about the disaster of the Aomori Fifth Regiment. During a march in the snow on Mount Hakkoda an entire company had frozen to death. I immediately composed the song, 'A Scattering of Snow,' and published it under the name of '*Tōkai kyōfu dan*' (or the 'Tōkai Society for Moral Reform'). Sales were extraordinarily strong. Reprint followed reprint as sales soared. I thought it was a pity to rely on just a couple of distributors when sales were so good.

At this point, Nakamaru recommended selling my song booklets through a bookstore. He had worked at selling printed material and books for a long while and was well informed about that world. I printed the original verses of 'A Scattering of Snow' on high-quality paper. I also used color in printing a cover and took the finished product to be sold at a bookstore. During the Seinen Club era, *enka* song sheets were typically printed on rough, low-quality paper. At the end of the month, I was surprised to hear Nakamaru's report from the bookstore. Virtually no copies were left. Send more, send more! Although the songbook 'The Snowy March' by Ochiai Naofumi and Ōwada Takeki directly competed with 'Scattering,' that work did not sell as well as mine. [13] One reason for this was that my work carried a low wholesale cost. The bookstore handling it perhaps used this to market the song subtly and advantageously. In any case, Nakamura became swept up in this success and even made a receipt book to use in his visits to bookstores.

I only went out a time or two to collect money from sales of the very successful 'A Scattering of Snow.' One day Nakamaru went out to collect the tobacco advertisement rates for *Nihachi Shinpō* ads for White Peony tobacco, produced by Chiba Matsubee (a man known as the tobacco king and also called the 'tengu' or long-nosed goblin of tobacco.) Nakamura left with the receipt books and never came back.

A Son and Chigasaki

My wife was soon to have a baby. Ishimaru's mother agreed to help prepare for the delivery by explaining with all kinds of examples drawn from real life. She also kindly helped by doing extra cooking in anticipation of the event. I wrote to the family back home to let them know.

As giving birth is an important task for a woman, the two of them discussed how my wife's mother would of course come for the event. We even thought that perhaps both of our mothers would be there together and looked forward to the prospect. Yet, when the time for the delivery had shrunk to less than a week or so my wife's mother betrayed our expectations. Only my mother showed up. The first thing she did was to explain why my mother-in-law failed to come to Tokyo.

My wife's mother's heart had leapt at the prospect of coming and there was no doubt that she wanted to be with us. Nevertheless, my mother said that something had happened back home and it was just impossible for the Hishinuma relatives to leave at this time. In short, my wife's elder brother had been swindled and fallen into debt. Ikeda, my elder brother-in-law, and others were now doing everything they could to deal with the problem and find some way to resolve it. My father-in-law in Hishinuma was a timid man without much capacity to handle the matter so now the family had been thrown into a thoroughly confused state.

My mother worked at cooking, sewing, and preparations needed for after the baby's birth. One day as the midwife was preparing to leave after her visit, she told mother and I that the baby would arrive before the night was out. My mother and I began to get restless. Over supper we talked about how the delivery would probably not happen until far into the night after all. My mother sat by my pregnant wife's pillow. I attended to straightening up the house and then left to bathe at the local bathhouse.

Try as I might I could not quietly enjoy a good soaking in the hot water. I hurried back home. Throwing open the *shoji* sliding screen I found my mother sitting in the middle of the *tatami* room. She turned to me and said, 'She gave birth. A boy.' She held the baby then now handed it to me. My mother's face beamed with happiness as tears came to her eyes.

I quietly took my baby. Held him. Embraced him gently. For a while I gazed into his face.

After giving birth, my wife did not feel the strain of that experience so much as the pain of rheumatism she had suffered in the past. She often patted her knees to relieve her discomfort. During her recuperation from the pregnancy, her knees began to swell a little so she remained in bed. As expected, her milk was insufficient. I had watched as the midwife gave the baby its first bath. I took on the important task of giving the baby its milk and then bathing it. The baby grew healthy and strong.

We named him 'Tomomichi' and made an official report of his birth ten days after he was delivered. Sumao, my apprentice, held the baby with a smiling face, one that resembled Ebisu, the god of wealth. At times he rocked him gently in his arms as he paced around the house singing:

> I will present you with two birds
> I won't need the burden
> A fleet-footed messenger will bring them to you
> I will present you with three birds
> I won't need sake to drink

and similar lyrics. The lines were new to me and it seems that they were lullabies from Kyushu. My mother, assured that all was well, returned to the countryside. Hana-chan, my niece who had ceased coming around, now came by to offer her congratulations on the baby's birth and to look in on my ailing wife. She also told us how my uncle had given up his job as a ship's engineer in favor of working as an engineer and foreman for Onagigawa's nail-making plant in Yasuda. Later, the Yasuda plant took in workers and gave them lots of work on a piece-rate basis. The laborers could earn two or three times the wages normally paid elsewhere and were happy to work there. But their mass production exceeded demand so much so that no nails were needed for several years to follow. As a result, all the employees were sacked and the plant closed. The owner made a huge profit. I would call this profiteering. The employees were dazed by what had happened. One of them, a fellow named 'Shige' was a friend to both Ishimaru and me. My uncle again changed jobs, this time moving to a flourmill.

My wife became able to get out of bed and felt well enough to walk around a bit. She once again went to the public bath, but was afraid to bathe the baby there. In the end she entrusted that responsibility entirely to me. [14] The Hachioji Oba-san came by to offer her congratulations with a gift of a half a skein of pongee silk. Heretofore, each and every time the Oba-san visited, my wife had managed to pay an installment for the cloth she had used. This time she did not have the money. The best she could do was to offer carfare and an apology. I thought a wife who could come up with an excuse to avoid paying a bill was truly a full-fledged wife, one who was becoming accustomed to the ways of the world. She had certainly become habituated to the difficulties of our hard life. I also began to consider what I might somehow do to make up for our insufficient income. I realized that we had to begin living a life of strict economy. If we intended to raise a child, I had to cut the quality of the tobacco I smoked in favor of a cheaper brand. I was born into a farm family, but from an early age my character was such that I was as spoiled as a little aristocrat. And I was lazy. When it came to food and other items I was also more extravagant than my peers. On becoming a father, I realized that I must completely reform such habits and become a reliable man.

My elder brother's factory grew ever more prosperous. He was especially keen on opening a new factory in Chigasaki and rounded up workers to that end. Before my wife earned her sewing certificate, she had done lacework. So when my elder brother in Ōiso opened the Chigasaki factory, he recruited her as one of the factory's women workers.

My elder brother-in-law often came up to Tokyo to visit his younger brother who ran a drapers business in Higashi-Ryōgoku and to call on his son, Masao, who now lived in the city. He wanted to talk over expanding the business in Chigasaki with a mind to letting me manage things there. But as he was well aware of my personality and my past, he avoided broaching the subject directly. He instead opted to mention the idea privately to my wife and have her discuss the prospect with me.

As I now had a child, I should rouse myself, first and foremost, to take on that factory, and make it prosper just as my elder brother had done with his business. I considered doing just this. But in the back of my mind,

I was struggling with all kinds of demons and could not easily come to a decision. Asai, a local neighborhood boss, who had never before visited me at my home now called. I knew immediately that something had happened. He explained, 'Kintarō hasn't shown up for the last three days. He has a debt and the repayment period has expired. Now the lender is pressing to be repaid. The guy is a loan shark, a not very nice loan shark.' Kintarō was Mr. Asai's son and he wanted to talk to me about acting as a go-between to handle the matter of his son's debt. We reached an agreement that very night and I went with the boss to Hirokoji in Ryōgoku to have a drink to seal the deal. It was there that the senior Asai told me tales of his days on the Shogun's police force. Afterwards, I returned home in high spirits. He soon learned where his son was living and he was able come to terms with him about the debt. But as he had to take on the son's loan, Kintarō became a liability and it became inconvenient to have him around.

I faced money problems of my own that caused the management of the *Nihachi Shipō* to suffer. Within less than a year we faced the sad reality that it must cease publication.

I was genuinely interested in going to work at the factory and gave up our first home in Banba-chō. Ishimaru moved somewhere and Sumao took his *enka* and left for the road. The day we left Banba, we gave a large bundle of goods that we would leave behind to Hana-chan and a potted mulberry bush to my uncle. Years later, that mulberry continued to thrive as a large tree in my uncle's garden.

We first went to Yokohama. If I was going to run a factory, I first had to master the basics of the job. I sought to accomplish that by stopping in at Ikeda's factory. He arranged our housing and we stayed there for forty days. We then moved to Chigasaki. It was the end of winter, 1903. Our new house was located in the front corner of an old building that had been a steamed bun store called 'Kamanari-ya' that stood in front of a railway station. Next door was a cheap inn called 'Sakana-ya' where several train conductors stayed on a rotating basis.

Many people turned out to celebrate the opening day of our new enterprise. Chigasaki's one and only geisha was summoned. A shrine priest, Sugizaki Nabenoshin, who was to work for the factory, sang local songs as he bobbed his head back and forth. Our hope was rekindled.

One morning I was still asleep in bed when I heard a rapping at the door. I arose to find my father from Ōiso. I blew out the paper lantern

96

that was still lit because dawn had yet to fully arrive. My father had made a beautiful wood and metal sink stand for us and had hauled it all the way to our house. I will never forget that image. Afterwards, my father remained at our still disordered place and moved about inside fixing this and that to help put things in order. My father-in-law from Hishinuma also came over. He sat by the fireside cheerfully drinking tea. Anyway, one and all gave us their cheerful support. All who had witnessed how Ikeda and of my elder brother in Ōiso had succeeded expected that I would of course succeed, too.

Despite their rosy outlook, things did not go well. We were able to secure about twenty workers, but found it impossible to find more than that no matter how hard we tried. From long before this time, Chigasaki had been a site for woodworking. Wages were better at our place, but the woodworking shops paid day wages. People who worked there were mostly the children of fishing families and the fishermen wanted day wages no matter what. We customarily paid wages on the last day of the month. I would go to Yokohama, collect the money, return, and pay it out. But employees did not want to wait. On this point, the situation was completely different from what held in Ōiso where the workers who had been brought into the factory were farmers' children. It was a fatal miscalculation.

Making matters worse was the problem of the poor quality of the workers. Of the twenty hands only three proved satisfactory. The skills of the others failed to improve. It required a lot of time and trouble to deal with these workers and the instructors found it hard to make any headway in increasing efficiency. A father of one of the workers was a rice dealer and we purchased our grain from him as well as commissioning him to provide meals and other services. Of the workers, he commented, 'Well, all you should be giving them is salt! They aren't worth much more than that.'

My niece, Oshin from Ogawa, came along to look after the baby. By the time she arrived, our new son was already able to sit in a baby carriage and play with a pinwheel. He always napped under the eaves in the shady corridor between the Sakana-ya and our house. I would sometimes peek in the carriage to find the pinwheel spinning.

Whenever the train conductors arrived to change shifts and take a rest at Sakana-ya they invariably looked in the perambulator and played a bit with the baby It was something I didn't think much about at the time. But one day I heard one of the maids at the inn shriek, 'Kanō-san, Not really!'

97

and looked out from out the side window to see someone in the uniform of a conductor, but someone who looked quite different from the others. Still, it was a face that resembled someone I knew.

'Hey, aren't you Kanō-kun?' Turning toward me full face I could see that he was in fact none other than Kanō Katsukiyo. I had not heard a thing about him since he had followed Hisada Kiseki and had gone off to Osaka. Now he had become a train conductor. He exclaimed, 'What the ... so this is your kid?!', as he dipped his head into the carriage and roared with laughter. Thereafter, he often dropped by with a gift of Kobe beef.

Kawakami's drama troupe visited. Tsukioka Kiyoshi's came, too. His wife took charge of wardrobe. The troupe suffered a string of setbacks that finally forced it to dissolve. The Tsukiokas, husband and wife, then came to stay with us. Somehow, rice was terrible at that time. It was being adulterated by mixing in Nanking rice, the cheaper grain imported from China. After eating rice prepared with a hefty portion of Nanking grain, the couple decided to return to Tokyo.

My work often caused me to go back and forth from Yokohama. Sugizaki Nabenoshin often went along. In the past he had composed haiku so we were able to talk about that while on the road. Soon I was writing haiku for the first time and had been admitted to a circle of haiku poets. Our circle invited Tochimandō Koyō to join us. He had written a scroll that contained the line: 'Pine shadows and the moon on the darkened folding screen.' As I did not think Ozaki Koyō or Tochimando Koyo were particularly great, the line did not leave much of an impression. [15]

In a half a year, I was finally forced to close my factory. We moved to one room of my wife's house at Hishinuma. My wife took a job at a school to teach sewing and accepted trainees at home. I departed on my own to travel around the Kansai region.

Notes

[1] The title for this chapter refers to Azembō's song, 'A Scattering of Snow.' The ballad tells the story of an incident in which poorly equipped troops on maneuvers died in a snowstorm. Nevertheless, the specific 'association,' refers more to Azembō's largely individual and largely unorganized crusade to organize and reform the *enka* songwriting and singing profession. In this chapter, Azembō writes of several groups that were both concerned with moral improvement (for example, the Sailors' Relief Association) and that experienced a loss of moral respectability (the Seinen Club and political parties), but these are the general contextual problems needing improvement that are background for his lackadaisical approach to the 'Eastern moral reform' of the world of Japanese popular music. Soeda, *Uta gojyū nen*, p. 32.

[2] Tokutomi Sohō (1863-1957) published *Kokumin no Tomo*, which became arguably the most popular and influential general magazine of the Meiji period. Although Tokutomi originally advocated a more open and democratic 'populism,' he later pushed for nationalistic and collectivist policies. His association with prewar rightist thought led to his house arrest by postwar occupation authorities from 1945 to 1947.

[3] The 'Marquis' and 'grand old man' refer to Itō Hirobumi, who headed the Seiyūkai as its first President.

[4] The reference is to Japan's involvement in the 1900 Boxer Rebellion and its aftermath in China.

[5] In fact, Nishizawa Sō insists that the strike never happened. See Nishizawa, *Kayōshi II*, pp. 2355-9.

[6] In the original Japanese-language text this expression is rendered in the katakana syllabary to read as '*Ai don noo*,' for 'I don't know.'

[7] The reference is to the 'inequality' of widespread acceptance of Western aggression in China (the land of the pigs) and condemnation of the pursuit of Japanese interest beyond Japan's borders.

[8] Kinoshita Naoe (1869-1937), journalist and novelist, worked to promote suffrage expansion. He took an active part in the Ashio mine protests, as did many of Azembō's politically engaged friends and associates. He also knew Azembō through their connection with the *Commoners' Press* and socialist causes.

[9] Azembō's comment is from the perspective of the early 1940s, when Japan's military policy centered on advance southwards (*nanshin*) into Southeast Asia and Oceania. Naval leaders advocated this strategy since World War I in opposition to expansion northwards pushed by powerful factions within the army. The attraction of securing vital natural resources was one motive for the choice to move southwards.

[10] Azembō is already married earlier in this chapter. In this passage, he elaborates on the circumstances of how his drifting life became more anchored.

[11] Most of these minor *enka* singers turned actors have been lost to history.

[12] See note 7 above.

[13] The scholar, Ōwada Takeki (1857-1910), wrote railway songs (*tetsudō shōka*) that were especially popular among Japanese young people.

[14] In nursing and bathing his infant son Azembō defies masculine stereotypes of Japanese men being uninvolved in baby care.

[15] Ozaki Koyō (1868-1903) is best known for writing *Konjiki yasha* or *The Golden Demon*, arguably the most popular novel written during the Meiji period. Azembō versified the story and turned it into an *enka* song.

Chapter Four

Before and After the Russo-Japanese War (1904-1905)

Travels in the Kansai Region

I got off the train at Nagoya with the *enka* songs I carried with me. I checked into a cheap inn called the Wata-ya to one side of the famous statue of the Bodhisattva of Mercy.[1] Most of the people staying there worked the shrine stalls and festivals and most were strapped for cash. There was one woman there called '*Chakasuke-bushi no obasan.*' '*Chakasuke-bushi*' meant 'strolling song' and they were popular in Nagoya.

> Nagoya is a great place because they serve *kaku oden*[2]
> Now isn't that good!
> Many believers come and many wait
> Birds cry
> Dawn breaks
> At the temple they strike the wooden fish *onmuku, onmuku*
> Until it sounds, there is no going home
> *Zuzudenzuno, zuttchakachakasuk*
> *Don don*

I heard that Sawai of Sangaimatsu was in Nagoya so decided to look him up. When I was in Yokohama unloading my family's land I had become acquainted with this *tekiya* stall-keeper while staying in the Matsushima-ya in Yokohama.[3] At the time, one of his friends was a retired boss in the Yorii family. He was given a welcome party when he came to the Matsushima. I had friends staying in the same place so I decided to go along. This wasn't a formal business-type assembly of *tekiya* pitchmen and hustlers but turned out to be a friendly gathering. Gen-chan of Iijima came to the party. He later became the top boss of barkers in the Kantō region. In those days he was known simply as 'Gen-chan, Gen-chan.' I recognized his face from having seen him before in Tokyo. His profile could often be seen at festivals. He spoke with kindness and had a gentle air about him. He possessed a virtue that enabled him to win over others quite easily.

Sawai made his base in Chaya-machi. Here he had a group of young guys sell ointment for chapped skin. They packaged the stuff in seashells. He had followers under twenty years old who had fine voices so I thought that I could compose some four-season *bushi* and other songs for them. I advised him to print up the song sheets on flyers and to have them sung here and there. They followed my sage advice and began making some money.

When I sang *enka* in front of the Ōsumon Gate one of the fellows who worked the festivals appeared to have one of the songbooks already. He said, 'This is a *mabu* so don't fret,' which caused Sawai to laugh. Among those in the business, a *mabu* meant a genuine article and a '*gamaseneta*' meant a fake. The hustlers had a clear conception of the difference. If they came across new items offered at one of the street fairs or religious festivals they might ask, 'Are these *mabu*?' or 'Are these for real?' and the asking would not be considered rude.

After singing *enka* I enjoyed trying my skills at a shooting gallery off to one side of Ōsu and for my efforts won a candy in the shape of a gold medallion. I carried this back to Sawai who took one look and said, 'What the hell did you bring? You get taken in by a bite of candy? That's what they call a consolation prize, ya' know. I guess once an amateur always an amateur.' He had a great laugh.

Everybody said Nagoya is a marvelous place so one and all recommended that I stay put. What this actually meant was that the cops were a lot more harassing to the west, so going there was no good. I was being counseled to stop a while in Nagoya. I had a Nagoya-style large padded kimono made for me. This kind of outerwear, locally called a *tanzen*, buttoned along the sides at the waist. It could be worn anywhere and you never needed to take it off. It was great as an overcoat for keeping out the cold. With the coat and a full stomach I could sleep anywhere. Even occasionally sleeping outdoors proved no problem at all. After a while I decided that there was no reason that I shouldn't go on to the west.[4] Dressed in that same *tanzen*, I sang *enka*. Yes, I remember that I also wore my *tanzen* when standing on platforms to give a speech or two.

A fisherman's boss from Isshiki who happened to be staying at the Wata-ya inn with me enjoyed my *enka* singing so much that he eagerly invited me to come to his home area and take the stage there. He practically pulled me along with him to the Kikyoza Theater in Isshiki. He settled all the details and then went through the town banging a *taiko* drum to roust out an audience. It was very much like a special solo performance.

Prostitutes and store manageresses came to the venue carrying blankets so that they could keep warm during the show. After I completed a song someone banged a drum and I came down from the stage to take a break. I sang many of the old threadbare standards and a few 'songs of happiness' in between. At the time I believed that the *sōshi* activist songs were completely out of favor, less suitable for singing in a small hall than for shouting on a street corner. In any case, guests packed the place and everyone got their money's worth. I performed in Nagoya, then in Tajimi, as I moved into Gifu Prefecture.

In Gifu I heard that Mashio Kanzaburō had become one of our roaming flim-flam artists. He had been a mender of chinaware. After that, but before settling in Gifu, he had gone around with Komada Yoshihiro showing pictures with a magic lantern projector. Komada was a fellow who had a habit of saying, 'exceedingly extraordinarily.' Some time after this, Mashio laughingly told me that in later years, Komada got into politics and even then continued as ever to use his trademark 'exceedingly extraordinarily.' It is fascinating how in the end he became famous for something like this. Tsutumi Jinshichi was another widely known as a *tekiya* in Gifu. He was also a member of the 'Tekketsu' or Blood and Iron Club.' Even when performing *enka* his associates regarded him as every inch the distinguished boss. I suppose that proves that character calls forth the treatment it deserves.

I stayed a while in Gifu and then moved on to continue my pilgrimage to the Grand Shrine at Ise. After visiting the shrine I checked into an inn. There I got acquainted with Watanabe, who was also called 'Prison Tarō.' He was skilled at speechmaking. He was staying at the inn with his wife and pleaded with me to help him write a speech. The boss at the Takita-ya, a local brothel, had gotten involved in staging *sōshi* activist plays and it was in this connection that Watanabe needed help with writing. It turned out that the plays were being given a rest so that his speech meeting could be held between the performances. Now he was pressed to come up with something for the meeting to be held that very evening. After enduring his pleas I decided to help him.

Prison Tarō's speech was no more than an attack on low-ranking government officials and policemen. For my part, I took up the conditions at the time of the Sino-Japanese War and the elevation of the great Japanese spirit. We also performed *enka* songs, 'His heart pure and true, he embraced the fiery engine to stop the leaking steam.' We sang another similar story about a navy sailor who saved an entire warship by hugging a broken steam pipe in the midst of smoke and fire. We also added the one about another sailor who jumped on an enemy torpedo that was closing on his ship and successfully changed its direction. These tales of sailors' exploits were a great hit.

At that time in the political center in Tokyo a debate was raging between the pro-war and the anti-war camps. Itō Hirobumi came up with the words 'sustained determination and perseverance' as a response to the situation. But since the Triple Intervention the weak-kneed diplomacy of the 'sustained determination and perseverance' stripe had been all we had.[5] It might serve for some other day when we could bide our time. But now things were coming to a head. A National Citizens' Rally had been held in Hibiya Park to protest the give-back of territory won in war.

My speech went over quite well and when I came down from the platform I found that Prison Tarō had made a quick exit and had disappeared with all the money collected as the price admission. Although I did not get my share, I was not upset at all. I could make money by singing *enka* so need not feel troubled.

I visited the port of Toba in Mie Prefecture and traveled around Wakayama and the Kishū region. I stayed at an inn called 'Tsuge,' a place where the famous poet Bashō is said to have lodged. I then set out for Osaka.

On my way, I can't remember exactly where, but I heard many children time after time singing something like '*Rosshia koi.*' I still remember their lisping, still not quite mature voices. It was then I decided to write the 'Russia, Bring It on Song' ('Rosshia koi-bushi'). In the space between Japan and Russia the storm clouds had at last grown menacing.

> To disrupt the peace of East Asia
> They put forward a far-fetched argument
> Russia, bring it on! Russia, bring it on!
> With faces that cry that the world's oceans are theirs
> Blue eyes brimming with insolence
> Russia, bring it on! Russia, bring it on!
> Now patience at its very end
> The sword of Japan honed sharp
> Russia, bring it on! Russia, bring it on!
> And the Liaotung Peninsula
> Where Japanese men shed their blood in torrents
> Russia, bring it on! Russia, bring it on!
> Why try to pander to all?
> As for me, I stand by my country first to last
> Russia, bring it on! Russia, bring it on!
> Now is the time, together we will go
> Saddle your horses, Japanese warriors
> Russia, bring it on! Russia, bring it on!
> Red-bearded black pouting pigeons cannot prevail
> Pasty faces, raise your white flag
> Russia, bring it on! Russia, bring it on!
> (Azembō)

Osaka and the Russo-Japanese War

I decided to stay at the Kawachi-ya, an inn near Sennichimae in Osaka. I roamed around the city for a time on the lookout for a suitable place to sing. The Sennichimae, Shinsaibashi, and Nipponbashi districts were all good but Dotonbori was the very best. Kaneko, a middle-school dropout, was also staying at the Kawachi-ya. The guy was really good and could sing anything, but was especially talented with songs like '*Hakata-bushi.*'

In addition to Kaneko, 'Gen-san' was another guest at the inn. He made his living by going around peddling decorative shrine cords wholesale. He was still in his twenties and came from up north, somewhere in Niigata. Although there are many merchants in Osaka, he was the first to hit upon the idea of selling the decorations. I suppose his prices were okay and this was one key to his success. But more than pricing or even timing, it was coming up with an idea that enabled him to be successful in the business. Selling shrine decorations suited Gen-san perfectly. Many other interesting types stayed at this inn that operated in a rather non-discriminating, open fashion. The old couple who ran the place even tended to call everyone 'Gen-san, Gen-san.'

By the time I became accustomed to how things worked in Osaka I had also made many acquaintances. Among them, Kaneko always stuck close by. He wanted to sing *enka* so followed me about wherever I went. I took him along as I traveled around the Kishū region. From the Kata inlet we crossed in an old-style Japanese boat to Yura. Midway across the water rain began to fall. As the small Japanese boat was not equipped with rain gear, we got completely soaked. In this instance, my aforementioned *tanzen* proved unsuitable for wet weather.

When it was all over, I came down with a fever and immediately went to bed upon arriving at the inn. I stayed beneath the covers for three days. A masseuse, one who could see, served clientele at the inn so I asked him to give my shoulders a light once-over.[6] He eagerly quizzed me on why I had come to this place. I told him laughingly that I thought I might make a speech, but it didn't look at if the prospects for doing that were good around here. He answered that if that was what I was up to, then I had best leave it to him. He would talk it over with his boss and something could certainly be arranged. I didn't think anything would come of the encounter. Yet, the masseuse acted as an intermediary and soon returned telling me that he had discussed things with his boss and that I should come soon to arrange my performance.

Who was this boss frequented by the masseuse? Upon meeting him, I discovered that he was a man's man, all sincerity and chivalry. The masseuse had been an effective bridge in making the arrangements for the speech meeting, but now a problem arose. There was a dust-up about the nature of a cedar reforestation plan. It appeared that cedar saplings had already been planted, but the opposition group had gotten so riled that it now wanted to uproot every last tree. The boss wanted me to include in my speech mention of how long it would take for the trees to develop. That problem aside, our clothes were not the best for making a public address so I was lent a *haori* half-coat and a thick white *obi* waistband of white silk crepe. For Kaneko, they bought a pair of *geta* wooden clogs and an *obi* dyed in the *Kanakin* style.[7]

The so-called meeting hall was nothing special, just a very roomy house. Nevertheless, the speech meeting itself turned out to be quite successful. Everything had been arranged and in the midst of the speeches money had been collected by making a round of the audience. All went so well that I was asked to do it again on another night. My new sponsors would cover the entire cost of our stay at an inn. When the time came to make our departure I went to pay my respects to the boss. At this farewell meeting, he asked the masseuse to escort us to Sumoto and requested that we speak again at the Sumoto-za Theater. He entrusted everything to the masseuse. Before we parted he said, 'Take this,' and turned to something like his household Buddhist alter cabinet from which he pulled out money sufficient to cover our expenses for the two-day speech rally. I said I could not accept all the money because he had paid for the charges at our inn and there had been other expenses he had covered for the meeting. But no matter. He wanted me to have it. I took the full amount and escorted by the masseuse, Kaneko and I departed. In the end, the Sumoto-za hall turned out to be reserved already so that was no good. We took our leave of the masseuse.[8]

At some point during the boat trip I read in the newspaper that war with Russia had just broken out. The paper reported extensively on the blockade of Port Arthur and the martyr's death of Commander Hirose.[9] I immediately set about composing an *enka* and returned to Osaka. I commissioned the Sumida Tenjin-dō, a print shop, to publish it.

The War Spirit, Lt. Colonel Hirose

A flower may fall but its fragrance remain
A man may die but his fame persist
How can a man, imposing, fully grown
Set out to lead a mediocre life?
Given the task of blocking the harbor at Port Arthur

A suicide corps undertakes its mission
Listen to their story
Our wondrously brave sailors
Sent out on the ships *Yahiko, Yoneyama, Chiyo, Fukui*
Their mission to sink these four vessels
Four squads of select braves
Board the four vessels
Among them, Lt. Colonel Hirose in the lead
He proceeds on the *Fukui-maru*
He faces the enemy position as bullets rain down
Unfazed by the fire
From stem to stern, he positions the boat perfectly
Explosives placed
And then he lights the fuse
An exploding roar echoing
Without a hitch his mission fulfilled
And then to withdraw with his band
He moves his men to the boats
But wait!
One is missing, one more sergeant
Sugino is nowhere to be seen
What then does the Lt. Colonel do?
'Sugino, Sugino!' he cries out
And again jumps back aboard the *Fukui-maru*
That ship is now on the verge of sinking
The depth of love for his men in his true heart
Means that he must search to the last
And only when no trace can be found
When nothing remains only then can he move to the waiting boats
Out of the blue an enemy shell
The Lt. Colonel is blown apart, shattered
His brains blown to the four directions
In the same boat his braves
Now soaked in torrents of their leader's blood
Boundless heroism, this honorable fall in battle
Ahh, how moving is this last moment!
Although his body is horribly crushed
His great undertaking will last
It will never vanish for a thousand, for eight thousand generations
How tragic, how tragic!
(Azembō)

108

I took along 'Russia, Bring It On!' and 'Lt. Colonel Hirose' and made the rounds singing these *enka*. The response was marvelous. Kaneko had already become quite good at singing and was on his way to setting out on his own. Meanwhile, the stir created by the new songs made my reputation. Sales soared, but only because what rises is that which has been lifted up.[10] My reputation spread quickly, especially in Osaka where the attendant fanfare became raucous.

Gen-san had become completely hooked on singing and had learned many of the *enka* by heart. He now demanded, 'Take me on, too', and followed me about. I told him that if he wanted to sing then he should do it according to his own lights. He consequently set out to do just that. His problem was his other job of selling shrine decorations; that was one kind of work, singing *enka* quite another. Unfortunately, he became completely absorbed in trying to balance them like two sides of a single carrying pole and the music suffered.

When it comes to war, the Japanese people have a nasty habit of using vulgar epithets to denigrate their enemies. During the Sino-Japanese War, we used terms like '*Chan, chan bōzu*' or 'Ching, chong, chinaman' for the Chinese and '*Rosuke*' or 'Russki,' and 'Blue-eyes' for the Russians. And there were many other similar terms flying about. Many people really got a thrill out of using such expressions. Eventually, I came to the point of feeling ashamed of myself for using the terms. Nevertheless, I wrote songs in that style one after another.

Song of Annihilation

Insult added to injury
That's Russia's plight now
A wrong righted, annihilation, annihilation
On sea and on land, battles all lost
The bandits grow frenzied
And worse still the nihilist party at home
Plunges all into civil war's chaos
A wrong righted, annihilation, annihilation
For long, oh so long, the land of the rising sun
Insulted as a minor country

The blue eyes threatening always
Boundlessly arrogant and insolent
To no avail, to no avail, annihilation, annihilation
Alexis has run away

There is no way for you Russians to righteously prevail
Realize as quickly as you can
That to surrender sooner is to surrender better
For if you tarry
All of Russia annihilation, annihilation.
(Azembō)

Song of the Russian Army

If you listen carefully to the Russian army song
Truly, you will laugh until water boils in your belly button
Advance, advance together all and one
We should be resigned to die as we advance
And when we encounter the enemy at that moment
Run away before you're injured
For such a tiny monthly wage?
It's silly to get hurt
And dying is even more out of whack
Advancing may be our duty
But running away is our right
Everyone on your own, flee!
But not before raping the women
Stealing the treasure of others
These things we must not neglect!
Military regulations be hanged!
An opportunity like this makes violence a virtue
Those strong Japanese troops
Should they find us then
Right away!
Advance to the rear, retreat!
To the place where the enemy is not, advance!
Yes, go in the wrong direction, advance to the rear
Although we are weak

If we never meet the enemy
We will never lose
Now isn't that happy-go-lucky?
(Azembō)

The Song of High Morale

For the nation's sake
Our men from the land of the gods will spare nothing
Ever victorious our forces
And our policies are best after the fight
Attention diplomats! We are relying on you

Faces come in all types, the horse face, the wigged face, the tiny face
There's the red face, the hairy face, the sulky face
But carefully consider the Russki's face and what do you see?
Hello! The weeping face of a blockhead!
(Azembō)

In this manner, existing conventional *kouta* ditties, one and all, were changed into war songs. The boss at the Tenshidō was another *tekiya* go-getter in charge of all sorts of resources so I relied on him to publish the songs. We discussed various tactics in working with itinerant peddlers of printed goods.

I also sang at a vacant lot opposite the Asahi-za hall in Dotonbori every night. Before I knew it, one or two people had put up booths around my spot. And then all of a sudden an entire row of stalls went up. A bit later a fellow who specialized in mending broken china began grumbling, 'That guy with the moustache singing *enka* is ruining this location.' Konishi Nobuyuki, a teacher of shield fighting, responded, 'Don't be stupid. That "moustache" is the one who opened up this place.' I overheard this and similar comments while hanging around there. Sensible people knew that I was the groundbreaker and respected me for that. Nevertheless, having fallen this far into the lower depths I ran into many troubles similar to this one.

By twisting around a bit, you can look out from the Asahi-za Hall to see where I was singing *enka* in the vacant lot in front of the Dōtonbori

River. And it was here that a patrolman strolled up to inform me that I was not allowed to sing on that spot. He warned me many times and I was finally hauled off to the station. On that occasion, one of the policemen complained at length about me. He said that this shitty guy, meaning me, says this then that, then that then this, and he's a real pain. In the end I was sentenced to pay a fine of fifty *sen*. As I had no money, they let me go home for the time being.

Once back home I ate a belly full of cooked rice and thereupon, still wearing my same old Nagoya *tanzen* coat, immediately returned to the police station. I told them that it was okay for them to lock me up for a night and that I preferred punishment to paying a fine. They responded that I should not say that kind of thing and they would accept installment payments. Then they sent me home again. In the end, everyone just let it go and patrolmen left me alone after that.

Both Konishi Nobuyoshi and his pupil, Watanabe, liked the speechmaking racket. Half in jest, they approached me with the idea that I would be the star performer playing the leading role while one of them took the part of a reformer at a speech meeting. With a sense of 'why not?' I lightly agreed to the idea. The first 'lecture series' was held in Kooriyama in Nagano. Again, the playbill was mostly speakers who expressed high regard for themselves as they shallowly criticized officials. This was the standard form for such performances at the time. I started my remarks with the observation that if you desire peace you must fight for it. It was something I had taken to heart after reading the *Short National History of Japan*. That work spoke of being forearmed to be forewarned and vice versa. Drawing on various examples, I talked about strategy. Konishi and Tendo were struck by my speech and told me how impressed they were in the way my talk had differed from theirs.

When we went to Nara, I thought the title of Konishi's speech might cause trouble and sure enough we were all hauled off to the police station and accused of insulting officials and being obstructive. Just before this we had asked the people at the Raku-ya inn to order something for us to eat and drink from a local eatery. Unfortunately, the commotion that followed shortly thereafter at the speech meeting meant that we didn't have time to pay the bill. We were mistakenly believed to have skipped out, a misunderstanding that resulted in some very rough treatment for us. At this point, these strains caused our roving speakers' bureau to dissolve. Gen-san and I returned to

Osaka and rented rooms in Namba-shinchi. Kaneko had already become an independent performer and was now sufficiently adept to travel about singing on his own, which is exactly what he did.

Six months spent in Namba-shinchi. One day in the blink of an eye my old reliable Nagoya *tanzen* half-coat was stolen by a burglar. Gen-san's purse, full of cash, had been left untouched where it had earlier been tossed on a table. It was strange that only the *tanzen* was gone. In the end, that coat never helped me to the extent that I had expected. I returned to Tokyo.

The Lamp House

I had decided to go straight back to Tokyo without stopping anywhere along the way. But when I got near Yokohama I suddenly felt like getting off the train and looking around. At Otani Tengai's second-floor room we talked the night through. Once back in Tokyo I sought news about Takahashi Sumao and learned that he was staying at an inn in Asakusa-machi and I went there to see him. He now had a wife.

For the time being, I wanted to partake of his hospitality to sort out a few things for myself. Takahashi himself was troubled by a lack of any good *enka* material. I showed him the songs I had composed in Osaka. He said they were great and that we must perform them right away. I gave him the stock of what I had left and then set out for Kobiki-chō to the office of Muto Printing, the company that had been the Seinen Club's printer. I asked them to print up the songs. Nukii Utakichi was there. He was a print shop worker who once, quite by chance, typeset *enka* for the Seinen Club. The experience gradually got him interested in singing and he later followed Suzuki Ichirō in performing *enka*. Heretofore, he had been printing only so-so songs that he sang on his own. Seeing my compositions set him to work immediately on mastering them for his performance. Takahashi's wife sold copies of counting songs such as 'One' or '*Hitotsu-tose.*' I composed new lyrics for her such as 'One, shining beam of the rising sun, one, one.' I soon moved to the second floor above Takei's lamp store in Kita-kiyojima-chō.

The number of singers performing *enka* rapidly increased. Many came to me for material for songs, but I tended to be away from home most of the time. I had made some haiku friends so I left the job of selling *enka* music

113

books to old Mr. Takei. One time I returned after being gone three days. The old man welcomed me by saying, 'Look at how many we sold,' and took the glass candy box from the shelf to show me the money inside. Sometimes I would take all the money from the box when I left. On such occasions Takei would open his eyes wide and declare, 'Well, I never … you're leaving again?'

The old man was uncommonly stingy. He sat in his store making a mosquito larvae dipper out of scrap or fixing metal fittings on one of the lamps.[11] He divided the money he earned into three categories, for expenses in categories 'a' and 'b', and a final pot that he vowed never to touch. He buried his savings beneath the floorboards so it would be all the more difficult to get out. If an official came to collect for the garbage pick-up he would argue against paying, saying that his house did not produce any garbage.

In a way he was right. I remember the time I cooked for myself in the upstairs room. I cut up scallions for soup, keeping the white part and carrying the green stems down to dump into the garbage box. On my way there the old man called out, 'Hey, are you throwing those away?!' as if doing so was the most extravagantly wasteful thing in the world. What's more, Mr. Takei took the greens and used them as the main ingredient in the soup he prepared for himself, his wife, and his mother. There is also something that happened later. When near death, he refused to take medicine for his inflamed kidneys. He claimed that the medicine wasn't worth the cost. Needless to say, he also regarded calling in a doctor a waste.

For all that, he was still an intriguing fellow. He often commented on various personalities who came to pick up *enka* materials. In those days *enka* singers differed completely from their predecessors. It was a transitional period and we had entered the generation of songs of suffering students. Iwaide Keishō was a tall man which prompted old Takei to dub him the 'heron.' He also called him the heron in the paddy. For example, he would say, 'The paddy heron showed up today in a fancy collar looking just like a lovely princess.'

Once Takei also told me that Iwaide had showed up complaining that he had no money for food and pressing for a loan. Takei replied, 'No money? You worked last night, didn't you? You did. Well where is that money? So you ate a *daifu* stuffed with sweet bean paste and then what did you order next? Well what did you have? You ate that much? Didn't you think about how much you were going to have to pay? Oh, but you wanted to eat, yes, I see, I see ... .' And the old man acted out the dialog just as if it had just taken place. At the end of the account of Iwaide he added to me, 'Mr. Soeda, that man Iwaide is not just an idiot, he's a fool!

I also learned that old Takei had a keen interest in rocks.[12]

Everyone who dropped in suffered at the point of the old man's sharp humor. One such episode happened when Takahashi Sumao came to pick up the first printing of some songs. According to Takei, he looked as happily relieved as a deity upon whose altar someone had suddenly placed a candle and offertory salt flowers, although he also had the air of a tekiya about him.[13] When those copies sold out, Takahashi came to the old man to get more. He soon told Takei that the printer was a real tightwad because one sheet out of hundred had come out unprinted. According to the old man, Takahashi's face went as white as that sheet of paper and he demanded that it be returned for printing. I had to burst out laughing as I watched Takei's expression as he retold the incident. The old man also complained about Takahashi's practice of sitting on the tatami mat with one leg stretched straight out as if holding a person at spear point. This was because Takahashi was slightly crippled and so had to sit in that particular way. I had gotten used to it and didn't mind a bit. Still, the old man's description of Takahashi was powerfully vivid.

Many people came by, Ishimoda Neigorō, Akiyama Yonejirō, Ishikawa Kyokuhō, and others.[14] Among them was a woman, 'Shibui Oba-san.' For long years she worked as a strolling musician singing the '*hitotsu tose*' counting songs, ditties called '*yomi*' songs back in the old days. She obtained copies of *enka* from a publisher and printer called 'Sanokin.' She often sang me her rendition of the counting song that retold Nishino Fumitarō's assassination of the Minister of Education, Mori Arinori.[15] She came to me saying she wanted to sing *enka*, but in the end she felt the lyrics were just too rigidly formal and asked me to write something for her that was a little less stiff.

I smiled bitterly. And then I wrote the 'Rappa-bushi,' 'The Bugle Song.' It was one part history and one part farce. This was the first time in *enka* that a toad, a kitchen maid, and a tomboy shared center stage. Later there were lots of comical *enka*, but this was the first farce to become a major

115

hit. It came out just as the Portsmouth Treaty to conclude the Russo-Japanese War was being settled and the war spirit still ran high. Nevertheless, farcical lyrics found much wider popular acceptance than did war songs. I had a kind of epiphany thinking, yes, indeed, this is the way things work.

The Bugle Song[16]

I lift my fallen comrade in arms
And lips to his ear call his name
He smiles, eyes brimming with tears
In his heart he is cheering banzai
Tokototto

Now the clock sounds eight-thirty
If we are late we're headed for heavy punishment in the brig
But we have next Sunday, don't we
Neglect your saber and it will rust
Tokototto

A sentry not easily moved
But by the sound of a marvelous flute
Was seduced as the light glistened on the swaying pampas grass
His tunic slashed
Tokototto

The snow falls and drifts and its cold cuts to the bone
Light cast beyond the paper screen shows a silver world
Where he is must be cold
And that thought brings tears suddenly
Tokototto

I am a pretty hasty person
And was happy to pick up a big-mouthed purse in the street
But returning home and taking a good look
Found it was just a frog flattened by a horse cart
Tokototto
I expect to land my father's inheritance
But his tea kettle bald dome is in the way

Would that I had a bucket handy
Every time he gets hot and ready to spout!
Tokototto
(Nomuki Sanjin)[17]

The song sold exceedingly well. Yet, I still felt somehow ill at ease. I sensed that I might be soiling the reputation of the Tōkai Moral Reform Society. It was only for these songs that I used the pen name 'Nomuki Sanjin' and published and distributed them jointly with Takei through arrangements he made with a print shop. Every morning a crowd gathered in front of our gate wanting to buy 300 or 500 copies per person. We limited copies to 100 or 150 per buyer but still found that the run was completely sold out within an hour or two so we had to dash out for more. At times things got so frantic that the printer ran an extra shift at night to keep up with demand. I had left these business matters to old man Takei up to this time and he soon developed such a taste for the work that he finally became an *enka* publisher.

Shibui Oba-san lived in Mannen-chō where Nagao Tomotari also had a place. Nagao's son Fukutarō was only seventeen or eighteen, but like so many others, he earned money by singing the *yomi* counting songs. Although his father never got beyond working the street stalls, the son was so talented that he had already played a minor role in Matsui Gensui's play, *Mae*, (the drama with that famous line, 'Yes, yes, that is so true.') Later he began to sing *enka*, but before that his younger sister started coming along to sing with Shibui Oba-san. The girl never said, 'let's go perform *enka*,' but said, 'Okka-san, by and by why don't we go do the I-don't-get-it?' By this she meant let's go perform *wakaranai-bushi* or 'I don't get it' songs. It had been Shibui Oba-san who had recommended the farcical songs and before she knew it she was gradually caught up in singing these popular ditties. In the end, she became a leader in this *enka* form.[18]

The Tide Society

I got in touch with my wife and son so that they could join me. This would be the second time we would try to make a life in Tokyo. My wife came beforehand to make the necessary arrangements. We found a two-story house to rent behind Takei's place. After settling the rental agreement, I had a photo taken of the three of us together. We then set out for Uenohirokoji just to take a walk with our four-year-old son, Tomomichi.

117

We walked through the grounds of a can factory. My wife held Tomomichi's hand as we strolled along. I was following immediately behind them when a man in an overcoat suddenly came quickly and loudly tromping up from behind. Tomomichi's hat was suddenly twisted, somehow caught in the sleeve of the man's overcoat. Tomomichi ran after the man. With his shoes on he kicked his little legs upwards twice at the fellow all the while swearing 'Damn you, damn you!' He then ran back to his mother's hand. As his legs didn't reach even the hem of the offender's overcoat, the target of the attack didn't feel a thing and continued walking toward Hirokoji. Tomomichi nevertheless looked satisfied at being able to wreak his revenge.

At this time, the 'Electric Railway Song' was in vogue and the age of the horse-drawn railroad ended. Oshin came from Yokohama to our new home. I designated that the second floor would serve as a boarding house for *enka* singers. A couple, the Akiyamas (they had gotten started with *enka* by following Takahashi), Ishikawa (a vendor of newspaper extra editions), Nakabayashi Denjirō, and a bunch of others loafed about in the upper room.

I paid a visit to Sakai Toshihiko in Motozono-chō.[19] I respected him. At our first meeting, he came out to greet me in his casual everyday clothes and said in a relaxed manner, 'I'm Sakai.' This left a good impression. At the time he published the *Family Magazine* (*Katei zasshi*). In a separate newspaper piece he had called for someone to write a new version of my popular 'Bugle Song.' The lackluster response prompted him to ask me to submit my own rewrite of the song. I accepted the offer and composed a new rendition called 'Socialist's Bugle Song.' He wanted me to call it 'The Socialist Party Bugle Song.' I hated the word 'party' but consented anyway.[20]

Up until that time I spoke easily in public. When making an address, my palms were open and relaxed. Now something had changed. I drew my hands into fists and spoke awkwardly. As I changed, Akiyama came to imitate perfectly all of my former methods of public speaking and he continually polished his skills. I saw him perform, making his impassioned speeches, beneath the huge clock that looks out from the side of Megane Bridge. At the time, newspapers typically carried articles that proclaimed, 'Beneath a winter moon, the young man, his eyes burning with intensity, expounded on the principles of his ideology,' and similar stuff.

118

It was also a time when Tokyo still had a lot of vacant land so we were never at a loss for places to perform *enka*. The Komusho field was a good place as was the empty land in Masago-chō in Hongo. Three or four *enka* groups would perform at these venues. There was one man who sang solo performances of his own songs immediately after the routines of the several groups of singers. He sang '*kinmai-bushi*.' I recall that one song was about spoiled girl students and was called 'The Voice of the Pines' ('Matsu no koe'). One refrain repeated, 'Alas, this dream world, this dream world.' It was about the only tune in his repertoire and was quite long. The audience laughed, saying, 'My, now that was one very long '*kinmai-bushi*,' and that set him off singing it again. He had stuck with that same tune persistently for about a year. Finally, it became something people talked about. The singer was Kaminaga Ryōgetsu. He had come up with a hit so other singers who had at first ignored him as a fool also started singing 'Voice of the Pines.' In the end the song became popular.

I could no longer stand the confusion and disorder raised by that group living on the second floor and took off. I left it to Takei to sort out the house and its occupants. I relocated to Naka-negishi without even taking the bedding or anything else from where I had previously stayed. Takei took complete responsibility, keeping track of costs by maintaining a daily accounts book. One day when I decided to return to Takei's to check on things he thrust the ledger at me complaining, 'Friend, you'd better take a look at this. Not a soul is making their daily payment.' It appeared that things had gotten even wilder since my departure. Every morning the Oba-san would look patiently up the stairway to be greeted by spiteful comments from the denizens above. Someone even said they should burn this place down and tossed down a lighted newspaper to underline the sentiment.

I joined a little group in Negishi called the Tide Society along with Satō Satoru from Sendai, Koizumi Uson, Hayashi Chikashi, and others. Hayashi belonged to the Salvation Army, which he claimed suffered harsh persecution at this time. When he went out to spread the gospel he was often welcomed with a hail of stones. He was full of ardor and each and everyone in the group shared a kind of common human purity.[21]

During this period I composed anew 'The Bugle Song,' 'Surrender Song' ('Akirame-bushi'), 'It's a Money World' ('Ah, Kane no yo'), and 'I Don't Get It' ('Wakaranai-bushi'). It was toward the end of 1906. It was at this time that I began calling myself 'Azen.' I was first known by that in the haiku circle, but added a 'bō' when I learned that another haiku poet used the same pen name.

In 1907, my 'Devil Wind' was cited as an infraction of the Publications Law and I had to pay a fine of five yen. I didn't have the wherewithal to pay but thought I might delay dropping in to begin my stay behind bars until the weather got a bit warmer. In the midst of that idea, an inspector called at our place saying, 'Is he here?' My wife answered, 'No, he's not.' He turned to leave but before he showed the back of his Inverness cape Tomomichi loudly blurted out, 'Mommy, Papa is here so why do you say he's not?'

I had intended to go to jail after the start of April, but I decided for the time being to go to the station in Kuromon-chō. I would put up there for a single night. Unfortunately, the police thought otherwise and they sent me to Tokyo Prison. Once there, I thought I might as well stay put, but Nukii Utakichi somehow put together enough money to bail me out and came to meet me at the lock-up. In the space of a single day I had suffered the double loss of serving jail time and paying a fine.

Traveling and Life at Home While I Was Away

Ah, It's a Money World

Ah, it's a money world, a money world!
To heaven? To hell? Depends on money
Laughing, money; crying, money!
First and second, money; and third, money, too!
Slicing the tie between parents and kids: money!
Cutting the bond twixt husband and wife: money!
Mock the immorality of those who grasp
Curse those blinded by greed
But words don't hurt and they don't itch
If it's something that can be changed to money
That's just rich
People's problems and troubles?
Keep your distance and don't knock yourself out
Ah, it's a money world, a money world!
What I seek is honest work

Yet, though I have arms and legs
I am bound by unseen chains
From morning to night without a break
Cruelly used and utterly tired
No time to savor life's flavor
Does this animal have freedom?

Ah, it's a money world, a money world!
If born a cow or horse
We need not bow our precious heads
Need not utter fawning phrases
But is seems once born a human
We are fated to pull a rickshaw
Its lantern shade shabby and torn
Shaking, trembling, wretched

Ah, it's a money world, a money world!
A factory belching poisonous smoke
We service its dangerous machines
Risking our lives to labor
Whipped by mortifying goblins
Weeping, weeping, seeking wage pay
Pale faces, eyes sunken
Hands covered with sores, feet festering
Not sick, no, not sick, no time to take sick leave
Listen all to this single song
If modern female factory hands are women
Then maidservants are princesses

Ah, it's a money world, a money world!
As long as the word poverty exists
Like sand on a beach thieves like Goemon[22]
Will be with us forever, eternal, ever present
And he whose task is to keep the thieves in check
He too is poor
On a snowy night thinking the thief might appear
Wrapped in a thin coat
His saber frozen by the cold
No time for the briefest nap

Under the eaves with a dog for a friend
At home his wife sleeps alone
She too is cold under her wafer-thin blanket
(Azembō)[23]

I Don't Get It

Ah, I don't understand, don't understand!
I don't understand this changing world
We call it civilized and enlightened
But it's all surface
I don't understand
Gas and electricity are great
Steam power convenient, too
But it's gilt work and gold plate
Gimcrack and fake
People weep and cry again and again
Hard times, hard times!
All year every year hard up
Ever scurrying, I don't understand

Ah, I don't understand, don't understand!
I don't get duty, I don't get love
All are blinded by self-interest
Duty schmuty, love schmove,
I don't understand this, I don't get that
Truly this is a money world
That's true for total strangers, of course,
But all the more so among blood kin
When the single word 'money' is mentioned
Suddenly our God of Wealth, becomes a demon
Eyes sharpen like those of hungry hawks and bears
Then the kin have fights, arguments, lawsuits
So this is civilization and enlightenment?!

Ah, I don't understand, don't understand!
Beggars, abandoned kids, for good measure throw in the insane
Pickpockets, shoplifters, and sneak thieves
Robbery, theft, fraud, appropriation

Sex crimes, adultery, forced double suicide
Union strikes and the jobless
Suicide, starvation, death by freezing
Wife-icide, parent-icide
Kill the husband, kill the boss
Facing unspeakable horrors unending
If we are still in the shadows, from some maw not yet emerged
How then call this civilization and enlightenment?

Ah, I don't understand, don't understand!
There are so many wise people
But in this world the fools
I don't know why
Become members of the national assembly
They're called representatives but it's just a name
Blockheads, asses, and cowards
Always woolgathering in their numbered chairs
Are they deaf? Are they dumb? I don't know[24]
(Azembō)

Song of Surrender

I'm dunned for the money I've borrowed
I can't collect what I'm owed
I guess that's the way of this drifting world
As for me, I always give up
(Azembō)

Song of the Four Seasons

An autumn evening at the paper mill
She takes a chance and slips out
The dewy grass, is it rain or tears?
Her parents beckon from a withered plain
Clouds cross the moon's face, the sound of geese calling

An autumn evening in the army camp a dream just starting to form
The illusion of home and its mountains and rivers
At the bugle's echo his eyes open
Looking out at the glow of a solitary moon.[25]
(Azembō)

Sales of these songs and others improved day after day. Many *enka* singers noticed the trend and flocked from all directions to buy music sheets. Some of them used the materials provided by Takei. Others staying at the lodge house at the rear of Takei's place came, too. Shibui Oba-san came. Ishikawa, Akiyama, and Ishimoda came together as a single group. At the time, they explained that they were the *enka* singers living on the second floor above the Iwata sweet dumpling shop. They later asked Iwata to work for them to provide the same services in the same manner that Takei had done for me. Among those people there were a few expert singers, men such as Katō Yoshio and Matsumoto Torajirō, who had grown bored with the same old songs. In the end, they called on me and once again I became a publisher of original music. I also spent a lot of time outside the house going around giving speeches opposing the increase in streetcar fares, distributing flyers, and participating in meetings. Sometime I did these things together with my wife. As we did so we found that our household expenses were gradually veering toward disaster. I was not producing the song materials that we needed to keep going.

During one of my father's visits from the family home, we decided that when he returned he would take Tomomichi back with him. In effect, we were practically leaving our son on his own. In the early summer of 1907 we had only a few song sheets left on the shelf and I lacked the capital to have more printed. I didn't do anything to better our straitened household accounts. On the contrary, I took leave of my wife and along with Satō Satoru and some *enka* music, embarked on a long-distance expedition that would take us from Fukushima on to Sendai

Along the way, Satō stopped off at his hometown and I went on to Aomori. We met up again and then crossed the straits to Hakodate. On the road I met an old neer-do-well called Ono and the three of us decided to travel around together. Ono passed himself off as an expert at the 'I Don't Get It' songs. After traversing throughout Hokkaido we had money left over as we prepared to return. This shocked my younger singing companion. It was good news but to my surprise he accused me of many things, of having a style too distinctly individual, being too old, and making it hard for him to perform with me in the smaller venues. He wanted to go on alone taking with him his share of the songs. Those who are split asunder will be joined again; separation and reunion are the way of things. As it turns out, we did reunite later when we once again crossed over to Hakodate.

I forgot about my family as I wandered about, but at times wondered how things were back home. I reflected on how strong my wife had become of late when faced with looking after everything on her own. She understood that I could not send any money home. As for me, I could make do, sharing a friend's lodging and willingly working when work was available. Such was my easy-going approach.

After traveling for such a long time, I at last came home to Tokyo. I returned unannounced, wondering how the family was faring. Arriving back, I found that the house had not changed a bit. On the shelf were stacks of newly printed music. I was relieved. I was also moved by my wife's economy, her ability to study, and skill at running the house.

Fall came and the winds gradually began to blow cold.

Those who came to buy *enka* songs usually came in the morning and certainly no later than noon to take care of business. This schedule emerged because we were apt to be away later in the day. One day I stayed later than usual because I expected a caller who would drop by after the others had stopped coming. My wife went out by herself. Night fell and she still had not returned. Just as I was thinking about how late it was getting Zama Shisui arrived to tell me that a speech rally had been held to protest the increase in streetcar fares. Sakai Tameko and my wife had been walking about outside the hall handing out flyers opposing steeper fares and this had led to their arrests. He had come all this way to let me know what had happened.[26]

The Tōhoku Speaking Tour

It came to pass that we would make a speaking tour through the Tōhoku region. Nishikawa Kōjiro, Matsuzaki Genkichi, and I would participate in the capacity of 'Tokyo Social Newspaper Reporters and members of the Tōhoku and Hokkaido Touring Speakers Bureau.'[27] We had this designation printed along with our three names on sets of business cards. After the cards were printed, Matsuzaki decided to drop out. I followed my own lights and departed on December fifth. Thinking that it would be good for the safety of the women if they stayed together while we were away, we closed up the Naka-negishi house and moved our families in together with the Nishikawas in Kinsuke-chō in Hongo.

Our roving speakers' bureau traveled to Morioka, Aomori, Hakodate, Morimura, Kutchan, Sapporo, Otaru, and Asahikawa. Supporters waited to welcome us everywhere we went. We met all types of people. Mr. Yamada Kinjirō, a *Tōoku Nippō* newspaper reporter, came to see us off at the harbor. In Aomori, I came across Watanabe Seitarō whose attempt to organize a commoners' farm had just failed. He was on his way home after giving up on the effort. He also made a speech at one of the rallies.[28] I talked with a nearly destitute journalist of the *Kutchan shinpō*. In Asahikawa I met Takemori Kazunori and Sakamoto Naohiro. The latter was the nephew of Sakamoto Ryōma and had become a Methodist. I also encountered Kishi Takanori, a Mrs. Tempoem, Takeuchi Yosojirō, Midorikawa Kikuo, and many others. I recall a whole series of faces met one after another. They left impressions that are still fresh in my mind. There was even one official from the Hokkaido Government Office who sang 'Ah, I don't get it, don't get it!' everywhere we went.

The chief editor of the *Otaru Shinbun*, Midorikawa Kikuo, went along with us to Sapporo and also took a stand on the speech platform. The title of his remarks was 'Asahi Cigarettes Have Risen to Eight *Sen*!' More than 500 people came to listen at the Sapporo-tei in Tanukikoji. This was a terrific hall for making a speech. Seating was laid out theater style and our supporters had prepared everything in advance. I thought that we might need a bigger place and advocated as much, but Nishikawa, a man of steadfastness, took a view that was as different as it was firmly held. Where I was excitable, Nishikawa tended toward passivity. I met Nishikawa's friends and teachers who knew him from his days at the Sapporo Agricultural School. But even as I sat with them I grew ever more impatient as Nishikawa gave a speech that essentially tried to make an old story re-bloom by repeating it yet again. Many of the people I met in Sapporo I would meet again in Tokyo. The wife of Midorikawa urged me to allow her husband to go with us back to the capital.

I also visited a free dispensary in Otaru and a charity hospital in Hakodate. I stopped at each bed in the clinic to talk with patients. All of them told stories of how they ended up in such places. Although the accounts differed in individual details, the general features of their stories were as if cut from a common pattern. Without exception, all had become a kind of human flotsam, the dregs of laborers who had been deceived. Some had fled from camps for convict workers and had fallen ill while on the road. Hakodate was a natural place for them to wind up because without resources there was no way for them to cross the Aomori Straits. While hanging about here they got sicker and sicker. In fact, many of them died in the streets.

In Aomori I visited the slum districts. At that time I met a fellow who specialized in buying people. He frequented the work camps in Hokkaido, in particular the Momijiyama convict workers camp. He told me gruesome stories about that place and tales of a camp in Kanaya that was close to being hell on earth. According to him, one bad fellow was beaten with a club, suspended from a pine tree, and slowly smoked over a pine needle fire before his body was dumped somewhere in a mountain recess. He had seen the bloody corpse. As I had had experience working in a labor crew, the pain of each story penetrated to my very core.

The Hokkaido journey was learning through living. Although many impressions have become mixed up, I do recall being in Hakodate after a major fire. I stayed at an inn constructed in that cheap barracks style. I remember going to sleep and watching snow fall into the room and settle near my pillow.

> Light glimmering from the lamp stand
> On my cheek
> Snow's icy bite

I wrote this haiku line some years later, but the impression is from that time in Hokkaido. Nishikawa turned his back to the blowing snow and muttered that we had come to a ridiculous place. Hakodate did have a horse-drawn tram, but it was said that it was second-hand and had been used long ago as transport for getting around Tokyo.

In Hakodate, I also encountered a man who owned three entertainment halls. Rumor had it that he stabbed someone in Edo. For all that, he was a fine and chivalrous old fellow and every inch a man. Usually, each hall featured

127

only *naniwabushi* recitals. He nevertheless kindly rearranged the schedule to open a place for our oratorical performances. He even stood in the ticket wicket and called out a pitch to draw customers to hear the speeches.

Shinozaki of the training school for the blind was privately a Methodist. In those days, circumstances were not the best for Christians. The problem after the great Hokkaido fire was that blankets and other relief goods had been sent from everywhere to help with the recovery effort, but they went first to Christians, second to converts, and only last and rather uncertainly to the poor. The feelings of the people who had sent those goods were repaid with something totally different than they had expected. In countless instances local people saw the giving as nothing more than hypocrisy.

It was snowing heavily when we convened our meeting in Otaru. Just when we said that tonight would be a washout many people nonchalantly trudged in wearing their heavy straw snow boots. The hall was filled. That evening I sang the 'I Don't Understand' song in the course of my speech. I had brought copies of *enka* sheets and people carried these around the hall to sell. They sold and sold and soon not one was left. In Asahikawa supporters put us up in a first-class hotel called the Miura, a ryokan inn. All along the hallway hung a row of little boards sarcastically advertising 'Tea for 200 yen compliments of Mr. Hara Takashi' and '150 yen compliments of Mr. Furukawa Ichibei,' and so on. Another board appeared a little below the others. It read, 'Pardon, but I cannot stay, Mr. Iguchi Ryōjō.' [29]

New Year's had already arrived. Nothing had been spared to make sure that rooms were kept warm, but when I awoke in the morning and pulled the bed clothes up a bit, I heard a *pari, pari* crunching sound. It seems that moisture in my breath had frozen my beard to the top edge of the blanket. The mandarin oranges had also frozen stiff. We lined them along the hearth, waited a while, and ate them anyway. At first it was exotic to eat semi-frozen fruit, but after eating too many of them we were bothered by scratches on our tongues.

Nishikawa sent a report of our activities to the newspaper. One excerpt from it noted, 'My preparations for the cold weather were inadequate, but Mr. Soeda's were more so. This morning his shoes continued to steam by the fireplace.' Sakai later commented on the article saying that, 'Nishikawa was a lousy writer but that part of the report was quite vivid.' In fact, my shoes soon came apart in places and I emitted squishy noises from my completely soaked feet. I was constantly by the hearth trying to dry out. The owner of the Asahikawa Club's hall, Mr. Baba, was also one of our supporters. The box office results were quite good there. Making a speech in a hall where the temperature was minus fifteen degrees Centigrade was a first for me. Despite that, we had an overflow audience.

Baba believed that even in socialism, extremists would not do. According to him, it was fine to go so far but ... . At that time, a view like his was sometimes called 'So-farism' instead of socialism. Occupying a middling, moderate position was Christian socialism of the stripe advocated in the pages of the magazine *New Age*. [30] Accordingly, the followers of this view were called the New Age faction.

We had a commemorative photograph taken with our supporters and at this point our tour was finished. Although I had planned on going on to the Yubari coal mine, where I heard something was going to break out, it turned out that I suddenly had to return. [31] Nishikawa had warned me not to stop at any dangerous places. To his own wife he wrote about all the travails of life on the road and even added that he could not have overcome these, 'without his wife's goddess-like spirit watching over him.'

We left Asahikawa on January 13. Although it had not been a sightseeing tour, we did see snow-capped Mt. Komagatake from the window of a rattling train. At the rickshaw parking area in front of Sapporo Station we were also treated to the bizarre sight of rows of rickshaws all standing with their wheels removed. They were being converted into sleds. At the time, I felt that Sapporo's streets were well laid out and in an orderly arrangement. Yet, I did not sense that Hokkaido itself would develop into an advanced cultural area.

In Morioka I was invited by Nakadate Umejiro of the *Shin Tōhoku* newspaper to dine with him at an expensive traditional restaurant. On a slip of paper he had written 'Kogiku' and something, something. He repeatedly glanced at the slip and it got me wondering what it could mean. I thought perhaps it was the name of special dish of some sort. I later found out it was the name of a geisha and her address. I knew that *morikkiri* meant a single helping of rice but here it seemed to mean a single rendezvous. Later I recall reading a line from someone's haiku in which *morikkiri* meant just that:

On a winter morning in Tono
A single meeting

With my lover
This morning our love rekindled

Thanks to our tour I at last understand the poem's meaning.

The Morning Glory House

We did not expect to make money on the speaking tour, but we did. On returning to Kinsuke-chō, Nishikawa tallied up our earnings. We both laughed with delight to find that we had more than twenty yen (of course, our supporters had paid for our lodgings and had invited us to stay in their homes). I used the money to move temporarily to a second-floor room over a leather bag shop in Minami Inari-chō. I think that the Haruki-za Theater had become the Hongo-za Theater around this time. It was there that Tochuken Kumoemon had become so popular for his recitations of *naniwabushi* done in a style that overflowed with the bushido warrior spirit.[32] Meanwhile, Koshige recited *naniwabushi* in a low, whispering, throaty tone at the Tanigawa-tei in Yokosuka. This was the first time that the lawyer and politician class began to favor the form. *Naniwabushi* consequently began to gain greater prominence.

In jest I said that maybe I would become a *naniwabushi* reciter, to which Matsuzaki Genkichi laughingly replied, 'By the time you're any good at it, *naniwabushi* will already have gone out of style.' While I was away on the Tōhoku circuit, my wife, Nishikawa Fumiko, Yoshida Katsuko, and others opened a women's speech rally. The press called them pioneers of a women's movement. Some time later, Fumiko chased after Miyazaki Toranosuke and got him to marry her. She and Kimura Komako organized the 'Women's New Truth Society.'[33]

Fukuda Hideko visited our second-floor place in Minam Iinari-chō to talk with my wife.[34] Instead of cakes with tea, we served sliced radish pickles.[35] Fukuda exclaimed, 'Delicious, delicious,' as she noisily crunched them down one after another. She left after finishing off an entire bowl. It was around then that I introduced a woman, the wife of Ishimoda Neigorō, to Fukuda to work as her maid. At that time Ishimoda had gotten in trouble after consenting to pawn some items for an acquaintance. It turned out that the goods were stolen.

130

The maid was an excessively timid woman and maybe a little unbalanced. When left alone in Fukuda's home, she became increasingly anxious about the *tansu* dresser drawers in the house. Finding it impossible to settle down she finally just fled the place. Fukuda scolded her and for good measure wrote me a note that read, 'The liberty that we are advocating is not at all like yours. If one is not responsible then there is trouble.'[36]

Our friends held a party at the Kingsley Hall in Misaki-chō in Kanda to welcome us back. The Kingsley Hall people worked to assist emigrants to America, published a magazine on emigrant issues and, on the lower floor of the hall, ran a kindergarten. The freelance writer Fujita was involved in the group. He had had a love affair with one of the women kindergarten teachers. When it went wrong he went into hiding. The affair was sufficiently notorious that the newspapers ended up writing about it. Fujita followed after me and sang *enka*. (Ōsugi and Satō Sannojō sang a little, too.)

Gradually, Katayama's friends seemed to distance themselves from him. Tazoe Tetsuji also left to join with Nishikawa. I wrote a new *enka*, the 'Tax Increase Song' that appeared in an extra edition of the *Tokyo Shakai Shinbun*.

The Tax Increase Song

The draft whistling through the paper-paneled door is freezing, *noya*
I want to show you
It's a hard problem, isn't it
Hell and hardships suffered
And a tax increase, tax

Carrying a child on my back and my belly as big as a *taiko* drum, *noya*
And now another load
It's a hard problem, isn't it
I'll go on and push my cart
And a tax increase, tax

During my tour I heard a version of the tax increase song sung by a beggar and it had stayed with me. I used a revision of that ditty here. Some years later Fujiwara Yoshie used the melody of my song for his 'A Gull Offshore.'[37]

131

I was once again broke. I had to go out to sing. One evening, songbooks in my pocket, I opened the window I was standing by and saw that it was raining. From behind me, Tomomichi said, 'Poor Dad.' Soon we moved to 37 Iriya-machi into a house next to a garden of morning glories. At the time the 'Iriya morning glory' was one of Tokyo's famous products. Close by was the Morihara milk store. That was where Katō Izan and Koizumi Uson worked. They were deliverymen. Koizumi eventually came to share our place.

Kuroku together with Kawada of the Aijin-sha press came to visit. At the pillow of my sick wife we somehow got into a row but it all ended congenially enough. Kuroku laughed heartily and then left. My wife looked up and said laughingly, 'Now there's an interesting person.' She had been listening to us. I went out to buy medicine.

At the side of the morning glory garden I bumped into Ikeda Keihachi. It had been a long time. He lived along the tram street that ran through Kurofune-chō in Asakusa. He had gotten into the business of designing acetylene gas lamps and had become rather successful (at the time the lamps were popular). He paid a sick call on my wife and brought a box of cakes. It was the first time he met her. Not long afterwards, a sake shop delivered an entire barrel of soy sauce to our door explaining that it came compliments of Ikeda-san. I met Ikeda Keihachi for the first time during the last days of the Seinen Club. At the time, I rented a room in Asakusa. He often trailed after me as I performed *enka*, but he himself never tried to sing. He came to hang out at my place and sometimes brought along an alarm clock. He worked at repairing clocks.

When evening came, a number of us gathered around my wife's pillow for a little haiku meeting. Among our members were Satō Gyōgetsu, Uson, and Izan. I can't remember who else. My wife joined us from where she was lying atop her futon. The theme was May showers and the summer moon. While we severally muttered 'summer moon, summer moon' over and over trying to come up with ideas for poems, a voice shouted:

In the skylight
Square and center
The summer moon

132

We turned to look and it was Tomomichi who was stretched out on the *tatami* looking out from a high window. Satō laughed, 'What? Tomo-chan said that?' We forgot about him and returned to our poetry. Tomomichi got up and took a fan out to try to stir up a cool breeze on his own. All the while he was murmuring to himself. He was seven years old.

My wife's poem went, 'The wind-swirled sand turned to May's falling rain.'

Kuroku dropped in. We enjoyed each other's company. One time he left five yen. It was a great help for me. (We later repaid him.)

Ah, Is the World a Dream?

Things got increasingly difficult. Akiyama said, 'When we sang "It's a money world" we were able to buy that cupboard and when we sang "I don't understand" we got the *tansu* dresser over there. Don't you think that's odd?' Despite the past prosperity, *enka* were not selling well at all now. At this point I brought out a new song 'Ah, Is the World a Dream?'

Osaburō's murder of Noguchi Neisai had created a sensation. The publisher Ikemura Shō who ran Shōyō-dō produced a little paperback called 'Midnight's Memory' by Yakumo Sanjin. Soon knock-off versions of Yakumo Sanjin's *enka* appeared. Shinmon Yasuji, a fellow who stayed on the second floor over the Iwata's print shop, came out with an all but identical text of the story and *enka*. I produced my own version.[38]

Is the world a dream?
In this prison I think that my sleep-time dreams
Are my waking thoughts
And looking around
A serene world surrounds me moving on

This was sung with the melody found in 'Natural Beauty,' a song sung in elementary schools. It sold wonderfully. Along with the song's popularity, Shōyō dō saw sales of their little book begin to surge. At the time, the paperback was called a 'beauty book' or '*bihon*.' Many people took this as a hint to produce something similar and lots of imitations were published. These were called red songbooks. Prices for them kept falling as competitors undercut one another. Nevertheless, Shōyō-dō did not try to cut costs by reducing the quality of paper on which 'Midnight Memory' was printed nor did the company reduce the booklet's price. The wholesale price was 1.5 or 1.6 *sen*.

I wrote another song, 'Dampened Sleeves,' intended to express the feelings of the wife of the condemned man. At the time, the lyrics were reprinted in Yamazaki Kesaya's *Hōritsu Shinbun*, a newspaper that focused on legal issues.[39] The poetic structure, in the form of a musical letter from Soeko to her imprisoned husband, was set in 7-5 meter. My version was inspired by a poem by Akabane Ganketsu.

Dampened Sleeve

A paulownia leaf announces autumn
Quickly two months have passed
Thrown into prison
How lonely you must be!
As the days come and go, I think of nothing else
Recalling in my bed alone
On my pillow hot tears
Dampen again and yet again
Autumn at long last nears its end
The leaves are red and gold in the surrounding hills
The sun shines shimmering bright
But what burns within your wife's breast
This fiery hue
Makes any color seem faded
In the ultramarine blue of the clear sky
I hear the call of wild geese
And I long for you locked away
Hearing the chirping of crickets in the bamboo hedge
I suffer at their cries
And can only weep
Falling to the grass in our garden
Countless times I cry there
You and I in this world
Share a mysterious fate
Bound to no others

The old morality
The cold rules of society
We have become outcasts from these
And have tasted this world's loneliness
Called a heartless woman of stone
Mocked in song as a woman unloved
I cursed the world and the people in it
From the depth of my being
But I have felt your warmth
Felt the love in your blood
And for the first time knew a woman's love

Soon you will go to the killing ground
And won't our shared fate
Vanish like the morning dew?
To hear such sad tidings
Cutting the bonds of our love
I shall never forget that cruel law
That rends me from you
My beloved, if left without you
What joy could possibly remain?
I will follow you
I will pluck out this pain that pierces my heart
In this cold world I am called merely
A wanton being, a criminal
Rather than suffer people's slander
If called a criminal then with a criminal
I will join hands with you and walk through death's door
We shall cross death's river together
Yet, even though so resigned
This world is one of violent storms and waves
How can I abandon your child to it?
It is said, a child raised without parents
Grows up and then
Is known as the child of the wicked, as an orphan
The child of the vilest demons
Scorned and abused by all
Thinking of the humiliation she will suffer
I who want to die cannot

I must make do for our child
My heart agonized by sorrow says
Die quickly, do away with yourself
But this suffering will not let me die
It is a sentence of fuller measure than yours
To make your wife continue to exist in this world
Understand my sin and grant your forgiveness
It is easy to abandon this world
But for your child's sake I shall not abandon her
I will continue this pitiful life
For the sake of our pitiful child
In this world, countless are those
Who weep because of a bitter fate
Your wife acts only unworthy
I cannot stop grieving, I cannot stop weeping
As the memories rush back ceaselessly
My tears fall without end.
(Azembō)

The song enjoyed a great public reception. At that time, the *enka* singer named Kuramochi Guzen, known for his passionate renditions, told me that he always had difficulty singing it because it was impossible to get through it without weeping. Akiyama was the first to sing 'Dampened Sleeve' but it became popular with many others. Even Shinmon said that it was impossible to sing the tune without tears dampening one's own sleeve. He liked the tune and came over by bicycle to trade his own 'Midnight's Memory' lyrics for my lyrics.

Around this time *enka* singers began carrying violins around with them. The first time I saw this was when I encountered Akiyama with the instrument on a festival day at the Suiten Shrine. I thought, what the heck is that strange thing he's playing? Kaminaga had brought out the instrument, but at first no one had the instrumental music to synchronize with the songs. We had to put ink marks on the strings and come up with other make-do solutions. The practice made for a wealth of funny stories.

It was the time of suffering student *enka* and the fever for those songs had taken over. Students had become ever more active in society around this period and were praised for their efforts. Influenced by the suffering student song, great numbers of young people flocked to Tokyo from all over the country. Many delivered newspapers or milk, or took similar menial jobs. Many among them also sang *enka* at night to make it convenient to study by day. All of a sudden the number of singers sharply increased. These *enka* singers customarily wore a *hakama*, a kind of formal man's kimono with a divided skirt, when performing. *Enka* began to be thought of as a kind of side job for working students. In the past, people when speaking of *enka* generally called the form *sōshi-bushi* or activist songs. Now they lumped the songs into a single genre called *shōsei-bushi* or student songs.

I recall that I once saw a bean curd seller dressed up in a *hakama* calling out 'tofui, tofui' in a stylized manner not unlike an *enka* singer. Anyway, it was a time of popularity for the suffering students. In fact, it was a great time for those who were not students but simply dressed up to present that image. Mixed among the *enka* singers were types many and varied. The old guard, those people who were genuinely suffering students keen on pursuing their studies, hated this trend. Many among them decided to follow other lines of work. Nevertheless, there were plenty other 'students' who were simply happy to carry around a violin and sing. Their type became as prevalent as proverbial mushrooms after a heavy rain. The public welcomed and embraced a new rage, one that made it possible to stroll down a lane in a red light district and be greeted by singers plucking these novel musical instruments.

Of course, the students did not please everyone. Some of new *enka* singers were reviled for using those deformed monster gourds and for making sounds that resembled drawing a saw across their instruments. Along with condemnation of the instruments came an onslaught of voices raised against depraved students, juvenile delinquents, and the like. The fact that many such people were indeed mixed in with the singers helped substantiate the complaints.

The Takayama Factory

Before long, we moved to Tabata. Ikeda Keihachi eagerly invited me to join him. His house was big. In front there stood a large gingko tree and in the spacious garden various trees were in leaf spring and fall. A gardener, Shimizu, lived there. In the back, in a small retirement cottage rented from the landlord, a widow and her son also had their place. The house had been thoroughly cleaned. Rice and coal had been sent by the Takayama Factory. My wife, Tomomichi, and I went for a walk side by side. In the distance above the Tabata highland we could see the beauty of clouds blown about by the summer wind. Tabata Station was right before us. When Tomomichi heard the steam engine give a shriek from its whistle after being uncoupled from the other cars, he declared, 'Ah, now the engine gets to play.'

I had a position during the afternoon shift at Ikeda's Takayama Factory (as in 'Takayama,' my wife's maiden name) as a kind of consulting manager. As the plant was near my house, a boy was sent running when there was something special someone wanted me to do. The factory produced machinery. At the time workers were trying to figure out how to copy an imported machine used for making pills. Ikeda was a small-time capitalist. The research on duplicating the machine was going forward, but only slowly. I was not particularly engaged for the time being. I felt carefree.

Katayama had a house at the rear of some wheat fields on the heights. The poet Kodama Seijin was also close by. Katayama went to Kanda from Tabata Station. As my house was on his way to the station, he stopped by to visit and to take a rest on the porch. The sun shined fully on the long veranda. In the garden the peach buds were beginning to swell. He said something like, 'It will be wonderful when those bloom.' We all looked forward to that, too.

One morning I heard the sound of pruning shears and got up to find to my astonishment that the peach tree, the one on the verge of blooming, had been cut back to practically nothing. Without even time to feel disappointed I realized that the place had been put up for sale. The neighborhood had shrines in the woodlands, a Buddhist hall (dedicated to Yama, King of Hell), and here and there, wheat fields. At night all became so completely quiet that my wife felt lonely when left by herself.

Kawada and Kuroku often called on me. When we ate together, Kuroku motioned toward Kawada and said, 'For virtue's sake, he eats nothing but bread.' Kuroku had a unique laugh. My wife called it the 'Kuroku laugh.' The workmen from the factory also stopped in. The son of Shimizu Reika, our next-door neighbor, came around because he wanted to learn how to compose haiku. When the conversation turned to making money, I sometimes got so involved that without noticing I started to rant. 'If I had just a little capital I could do this and that and make a bundle,' I would say as I got swept away.

138

On those occasions, my wife would titter out loud and say, 'Now that's rich! For you to talk about making money!'

My elder brother-in-law and the rest of the Ikeda family moved to a house not far from ours. A change in fashion and shift in international trade had brought the once prosperous business of making lace, handkerchiefs, tablecloths, collars, cuffs, and other items to a dead stop. For the time being my elder brother-in-law would work at the Takayama Manufacturing Plant. Masao and my nieces came to play. The research on the pill making machine was turning out to be rough going. Workmen busied themselves killing time, greeting one another or engaging in banal conversations about a broken spring in some machine. Factory business aside, a certain Mr. Kin who lent money to Ikeda now frequently came to the factory. At home we often had *soba* buckwheat noodles. But they tasted so bad that they were barely edible.

Ikeda Keihachi's woes gradually increased and our rice supply declined. We had one large bale of glutinous rice left and with some of that we mixed red beans to make *sekihan*, a dish usually reserved for special celebrations. It filled the bill. When guests would come we could drizzle a little sesame oil and salt over it and serve it just like that. At first, the workmen who stopped by felt that they were being given a festival treat and commented on how good it tasted. But, as might be expected, day after day of *sekihan* left them saying, 'Ah, I really want nice plain rice.' Despite their complaints, they nevertheless managed to eat through the entire bale of glutinous grain.

Three men had established the factory by jointly putting up the capital to get it started. Now one of them, his patience at an end, looked almost ready to give up. 'Until dividends are produced I will leave the running of the place to you two. Do as you see fit.' After so declaring, he no longer showed up. At long last, the pill making machine was on the verge of success. Unfortunately, Ikeda's spear was broken and his last arrow already shot. He now had to transfer his rights to the machine to a creditor. When it became clear that failure was certain, Mr. Kin, sniveling a bit, noted, 'Ah, those *soba* noodles, we certainly had our fill of them.'

The Ryōmoto-dō Incident

Kawada and Kuroku became junkmen. Kuroku rented a place in Dōzaka. I went over to look in. He had posted the word 'Entrance' in large letters above

139

his shoji sliding screen entryway. Even without the sign one could tell there was no other way to get in.

Kuroku got quite excited when he heard some inside information from his fellow ragmen. The story concerned a decrepit-looking old woman who often showed up at the rear entrance of the Ryōmoto-dō, a tea store in Ueno. She was treated like a beggar, but the rumor was that she was the proprietress of an old store in Nihonbashi and had once made a handsome living. She, in fact, had good reason to show up at the Ryōmoto-dō's rear entrance because Kondō, who ran the Ryōmoto-dō, was actually just the shop's former clerk and a kind of caretaker of the establishment. When the real owner died, Kondō went to pay his respects to the widow. The visit resulted in her relying on him to run things. The more kindness he demonstrated the more he was asked to do. He became a guardian of the enterprise and looked after its accounts. In this way he was able to oversee matters in the wake of the owner's death and to help his family put their household affairs in order. (The original master had an eldest son but he was mentally defective.)

The outcome of settling up the storehouses, land, and rental properties yielded more than 20,000 yen. Kondō was given charge of the money, from which he was supposed to send the widow a small amount for her monthly allowance. But the money that Kondō kept he used to dabble in speculative ventures. These failed and within ten years he had suffered major losses. He used what money remained for running the Ryōmoto-dō shop and a tea room in the natural history museum. Kondō thought that he could use the income from these to handle the old woman, mollifying her with a monthly allowance for the rest of her life. Meanwhile, he would keep a comparatively larger sum that he would receive through liquidating the inheritance. Now he had decided that even the widow's monthly stipend was too much. He turned to putting off the old woman with ill treatment and simply giving here a quart of rice and bag of charcoal whenever she called at the rear entrance to the business that her family had once owned.

Kuroku's righteous indignation burned when he learned the details of what had happened. I became his partner in his plan to help the old woman. First, Kuroku had to pawn his belongings to provide money to feed and care for the old woman's forty-year-old idiot son. We then took two months to collect information about what had befallen the Ryōmoto-dō. We intended to go to the Ryōmoto-dō to confront Kondō, but he seemed always to leave the shop to others while he was out running around somewhere. It was said that he was heavily into gambling. We wanted to seize him by the neck, but never knew when he would return and it wouldn't do to be loitering about his house. At this point, we assigned Masao to stand watch near the statue of Saigo Takamori as Kuroku and I watched from the car stop area in front of Ueno Station. It was the second day of our watch. It began snowing lightly in the evening. Suddenly our scout Masao ran to us and said, 'Now! He's gone in just now!'

We immediately marched into the enemy's camp, but Kondō controlled the discussion as he skillfully evaded responsibility, claiming, for example, that he was not obliged to inform the old lady of financial particulars and the like. We pressed him on details but he asserted that according to his accounting records he had in fact even overpaid the old woman. When we said we wanted to see the calculations he pulled out an old ledger. Of course we knew that it would be some made-up balancing act, but we did discover that even with this cooked book, something over 100 yen remained due the old woman. We demanded that he give us a written statement of the balance. He responded that he didn't have the money with him. We then arranged to meet again on another day to settle things and went home for the night.

The snow piled up. It was cold and we got something to eat. Then Kuroku rolled up his the sleeves on his Inverness cloak. It was supposedly the '300 model' but it was a rather irregular Inverness, as Kuroku like to say. He pulled up his hands and waved them over his head and cried out, 'Please help me O Great Spirit of the Ryōmoto-dō!,' and then did a little jig. He was in a great mood and explained that his performance was called the Ryōmoto-dō dance.

On the promised day we went at the appointed hour. This time it would be at our turn to do the talking. Kondō began with a story that was just impossible to understand. Gradually my own voice became louder and louder. Kuroku slowly began to roll up the sleeves of his kimono. At that moment a sliding door in the back gently opened, and someone said, 'Now, now, as I am sure I certainly don't want to embarrass two fine young fellows like you two ... .'

The speaker was a portly man with a metal chain hanging from his thick *obi* waistband. We hadn't even considered a turnabout like this. It was Osawa Tsunemasa. He was the fellow who had taken care of registering transactions when Kondō consolidated his master's family's assets. As we talked things over, we found that Osawa was of the old school and possessed

141

a strong sense of justice. He also said he was a friend of Enomoto Buyō.[40] At last he turned to Kondō and told him that he was wrong. As for Kondō, he expected that Osawa would support him, but he did anything but that. In the end, he mediated a settlement of 450 yen to be paid to us, which Kondo was to provide by selling the teahouse in the museum.

The old lady thought she would never be able to recover her money. When she got a glimpse at the cash a look of selfishness spread across her face. We had called the old lady to an eel restaurant to settle matters. We could read her thoughts as she gazed at the cash. From the start we had intended to help her so it was fitting just to give her everything, but between ourselves we had also agreed to split the receipts. After all, we had gone to a lot of trouble to pull this off, what with pawning goods to feed the old lady and all. Finally, we decided we could be neither evil nor saintly. It is really difficult to express the subtlety of our mental state at this time. We took 200 yen and gave the rest to the old lady. She looked at the money with a bit of wistful regret and then said, 'Okay, but you two pick up the tab for this meal.' Later we split the remaining money fifty-fifty, except that Kuroku took five yen off the top saying that, 'If I don't collect the five you owe me now, I'll probably never be able to collect it, ha, ha!' This all happened while I lived at the place in Iriya.

The secret information had emanated from the junkman's house and it was from trash that the 'Ryōmoto-dō Incident' took shape. When he saw me off that night I stood around a bit and Kuroku asked, 'Well, aren't you going on home?' I replied that I would go out and sing *enka*. He said, 'What pluck!' and walked away. After singing, I went home, too. Not long after that I got a letter from Kuroku. I couldn't guess where it was from and was amazed to learn that it came from distant Okayama. I don't know what he had gone there to do. He only mentioned enigmatically that 'thanks to you my purse has become lighter.'

My Father's Death and My Mother

I received word from my hometown that my father had died. I borrowed a swallow-tailed coat from Ikeda Keihachi and carried that with me when I returned. My father had a good expression on his face. His body was already cold.

When we lived at the Naka-negishi place, I invited my father to our house and provided all the hospitality possible. But he was no longer able to drink. When he was healthy he could easily put away a one-*shō* bottle of about two liters. But more recently, after just two drinks, he would say, 'Ah, I will leave the rest to you,' and refused to drink no matter how often we offered. While with us in Tokyo, he decided to go out to look at Iriya's famous morning glories. But he lost his way and did not return until close to noon. Akiyama and many others split up to help search for him. No matter how hard we searched we couldn't find him. Long after the noon hour had passed he came dragging in alone without the guiding hand of anyone to lead him. When he returned to the countryside I had to accompany him more than half-way back. After worshipping at the Daishi Temple in Kawasaki and making a call on the God of the Harvest, we parted at Kawasaki Station.

That was our final parting.

My father undertook all kinds of work for the sake of the village. He was a believer in Narita and a leader of the Fujikō sect that believed in the efficacy of prayer at Mount Fuji. [41] He took care of our local temple. He led his fellow villagers to worship mountain spirits and perform the *otakiage* ritual, whereby the Fuji believers find healing by warming themselves at a blazing fire. [44] When they returned from a mountain pilgrimage he escorted them back home. He was always working and bought himself a fine set of tools. He disliked anyone touching his toolbox. He would work away out in the storehouse, slow but sure. When I returned home to take the army induction physical I peeked into the second floor of the storehouse to find that he had built an enormous wooden tub. When I asked what it was he just said, 'Oh that ... .' In fact, he had built his own coffin. He was a man who enjoyed working properly. We put him in the coffin he had built for himself and he was gone.

Before my father died, a shelter for indigents had gone up on the other side of the railroad tracks. But the new construction had not resulted in everything being pulled down. On the edge of our neighbor Michigoro's property two huge trees still stood. They were so big and full that they obscured any view of the fields behind them. Their roots were beginning to be exposed, something that greatly worried my father. 'If only they weren't out like that, if only ...,' he used to say. After my father died the two big trees withered as well. Earlier, I mentioned the decline of the lace business. Of course, my elder brother's enterprises also went belly up. Nothing could be done. He sold the house and land to Watanabe Heibei. With this final step, my family was now financially ruined. Zenjirō returned to take care our mother. My elder brother lost the house that he thought he would inherit with my father's passing. Making matters worse was the fact that he had a family of seven to support. He simply had to eke out a livelihood somehow. Yoshigoro, my younger brother who had ruined our family, took off. In all of this, my situation was not really taken into account. My elder brother left for Yokohama, putting our mother and his eldest daughter Oyuki, a girl cherished by her grandmother, temporarily into the shelter across the tracks. Zenjirō had been planning to teach school in Ōiso to enable him to look after our mother. But he changed that plan when hired to be the household tutor for the children of Viscount Suematsu Kenchō. [43] Mother, wanting him to succeed in the world, consented to his taking the position. And so Zenjirō also went off to Tokyo where he lived at the Suematsu estate.

My mother finally rose to the post of maid in waiting in the house of the nobleman, Hayashi Daigaku. For her, working in a nobleman's house was her own version of achieving worldly success. My mother told me the following story of her experiences during the 'maid-in-waiting' years. The maids themselves got together to write haiku. My mother wrote, 'A fluttering against the shoji's paper panel, the reflection of a butterfly.' I told her it was a terrible poem but she just laughed and reminded me that my haiku friend's line, 'The first snow and wild geese and ducks driven down,' was even sillier. Anyway, when guests passing down the corridors at the mansion saw that even the maids composed haiku they commented, 'Well after all, the maids at the Rinke house are indeed quite different from our own.'

Mother also served Count Matsudaira's family.[44] The Count had strict rules about how the servants should speak and refer to specific objects. They could not, for example, call a broom a broom but had to refer to it as a stroke. My mother, well, she had a refined character that did not match her country background so she fit in. She also had her peculiar ways about her. If someone said that a certain man was rumored to be a truly admirable fellow, she seemed to listen and agree with a 'Yes, yes,' and an 'I see, an admirable fellow.' Then she would suddenly say, 'But what is he really?' She inevitably added something like this.

Thus, my mother and Oyuki had been left behind in that shelter in the country. Soon thereafter I thought it was a good arrangement that would allow Tomomichi to go to school. I asked my mother to take care of him and

Oyuki. I thought that if she was taking care of one child another would not make a difference. And thus Mother also accepted Tomomichi into her care.

As for Zenjirō, achieving a degree of 'worldly success' corrupted him. He attempted to emulate the ways of high-class living. On one occasion one of his creditors, the owner of a Western-style restaurant, showed up saying, 'Regardless, even if it's Western food, you have to eat a lot of it to run up a tab of 100 yen!' He seemed genuinely impressed with my brother's wastefulness. Of course, there was no way my brother could send anything to our mother. He sent her a little money at first, but that suddenly and completely came to a stop. My older brother suffered the utter misfortune of losing the house he deserved to inherit. His first priority became supporting his wife and children. It was all he could do to accomplish this. He had not a moment to look after the welfare of others.

Notes

[1] The statue is one of the bodhisattva, Kannon.

[2] As assortment of boiled vegetables and products of yam and fish paste served in broth and skewers, and often on the menu at outdoor night stalls and other eating places.

[3] The *tekiya* designation originally referred to a low-class of itinerant peddlers during the Edo period. Its more recent usage straddles the region between legality and illegality in referring to a stall-keeper, huckster, runner of petty gambling games, and seller of good of questionable quality and dubious provenance. *Tekiya* often led a drifting life working the entertainment stalls of local festivals. They sometimes cooperated in loosely organized groups of fellow *tekiya* and had ties with *yakuza* groups.

[4] Azembō is beginning to think like the homeless wanderer he was always on the verge of becoming.

[5] The Triple Intervention refers to the action of Russia, Germany, and France after the Sino-Japanese War (1894–95) and following the singing of the Treaty of Shimonoseki to force Japan to return the Liaotung Peninsula to China. The Japanese government, recognizing the threat implied in the European powers' advice, complied. After the Japanese government acquiesced, Russia immediately occupied the peninsula. In Japan, this created a widespread sense of national humiliation and demands for revenge that culminated in the *gashin shōtan* policy of persevering through any difficulty to achieve revenge. The Triple Intervention thus created public support and the political will needed to push public spending for military strengthening and heavy industrialization. The policy appeared successful when the Japanese won the Russo-Japanese War (1904–05).

[6] The occupation of masseuse was typically one pursued by a blind person.

[7] *Kanakin* is a Portuguese loan word given a Japanese pronunciation and used to refer to calico and other cloth types.

[8] Azembō is moving westward around the Kansai region after departing Nagoya and the Chubū region. He has now passed through Osaka, Mie, Wakayama, and Kyoto prefectures.

[9] Hirose Takeo (1868–1904) became a hero of the Russo-Japanese War when killed attempting to use several small ships to block Port Arthur. His death, remembered in song and mass-produced prints, was also one of the war's most highly publicized events.

[10] In other words, the product was good because of the effort Azembō put into creating it. He has found a modest way of being immodest about his skills at songwriting.

[11] The dippers were used to clear mosquito larva from the ceramic or metal equivalent of rain barrels. Japanese homes used rainwater that was passively collected from roof runoff and downspouts to dampen the dust in front of the home, water flowers, and other purposes.

[12] The sentence is its own paragraph in the original text. It appears to refer to the hobby of collecting rocks and stones that are distinct by their odd or fantastic shapes.

[13] Flowers made of paste and salt in the shape of a lotus flower were placed on the Buddhist altar as an offering to a departed family member. The practice continues in many parts of Japan today.

[14] All names mentioned here and in many places elsewhere in this chapter are those of minor *enka* singers and street performers. Most were known to Azembō, but have been lost to history.

[15] The diplomat and statesman, Mori Arinori (1847–89) is best known for his work to establish the Japanese educational system to serve state needs. He served as Minister of Education in the 1880s, after establishing the Meirokusha (or Meiji Sixth Year Society) and worked

to disseminate Western thought and customs, including ballroom dancing. On February 11, 1889, the day the Meiji Constitution was promulgated, he was attacked by the ultranationalist, Nishino Fumitarō, who was outraged by Mori's alleged disrespect for Shinto proprieties.

[16] Here Azembō appears at his most disingenuous. Yes, there was a farcical version of 'Rappa bushi,' but it was not the one for which he is best known and the song sometimes called 'Socialist Rappa Bushi.' See the Introduction at the start of this study.

[17] This is another of Azembō's pen names.

[18] Azembō is again passing off as farce some of his most biting and politically loaded satirical work. See his 'I Don't Understand' ("Wakaranai bushi") that appears later in this chapter.

[19] The socialist leader, Sakai Toshihiko (1871–1933), co-founded the Japan Communist Party. Sakai became a reporter and in 1903, together with Kōtoku Shūsui, started the weekly paper, the *Heimin shimbun* (*Commoners' News*). He was arrested for espousing pacifist beliefs during the Russo-Japanese War (1904–05). He continued active in socialist causes after being released.

[20] See Introduction for one of Azembō's versions of the 'Bugle Song.'

[21] Azembō begins to spend much of his time in composing haiku, but it appears that the Tide Society was more than a literary group. The late Meiji years also saw him engaged in leftist causes and reformist work. This perhaps explains the mention of Hayashi and the Salvation Army band of social reformers in this passage about the group.

[22] Ishikawa Goemon (legendary *c.* 1558–94) is Japan's version of Robin Hood. According to legend, this most famous thief was put to death after failing to assassinate Toyotomi Hideyoshi. When placed along with his son in a cauldron to be boiled alive, he attempted to hold his son above the heat for as long as he could. A large iron kettle-shaped bathtub is called a *Goemon-buro* after him.

[23] This version of the 'It's a Money World' reproduced in a 1999 reissue of *A Life Adrift* omits stanzas in other existing versions of the song. The references in the unedited version refer to the leader of popular anti-Tokugawa peasant uprisings (Sōgorō), a famous samurai rebel (Ōshio Heihachirō), and Karl Marx. Here are the missing verses:

Ah, it's a money world, a money world!
In the cold emptiness these flimsy clothes
Unbearably hungry, only half alive
I must watch without blinking
My parents decrepit, my wife sick
Children crying from hunger
The pain of wanting to die but unable
Ah, it's a money world, a money world!
What can save people from such misery?
From the fields of precious wisdom
The selfish draw off the water even from there.
Why? Why for money of course
Ah, this wretched money world.
Chōbei, Sōgorō, where are you?
Ōshio, Marx, where are you?

Ah, it's a money world, a money world!
Mutually bloodying and bloodied
We are dog-eating dogs contending
And the losers?
They become beggars and thieves

They die by the roadside or drown
They are run over by trains, hang by their necks
For them, no other road,
Just death
Ah, it's a money world, a money world!

[24] Other versions of this song complain about labor conditions and class exploitation. Azembō wrote other songs not included in *A Life Adrift* that attempted to more clearly define what ailed society. One of his most ringing commentaries is a kind of Devil's dictionary titled *A Dictionary for Today's World* that sardonically provided a guidebook to contemporary ills. In it, he notes gaps between advertised claims and the bleak reality that contemporary language attempted to hide. Here are few excerpts from Soeda, Uta gojyū nen, pp. 66–7:

'Unprecedented and hereafter never again' means 'something all too frequent'
'Prize winning' means 'bait for blockheads'
'Love' means 'to cheat out of money'
'A never-married virgin' means 'the divorced woman once again living at her parent's home'
'Average looking' means 'the face of a monster'
'True blue indigo' means 'colors guaranteed to run'
'An honest person' means 'one not suitable for real conditions'
'A wage earner' means 'a tax slave'
'A gentleman' means 'one who loves to play'
'A maid servant' means 'a secret mistress'
'Selling one's bottom' means 'a prostitute'
'Selling one's life' means 'a worker.'

[25] 'Song of Surrender,' and 'Song of the Four Seasons' also appear in truncated versions of *A Life Adrift*, perhaps because of implicit antiwar sentiment and the tension between classes apparent in these songs.
[26] 'Mrs. Sakai' refers to Sakai Tameko, wife of Sakai Toshihiko, and herself a socialist leader. The women had joined thousands of other Tokyoites to protest plans for higher streetcar fares in the city in 1906.
[27] Nishikawa Kōjirō (also known as Mitsujirō, 1876–1940) began in politics as a Christian socialist and member of the Commoners' Society. His attempts to assist in union organization resulted in a two-year prison term and upon release in 1910 he turned to self-cultivation based on the study of the Chinese classics.
[28] Watanabe Seitarō (d. 1918) was an anarcho-syndicalist associated with Ōsugi Sakae and other anarchist writers and activists. In Tokyo in 1915 he organized a study group and later helped edit *New Society*.
[29] Hara Kei (or Hara Takashi, 1856–1921) was Japan's 'commoner' prime minister, who came to power in 1918 following a period of rapid inflation, and was assassinated in 1921. Furukawa Ichibei (1832–1903) created the Furukawa *zaibatsu* or industrial clique that controlled the infamous Ashio Copper Mine. The joke is that these erstwhile leaders were responsible for the astronomically high prices.
[30] The Christian socialist, Abe Isoo (1865–1949), started this journal in 1905. Abe grew more moderate later in his career and served as a Diet member in the late 1920s.
[31] Azembō is referring to the miners' strikes and actions termed 'riots' by the authorities at the Ishikari coalfields in Yubari, Hokkaido in 1906.
[32] Tochuken Kumoemon was an early popular music singer who managed to cross over to become a recording star.

148

[33] Nishikawa Fumiko (1882–1960) was a member of the Commoners' Society and advocate of greater political rights for women as editor of *Shin Shin Fujin* from 1913 to 1923. Kimura Komako (1887–1980) was an actress, dancer, and activist for women's rights.

[34] Fukuda Hideko (1865–1927) participated in the Liberty and Popular Rights movement in the 1880s, and in the Osaka Incident, which resulted in her imprisonment. After her release she became active in the Commoners' Society and edited *Sekai Fujin*, a journal that advocated expanded political rights for Japanese women.

[35] These were *takuwan* pickles, a very common condiment usually made from daikon and served with other dishes.

[36] Fukuda's comment about liberty appears to make the point that political freedom is not to be confused with personal irresponsibility. It is clear that Azembō considered her to be a bit too tightly wound.

[37] Fujiwara Yoshie (1898–1976) founded Fujiwara Opera in 1934 and produced Japan's first full-scale Western-style opera. He sang roles in both Japanese works and the standard Western repertoire, including performances for Seattle's Nippon Kan Theater.

[38] On an evening in late March 1902, the body of an eleven-year-old boy was found in a vacant lot near Yotsuya Station in Tokyo. An autopsy revealed that the boy had been smothered, but also noted a wide strip of flesh missing from his left buttock. Although the case was never proven, police identified Noguchi Osaburō, a university dropout who was later executed for another murder, as the main suspect. The convoluted case has been variously interpreted. One version says that Noguchi supplied the flesh to his beloved's elder brother so that he would give his permission to marry his sister. The human flesh was allegedly served in a soup that the elder brother needed to remedy his leprosy.

[39] Yamazaki Kesaya (1877–1954) worked as a socialist, labor reformer, and publisher.

[40] Viscount Enomoto Buyō (1839–1909) was the first officer sent by the Tokugawa government to study naval science in Europe. He is best known for an unsuccessful attempt to resist the fledgling Meiji by creating a republic on Hokkaido. He later received an important post in Hokkaido in the very government he attempted to resist. He held many key ministerial positions in the central government thereafter.

[41] Since ancient times, mountains in Japan were seen as divine manifestations, or sacred objects of worship, and thus off limits to most people. Mt. Fuji was one such mountain that had its own sect of pilgrims, the Fujikō, of which Azembō's father was a member. Believers would purify themselves and were allowed to enter the sacred terrain of Mt. Fuji to seek contact with the mountain's deity. Such contact was said to protect their families and cure illnesses.

[42] *Otakiage* is a ritual to burn New Year's decorations and old charms and thank the gods for their protection. People stand around the fire to be cleansed of evil.

[43] Suematsu Kencho (1855–1920) graduated with a law degree from Cambridge in the 1870s, after which he enjoyed a multifaceted career as statesman, historian, journalist, and politician. He wrote the first English translation of *Genji Monogatari* and traveled to Europe in 1904–05 to fight anti-Japanese propaganda and fears of the 'Yellow Peril.'

[44] The Matsudaira family had a long lineage dating back centuries and became members of the new Meiji nobility. Azembō does not identify which Count employed his mother as a serving woman.

149

Plate 1. Soeda Azembō in his prime, 1904.
(Courtesy of Kanagawa Museum of Modern Literature Research)

明治26年 赤本の表紙画　演歌壮士の風俗と情景が見える　手に持つのが歌本

Plate 2. Cover of *enka* song booklet depicting clothing style of *sōshi* singer, 1893.

151

壮士の歌う姿　ふとこ
ろに歌本を入れて

Plate 3. *Sōshi* singing on behalf of liberty and popular rights, originally a songbook cover illustration.

Plate 4. Caricature of professional *enka-shi*.

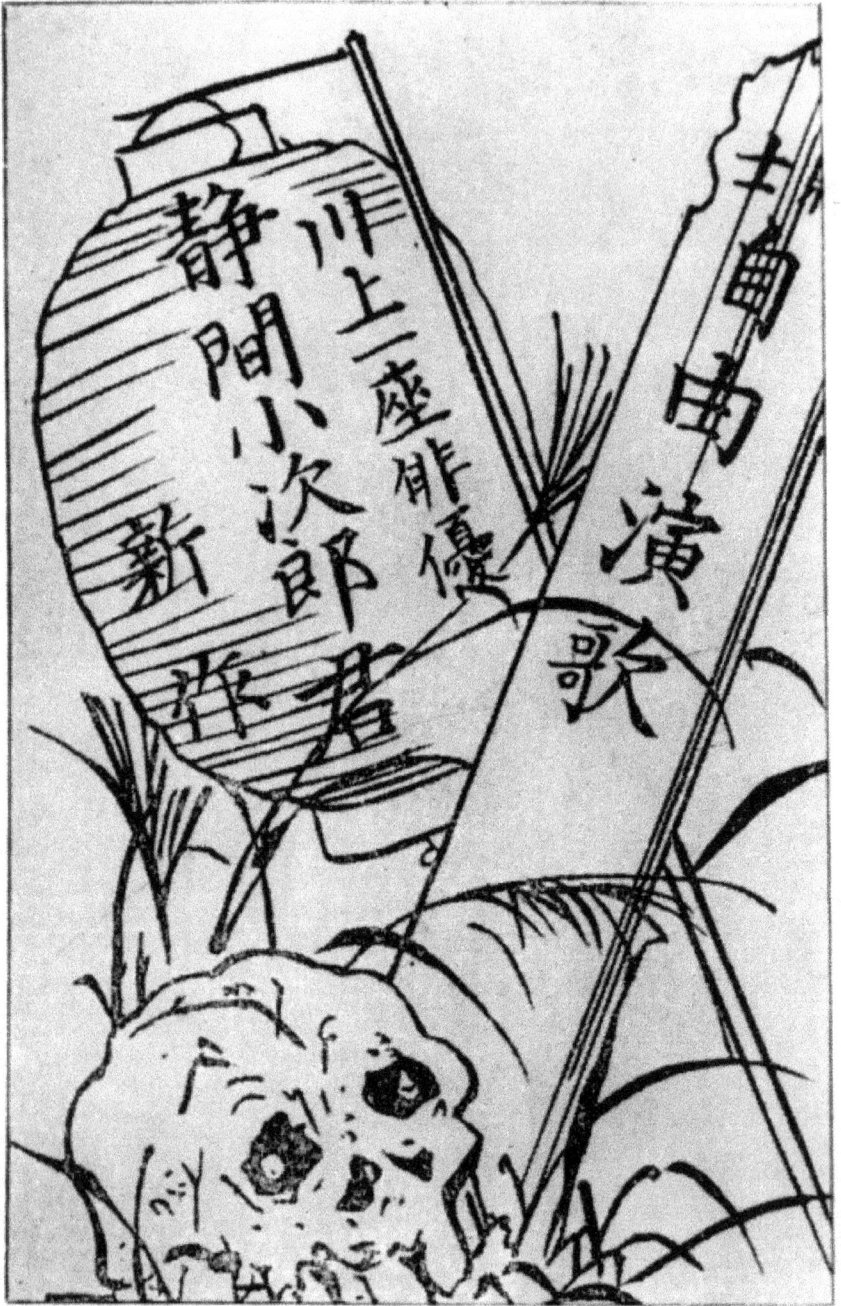

初期ウタ本のカタをのこした野ざらしの表紙

Plate 5. An early *enka* songbook cover offering a paean to liberty.

Plate 6. Late Meiji period songbook covers.

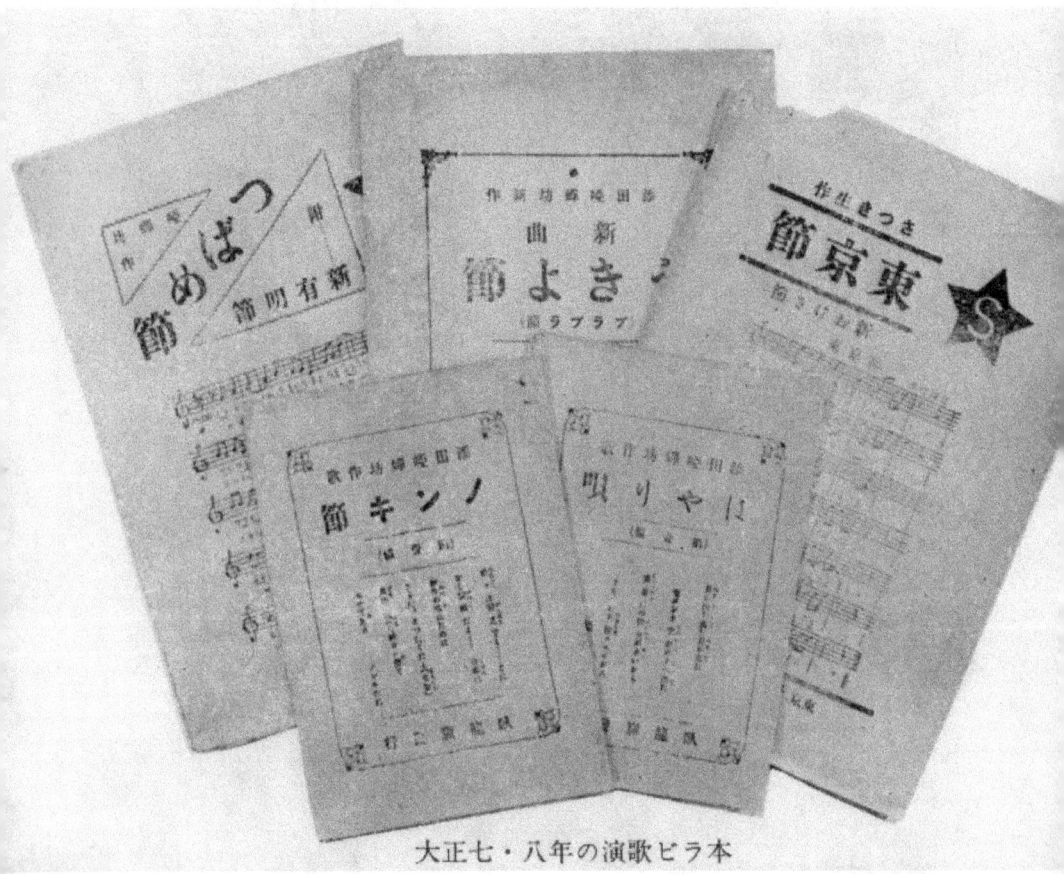

大正七・八年の演歌ビラ本

Plate 7. Professionally printed songbook covers, 1918-1919.

Plate 8. The violin-playing student *enka* singer.

男女づれになっての流し

Plate 9. Women singers emerge, late Meiji-early Taishō.

158

Plate 10. Soeda Azembō, 1920.
(Courtesy of Kanagawa Museum of Modern Literature Research)

Plate 11. Azembō in Takahashi Shōsaku's junkyard, early 1940s.
(Courtesy of Kanagawa Museum of Modern Literature Research)

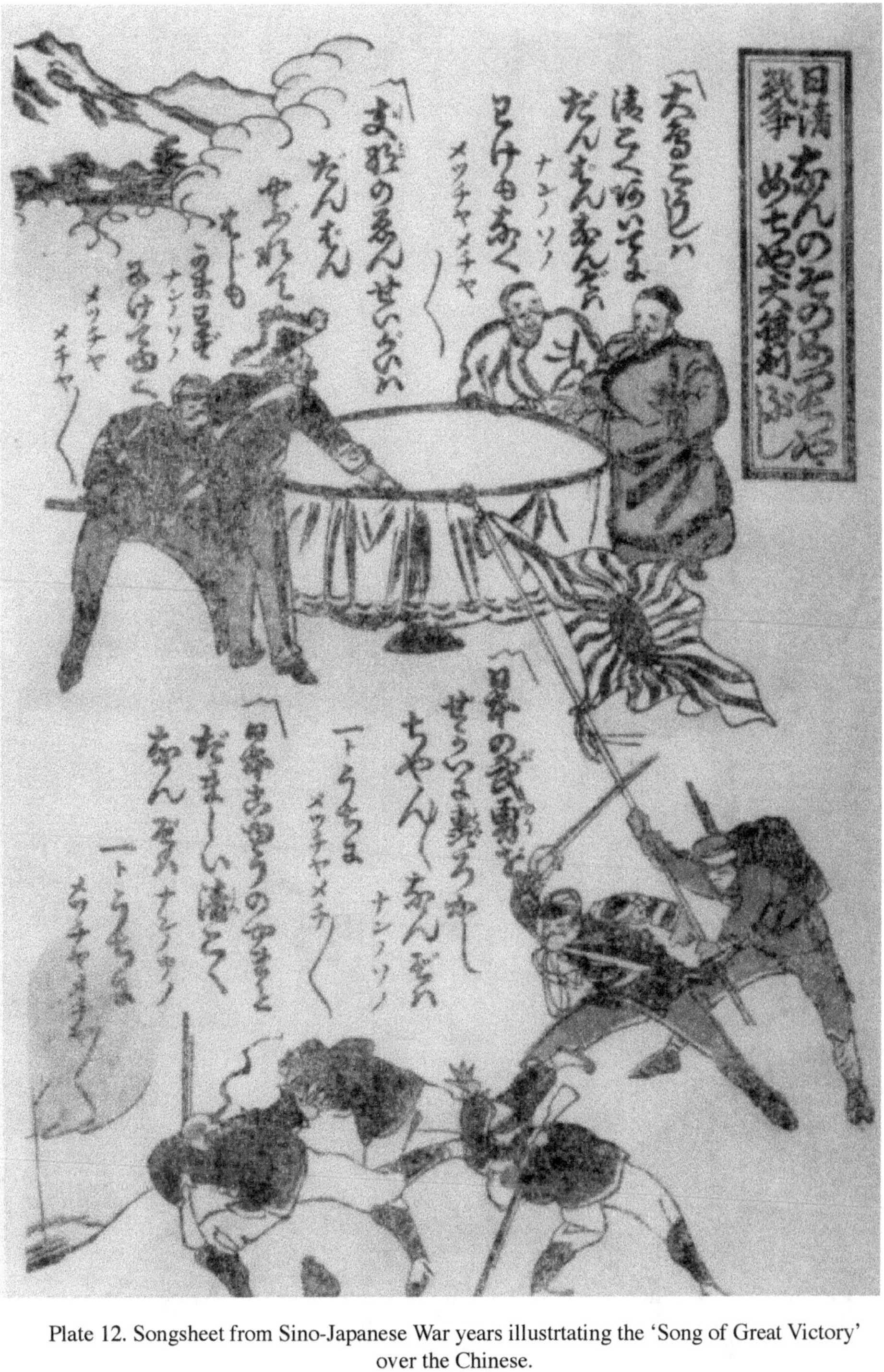

Plate 12. Songsheet from Sino-Japanese War years illustrtating the 'Song of Great Victory'
over the Chinese.

161

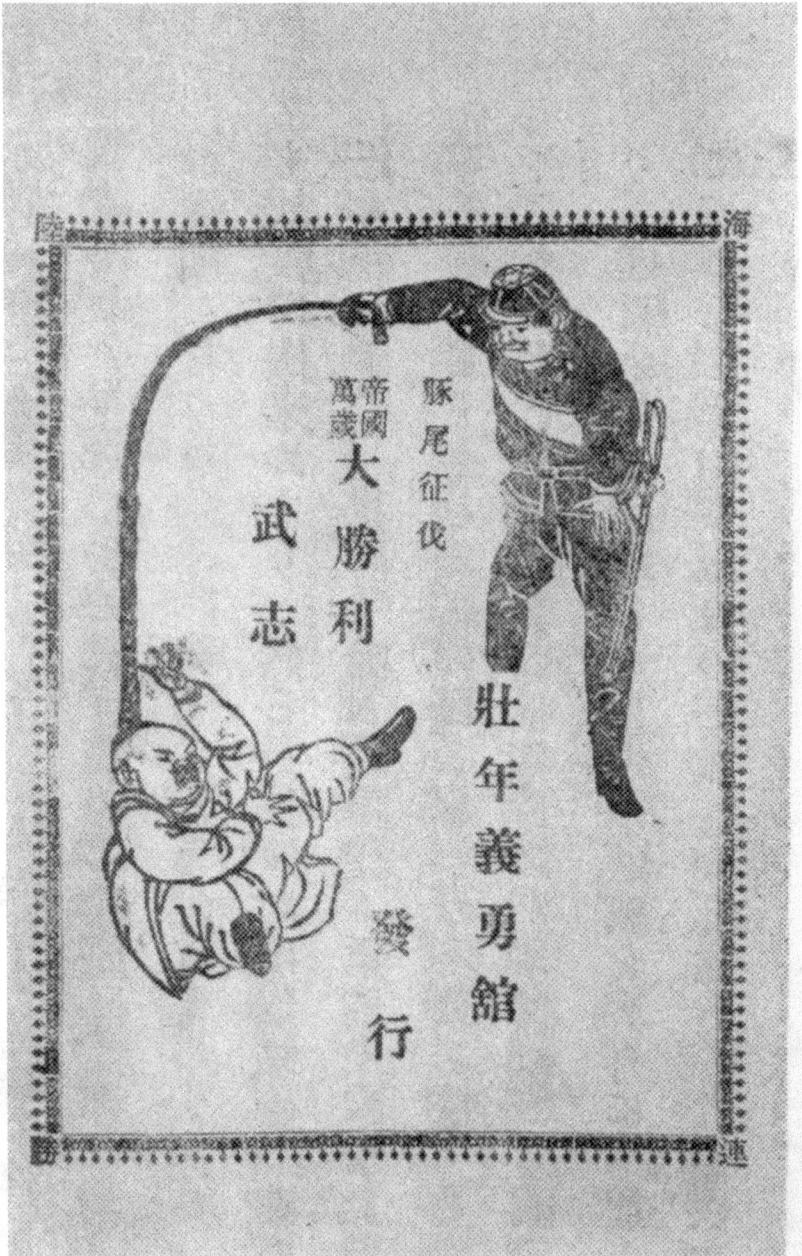

Plate 13. Song sheet from Sino-Japanese War period illustrating Japanese victory over the 'pigtailed' race.

Plate 14. Infant Soeda Tomomichi with mother, Take. The elderly woman is not specifically identified but is probably Azembō's mother and Tomomichi's grandmother, Soeda Tsuna. (Courtesy of Kanagawa Museum of Modern Literature Research)

—明治三十七年二月、大川屋版—

Plate 15. Songbook cover for 'Conquest of Russia' 1904.

164

——明治三十七年三月、萩原新陽館版——

Plate 16. Songbook cover for 'Russia, Bring it On!'.

Plate 17. Speech rally to promote the Socialist renovation of Japan, 1914.
(Courtesy of Kanagawa Museum of Modern Literature Research)

Plate 18. Azembō with friend and collaborator, Kuramochi Guzen, 1933.
(Courtesy Kanagawa Museum of Modern Literature Research).

Plate 19. Azembō with Kuramochi, late 1930s.
(Courtesy of Kanagawa Museum of Modern Literature Research)

Plate 20. Unveiling of monument to Azembō at Bentenyama Temple (within the Sensōji
Temple precincts), Asakusa, Tokyo, 1955.
(Courtesy of Kanagawa Museum of Modern Literature Research)

Plate 21. Soeda Tomomichi standing before the Mokuba-kan comedy theater in Asakusa, 1975.
(Courtesy of Kanagawa Museum of Modern Literature Research)

Plate 22. Soeda Tomomichi and wife, Kiku, at the grave of Azembō and his wife, Take, at Kodaira, in suburban Tokyo, 1956.
(Courtesy Kanagawa Museum of Modern Literature Research).

171

Chapter Five

Enka, A New Style

Filial Piety

My wife showed signs of being pregnant. At the same time, I was somehow taken with the idea of trying one more time to be a dutiful son to my mother. We had left her in the countryside with many kids to look after, but no one to look after her. Each of her own children had their own reasons for not being able to take care of her. Those reasons aside, my wife thought the neglect was just too terrible. She somehow exempted me from the ranks of the neglectful, perhaps because I often went along with her when she went to the country to visit my mother. My mother was less forgiving. When I went along on the visits, she would screw her face into a grimace and declare, 'Dear me, you've gone and pulled him along again.' My wife would say, 'I didn't pull, he followed along on his own.' I laughed at such exchanges. My wife worried about my mother being neglected while my mother detested her son tailing after her.

We had left our son, Tomomichi, in my mother's care so that he could go to school in Ōiso. We now decided that it would be best if we also went to

Ōiso for the delivery of the new baby so my wife moved in with my mother as well. It came to pass that I had to give up our house in Tabata. I called a junkman and brought our household belongings out into the garden. My friends Kawada and Kuroku stopped by and set prices on each item before the used goods man arrived. The sale made more money than I had expected. Kawada and Kuroku smiled and commented, 'Goods sold this way don't make the junkman any money.' After the baggage-laden cart had departed, we carried a number of small items to Kawada's place. I then left for the countryside.

After a while there, I left my wife in Ōiso and returned to Tokyo. Kuroku had a business in his hometown in Yamaguchi and I decided to go there with him. On my way to Yamaguchi Prefecture I again dropped by Ōiso. That night my wife, son, and I, just the three of us, strolled around behind the Sōraku Tower singing the song, 'Gojōhara.'

I left the next day. My wife came to see me off at the station. Just as the train was pulling away from the station, I could see Tomomichi, school bag over his shoulder, standing outside the fence. He had come to see me off on his way home from school. Pushed by people bustling behind him, he started to cry. I could see my wife had left the station and was running to him. And then the train pulled away and they disappeared from sight.

Hiroshima, Iwakuni, and then on to Tokuyama. Kuroku and I went by rickshaw to Kuroku's hometown of Tomioka. That was the first time in my life I bathed in something called a *goemon-buro*, a huge metal bathing tub with a heavy lid used when heating it. I also played around at Takeshima. They have hot salt baths there and the Takeshima Library. During the night I slipped out to the salt bath hot spring after which I rowed around the island in a small boat. It was June and the moon was lovely.

It was in Takeshima that I wrote the song 'The Golden Demon' ('Konjiki Yasha'). I intended to make some money. [1] Kuroku picked up my draft of the song, took one look at the part about Kan'ichi's love agonies, and gave a great reverberating horse laugh. I actually felt the same way. Yet, one side of me also wanted to create *enka* that had depth of feeling. We needed good songs. For some time I had been thinking of nothing but this. Good songs required good composers. We needed artistic merit. I thought we should be able to expect those things from the ranks of professionals in the business.

Now, late in life, I realize that such poets are under exclusive contract to the record companies. My dream of a world of creative musical professionals has ended up being just that: a dream. As for me, these were my years of groping in the dark.

The Golden Demon

Mists shrouded the sky
But the moon's reflection glimmered over the wide sea
The water's as glossy and calm as shimmering oil
The sound of the fisherman's oars echoed
Far out at sea their fiery lures[2]
Dyed red the enveloping mist
As if a dream unfolding
Atami's night beach in springtime
Pines hazy in the mist
They walked here and there
I sing of Kan'ichi Hazama
And Kamosawa Miya who suddenly
Appear so filled with worry
In the eyes of others they look so unmistakably like lovers
All the while feigning that they are not
He looks to her and speaks
You said our love would be forever unchanging
But you have thrown that pledge away
To follow a rich man in marriage
Like the mountain rose that blossoms but bears no fruit[3]
Awake from your golden delusion
Open your eyes to sober reality
Let us share an honest and simple life
Kan'ichi thus poured out his heart cajoling
But his beloved's heart was a drifting cloud
Now captured by the winds of wealth
Miya unmoved by compassion
Had forgotten his faithfulness
Yearning for ephemeral wealth
This mean-hearted woman
This cold-hearted woman!
Until today he never knew

He thought her so pure
The utter baseness of his beloved
Unchaste, abominable woman
Unable to bear any more Kan'ichi
His eyes bulging and bloodshot
Blood boiling as if to rend his chest
In such utter suffering, Kan'ichi
His lips so firmly set
His face as if steeped in blood
His whole body shakes with anger and despair
He falls backwards, collapses
And even Miya is surprised
She embraces his sand-covered form
From Kan'ichi's clinched eyes tears
Fall like sheets of rain
Glowing gray his cheeks
Even the moonlight looks sad
He cannot catch his breath
She feels the blood pounding in his breast
Miya comforts the sand-smeared Kan'ichi
She wipes his tear-stained face
'All this is my fault'
Her face on his shoulder
Trembling she entreats
She encourages but the words cannot win
Kan'ichi his strength ebbing, ebbing
He takes the hands of Miya who clings to him
Miya! Never forget January
Always remember its seventeenth day
On that night you were together with Kan'ichi
And now there is but tonight to speak for a last time
To enjoy the comfort of your touch
Come what may, we have only tonight
I will give up my studies
I will break with my dear friends
And come next year, this moon
No matter where I behold it
I will never forget this night
The moon must forever
Be clouded by the tears I weep

And when its face is misted over
As it is tonight, Kan'ichi
Tormented by bitterness of a depth unfathomable
Will remember and weep with the moon
(Azembō)

From Osaka, I dropped in at Yokohama where a group of *enka* singers had organized their own seven-man association. All used the violin and sang cheerful songs accompanied by their instruments. I was the only one who quietly sang the 'The Golden Demon' and who did so without a violin. Despite that, I was able to chalk up the best results. This prompted Watanabe to ask, 'How did you do that without the o*rin*?' After that they followed me about to observe my routine. (Oh yes, the violin was called simply the '*orin*.')

When I stayed in Tajimaya inn, Ishida Shikibu happened to be there, too. Ishida was one of Takei's intimates. He was the one who came up with the 'English Language Conversation Rapid Mastery Method.' He believed that while classroom English might be an academic subject, it was not at all practical for becoming a proficient speaker. To test this view he encouraged people to try actually speaking to foreigners and to notice how difficult it was to get anything across. He contended that the difference was found in the classroom approach versus the practical, and the art of conversation came from the art of conversation. If you had the knack you could speak fluently and immediately get your point across. This was his position and he wrote it up in a little booklet. It was still selling well. Sometime later, the peddlers and stall-keepers made the book a staple among their wares.

My Wife

After returning to Tokyo I received a letter from my wife saying that she had something to discuss and wanted to see me. Upon arriving she said, 'Let's walk.' and we went out. For a while, we strolled in line parallel with the railroad tracks. Fireflies were in the air. At last, we squatted down on our heels and talked. My wife said that, after all, it was simply no good that she continue staying in Ōiso. She just could not get along with my mother. My wife acknowledged her own responsibility. She had gone there on her own knowing everything about the situation beforehand. But my mother was a woman of another era. My wife had breathed new air and there was clearly a

177

difference in their generations. Despite that, because my wife had experienced hardships in her own life, she felt fully confident that she could put up with my mother's peculiarities and make a go of things. Yet, after trying for some time, it was not going well. She felt that her attempt at her own form of filial piety had failed. She asked rhetorically if it wouldn't be better to leave my mother on her own and perhaps send an allowance, no matter how much? She didn't see any other way out. Let's go back to our life in Tokyo once again, she urged.

On the way back to the capital, we stopped in on Ogawa, my wife's brother-in-law, who lived in Hiranuma. My wife's time to deliver had drawn near and it turned out that we would stay at her younger sister's house for the baby's arrival.

Our first-born girl came into the world. My sister-in-law looked after the baby. My wife's postpartum recovery went well, too. Shortly thereafter I had to go to Bōshū because my brother-in-law's family wanted me to meet with Oshin, Ogawas's eldest daughter, who had relocated there.

Upon returning, I found that my wife's condition had deteriorated. She had a weak constitution and was taking a long time to recover from the birth of our daughter. She was doing well up until twenty days after the delivery, but then the midwife showed up telling her that she needed to get out of bed, hold the baby a little, and walk a bit in the garden. She roused herself and putting the baby on her back in a warm carrying coat, went out into the garden. The effort resulted in her catching cold.

The doctor examined her swollen feet and twisted his head, looking puzzled. I was in constant attendance taking care of her. We tried all kinds of medicines. We even tried a cure that promised, according to the list of efficacies that came with it, to 'give the patient energy equivalent to the ingesting one bale of rice.' At last the doctor simply shook his head in resignation.

I was resigned, too. I thought it was her last and I tended to her as long as I could. I called to have Tomomichi brought to see his mother. Day by day her condition worsened. All my son and I could do was to watch her minute by minute, helpless to do anything to make her better. At night we would put our legs under the warming table and doze off as we stayed by her side. I wished that someone, anyone, would take my place. Just an hour would be fine. How I wanted to stretch full length on the *tatami* and sleep.

I felt so exhausted that at times I could only think thoughts like these and nothing else.

Then came a day when the patient said she felt extraordinarily well. It was the first time since becoming sick that she said she felt so completely refreshed. My wife's expression was as if a burden had been lifted and she said she wanted to look outside for a while. I opened the heavy sliding screen near her pillow. Snow was falling. My wife watched and said, 'Ah, the snow at Tabata was wonderful.' From discussing Tabata we went on to talk about this and that, one thing after another.

She said, 'Tomomichi is alright now. Don't you think we should leave Toshie to someone else to raise?' We had named our eldest daughter 'Toshie.' My wife decided on giving her up out of consideration for my circumstances at the time. She said, 'You have taken such good care of me and I've been such a burden.' These were her last words. She said nothing after this. Two days later during the night she left us. When the time was near, I woke up Tomomichi, who had fallen into a deep sleep. He was crying and cranky. But he was still able to give his mother a last ceremonial drink of water. Perhaps he felt he was still in a dream.Sick in bed for seventy days. January 11, 1910. Twenty-nine years old.

My wife, who was by nature frail, had had her body worn out. I had cruelly dropped her into poverty. She had somehow passed through all manner of storms. In the midst of it all, she even studied. She had started to learn English. And now my wife was dead. Did I kill her? Did society? These were the only thoughts that kept circulating in my mind. I found I could no longer laugh.

I went to an undertaker with Yoshigorō. As soon as Yoshigorō entered the shop he said, 'So, how's business?' The boss of the place shook his head and in a serious tone replied, 'Not good, not good at all.'

Everyone from the countryside came to the funeral, but it was almost as if they had come to do a chore. On finishing up the business they needed to rush immediately home. It was as if they were reluctant to sacrifice the time. I suppose it could not be helped. I was surprised to find that Sakai Tameko sent a postal money order for fifty *sen* along with a note of condolence. I myself had not informed anyone about the funeral. There had not been time. I wondered how Sakai had learned about what had happened. Her letter was a heartfelt and special remembrance of my wife. It made me happy.

I thought I would settle in Yokohama and put Tomomichi in school there. My wife's will instructed me to give care of Toshie to her younger sister. Unfortunately, they in turn left her in the care of another family. [4]

I rented a house. I had to go out to perform *enka* at night. Tomomichi, who was left on his own, always said, 'You will hurry back, won't you?' His voice pierced my heart. This won't do, I thought. I used a hot water bottle when I went to bed. A burn from that same hot water bottle caused an injury that took ten days to heal. We gave up the house at the same time my convalescence ended. Once again I placed Tomomichi in my mother's care. And once again I left, this time for Tokyo.

A Ghostly Haiku Meeting

Upon return to Tokyo, I learned that Shibui Fukutarō had cheated Iwata and sold all of my old *enka* music and drank away the proceeds. I had left a bamboo trunk in Iwata's care and before anyone knew better, Shibui had gotten hold of the songs and had them reprinted.

As Kobayashi Reitei had his own house in Mannen-chō, I stayed there. I spent time at Akiyama's place in Fukagawa, too. Late at night I was haunted by my wretchedness. What should I do? I myself had no idea. I hadn't had time to feel sorrow before, but now it hit with full force. I wanted to express this loneliness to someone and thought that when dawn came I would immediately rush off to ask somebody what I should do with myself. Yet, when the dawn came, some diversion would pop up. Then it would be night again and I would once again be pressed by the same loneliness.

Haiku gatherings were held. I attended. I went around to collect the poems. I made that my job. I published a little poetry magazine called *The Tide*, and came to know many haiku poets. My own pen name was 'Bonjin' or 'Common Man.'

Raidō Ryū had heard of my *enka*. He worked the front counter at the Nakagome house in the Yoshiwara pleasure quarter. A woman ran the place. She was the original owner's mistress and looked after his wife after he died.

She would take the sick woman to the Shizuka-za Theater to enjoy the plays of Fujita Reisai. Later on, the mistress became a believer in Tenrikyō, which prompted her to emancipate the prostitutes and close up shop. Four other houses then joined to buy the place and it became the Fuji-rō.[5]

Raidō also owned a tobacco shop near the riverbank in Senzoku. Later he opened a bookstore. His father was Raidō Ryūkin. The son was Asakusa born and bred, and born and bred to be a haiku poet. Asakusa's haiku circle revolved around Raidō. Ashiyama, Akigiku, Ōmura Kishō, Dōki Hō, Ishii Jūriko, Gekka, Settchū Gantōshi, Hattori Rantei, Hattori Kōseki. Kawamura Togyū, Tsuji Kei, Edo Ryū, Tai U, Seiten, Kōgyo, Bayū, Shirō, Kokusen, Kōji, Kōrō, and others were among its members. In addition, there were people from the Kikaku-dō school, such as Shigu Ran and Ukan, who was the last of Settchū Ran's followers. I got to know many poets as I wrote as the 'Common Man.'[6]

The owner of the Koizumi Print Shop in Kitakiyoshima-chō printed *The Tide*. His pen name was Kōgyo and he was entirely devoted to haiku. Despite his enthusiasm, his print work was always slow and we all craned our necks for sight of him as we impatiently waited for Kōgyo to carry over the freshly printed copies of the latest issue of our magazine. No matter how long we waited he never seemed to come. Finally, I decided to go to his place to see what was up. He explained that he wanted to get to the haiku gathering as soon as he could, but then he realized that he had not completed an important job. So now he was still at it, running the press with a clang and a clang as he puffed and panted trying to finish up.

My tie with Kōgyo was a little strange. Sometime before this, I was in Sannowa one night singing *enka* when someone came up and said, 'You're Soeda-kun aren't you?'[7] It was Koizumi. He said, 'In your line of work it is essential that you decide on one printer to handle jobs for you.' I thought that that was certainly true and as I listened to him talk I realized that he was really talking about his own printing business.

In the past Kōgyo had been an itinerant peddler of books and printed materials dealing in *furimono*. These were sensational, lurid, and usually inaccurate accounts, cheaply printed and cheaply sold, of events such as the great Nōbi earthquake, the eruption of Mount Bandai, and similar disasters. He sold these works by traveling about and delivering a puffed-up street speech that touted his wares and encouraged people to buy. One *furimono* subject was Oroku, the bandit queen of the crescent moon (*Mikazuki Oroku*). The spiel about her went like this:

> Listen up, listen up to learn the detailed circumstances, from first to last, of the arrest of that great rarity in this age of Meiji: the infamous woman bandit! To begin at the beginning, that woman was employed as Shiragiku, well known among those girls at that famous Yoshiwara brothel in Tokyo, the Daimonji-rō.

He would then go on to recite everything he had memorized about the woman robber and her circumstances.

> And that, my friends, is how she at last came to be arrested and sentenced to death. Despite her reliance on the famous lawyers Ōi Kentarō, Okamura Teruhiko, and attorneys x, y, and z for her defense, in the end it was death! Read about it from start to finish. Part I and Part II, two volumes! Nothing left in the middle! Printed in our hiragana syllabary free of those hard-to-understand Chinese-style ideographs! One volume for two *sen*; both volumes for three!

And so it went. In that long verbal advertisement, the barker covered everything contained in the booklets. Buying them after listening to the speech invariably revealed that there was nothing new to be learned.

As the story of Mikazuki Oroku was a total fabrication by the writer Takahashi Suiyō there were, of course, no real details; no root, branch, or leaf to tell the tale. When the public was bereft of genuine sensational incidents, some enterprising writer would simply create this kind of put-up job. Despite that, the story of *Mikazuki Oroku* was later even made into a movie.

Koizumi had a Roman nose, so was nicknamed 'Nose-Nose.' His haiku penname was Kōgyo. He lived in Hashiba where there was a house, long vacant after Odake Kokkan moved to Negishi.[8] It was rumored to be haunted by a husband and wife pair of ghosts who were said to appear from time to time. A fellow charged with taking care of the empty house saw the ghosts, became sick, and had to be hospitalized in Meiji Hospital.

It came to pass that that was where we would hold a haiku gathering. We called it the 'Ghostly Haiku Party.' A wide river ran behind the large house with its many rooms. We used candles for light. An unusually wide and tall staircase led to rooms upstairs. Passing through a long and curving hallway we found firewood near the kitchen. We put the catchphrases, which served as the subjects of our poetic compositions, in that room. Each of us had to go to the room to take a title and then return to compose in silence. This added to the dead silence that already filled the house.

As every new member of our party arrived, we took turns going out to the main entryway to meet them. My hair was quite long and when it was my turn I spread it out so that long strands fell out over my face. I then took a candle and let loose a terrifying shriek as I jumped out at the new arrival, Ryūdō, our haiku master.

About twenty members gathered. Grouped in one room, we silently concentrated on composing poems. No one said a thing and a single candle did little to relieve the gloomy darkness. As everyone grew more and more afraid by the eerie mood, there was suddenly a clattering noise on the outside shutters. Kishō spontaneously shouted, 'What the ...,' and yelled that this was no way to compose poetry and before anyone else could accuse him, he admitted that, yes, he was a coward.

Someone said, 'Maybe it's a river otter.' I got up to take a look and a tiny voice whispered, 'Danger, danger' and 'Stop, stop.' The others stopped me from going further, but I did manage to throw open the shutter and look outside. The only thing that I could see was the silently flowing river. I closed the window and returned to the room. After a while, once again we heard the sound of rapping. It seemed that something was knocking on the outside of the shutter. Everyone remained silent and then began asking each other what it could be. I commanded, 'Quiet! Quiet!' And then everyone kept still for the longest time until a feeble voice was heard saying, 'Kōgyo-kun.'

We looked at each other, bewildered by the voice. And then someone said, 'Isn't that Bayū?' A relieved expression spread across everyone's face. Kurokawa Bayū had slipped out into the garden intending to play a little mischief. But when the house suddenly grew quiet and no one responded to his rapping and tapping, he became impatient and decided to reveal himself.

We did not, in fact could not, write any poems. As we talked together, a drowsy spring morning dawned upon us. With daylight, we made a thorough tour of the house and then went home. That house always remained vacant.

Raidō created a new school of haiku in Asakusa. He was well known as poet of linked verse. But aside from Kōseki, Shugiku, and a few others, no more than might be counted on one hand, belonged to Raidō's school. Somewhat later, some younger poets keen on breaking from the old school became swept up suddenly in Raidō's approach.

New school members took no account at all of the old artists who worked in the same stale rut. The new poets also acted with outrageous arrogance in ignoring even commonplace conventions such as removing one's overcoat before sitting down or taking off one's hat. Such people asked how they could possibly be expected to understand old poems. Rokusan said as much as he stretched out casually resting his head on his elbow. As a rule, members of this group did not care much about clothes or appearances. When well-mannered poets of the old school, men who were lead poets (*sōsho*) of a group, showed up at haiku gatherings, the young Turks grimaced and acted terribly put upon.

I was second to none when it came to acting ill-behaved. I rested my head on my chin and looked bored, too. Later, I reflected on my actions and now realize that my behavior arose from my poor physical and mental state, which made it unbearable to stand people who overstayed their welcome. Stretching out completely all of a sudden became a habit. If the gathering looked at all like it might become somehow formal or rigid, I was known for soon throwing myself down and using my cradled arms as a pillow.

There was a major haiku meeting at Shiobara in Uguisudani (hosted by Tōshi). At that time, three rows of seats were prepared in a large hall for the 150 or 160 participants. In another room the famous men gathered together. Among the select were Naitō Meisetsu , Iwaya Konami, and others.[9] They were dressed up in formal *haori* jackets and *hakama* skirts or in formal Western suits. I took a seat somewhere near the center of the middle row. Later Raidō laughed at me saying, 'I thought our old "Common Man" would probably end up doing the elbow pillow thing and sure enough he did.'

The *Enka* Crowd

The old man Takei passed away without my knowing about it. All of a sudden his funeral was over before anyone had been notified. It was sometime after he died that his wife followed him. She had continued to publish music and provide sheets to singers, but the business gradually went south and she gave it up. She then married Matsumoto Yumeka, a good-natured guy skilled at the violin. The *enka* singers called him by his nickname 'Pon-chan.' At the time all the *enka* singers used nicknames among themselves.

There were two Watanabes. There was 'Dobu Wata' or 'Gutter Watanabe' and 'Genko Wata' or 'Watanabe the Fist.' There were also several Gotōs; 'Rad Gotō' for Gotō the radical, and 'Gotō the Dandy.' There were just as many Saitōs, including 'Kara-san,' so named because he seemed to eat only caramel. Yūtei was called 'Gacha' because he always made a kind of '*gacha, gacha*' clattering sound. The long-legged guy was 'Mr. Long,' the fellow with the slender build was 'Mosquito Legs.' The tall Ishikawa was called 'Noppo,' meaning 'lanky.' Virtually everyone among us used the nicknames to refer to one another. Perhaps the practice can be construed as a lack of seriousness, an approach to life that some might consider disrespectful or even slovenly. But it just as surely also reflected the closeness we felt toward one another.

Later, Pon-chan manufactured a lot of violins in Kyushu and then died young. It is unclear where his wife went after that. According to Ōshima Akizuki in Kyushu, she relocated to Gifu, but according to Ishida Shikiba of Gifu, she became the second wife of a rich farmer in Mino or Owada. He said he even enjoyed a warm welcome when he visited her in her new home. Women are certainly changeable. Takagi Seiyō took Iwata's daughter for his wife.

About that time I visited Iwata's place to join Aoba, Gingetsu, Genkō, and Yūtei in a second-floor room where we entertained ourselves by composing haiku poems. Some of the lines that flew through the air were perfectly awful, for example:

Spring rain
And there we see
The signboard of the wooden clog shop

This threw the party into an uproar. Someone shouted, 'Let's vote on the worst; read them aloud!' Just then Iwata's father came up to the second floor and looked at us anxiously and said in a quiet voice, 'This won't do. The police will raise hell. Stop this business.' Someone spoke up saying, 'Don't worry, this stuff is perfectly innocent.' Unconvinced, the old man said that this was still no good as he turned to go downstairs. It turned out that he thought we were running some kind of gambling game.

One day the old gentleman got into a quarrel with one of his customers. When the customer got so angry that he became violent, the old man said to his wife, 'Run to the post office and swear out a complaint!'[10] Sometime later he learned the difference between the post office and the police. But no matter how we tried to explain haiku to him, we never got through.

On another occasion the old man said, 'Sir, please take a look at this. Now aren't there just some wonderful poems in this. Shibui-san brought it over.' So saying, he carefully took out something wrapped in paper. He opened it to reveal an old magazine that had been vertically folded and then ripped into a thousand small pieces. Once again, the old man had fallen for one of Shibui's tricks. It was at this shop that I met for the first time Shimizu Raijirō and his wife. He both sold candy and sang *enka*. I also saw the great 1910 flood from Iwata's second floor.

Among the tunes being sung at the time were the *enka* 'High Collar Song' by Kaminaga; 'The Hills of Hakone,' a parody of the 'Scholar's Song'; Asai's composition, 'Coarse and Rough,' another parody, this one of the 'Song of Countless Foes;' and my 'Recollections.' Soon everybody was using the expression 'What perfect timing!' Takeishi Muson used the refrain in his song 'Good Timing,' which also became a popular hit. At the time, I did not feel like singing *enka*. It was only after Nagao repeatedly invited me, saying, 'Let's go,' that I finally went out. We strolled around the twelve-story building. I sang 'The Golden Demon.' About that time Kuramochi, Nagao, Kobayashi, Ishikawa, and others advocated bringing together the *enka* singers who were dispersed all over the place. In Koishikawa, Shirota Keisui and others in the group sang the 'suffering student' songs. All of these people came together in a newly formed 'Tokyo Seinen Club.' As for me, I felt that the new organization was just an extra burden. In any case, I was too distracted to pay much attention.

High Collar Song

Gold-rimmed spectacles and a high collar
In Mejirodai in the fashionable west of Tokyo
A student at the women's college
In one hand the poetry of Byron and Goethe
On her lips holding forth for naturalism
And the wind murmurs *saara, sara* through Waseda's rice stalks
A magical breeze, love's wind softly stirring
(Kaminaga Ryōgetsu)

The Scholar's Song

What the? Kanda Bridge over the Kanda River
Gaze across it at five in the morning and see
A man in tattered Western clothes, lunchbox tied to his waist
Walks trudging along considering his nine yen a month
He spies the gentleman flying by in a car
And his tears begin to trickle forth
He wails, 'Oh spirits, oh Buddha listen to me!'
Even a once prosperous Tempo era samurai[11]
Cuts a miserable figure today
At home his house-bound wife ties off hemp threads as piecework
His fourteen-year-old daughter is a hand at the tobacco factory
But though he can smell cut tobacco he can't afford to buy anything but plug
Always his money must go to the Home Ministry
He never has any money to live his life
And play out this struggle for existence
(Kaminaga Ryōgetsu)

Coarse and Rough Song

There are thousands and thousands of sweets
All are of made of sugar
But even if not made of sugar
They are none the less sweet, oh so very sweet
Buns filled with bean paste are unbeatable
But macaroon cake and sweets of chestnut cream
Everybody longs to eat these
We search out the money box
For our searching we are scolded
There are goodies we cannot gobble down
There are goodies we cannot even taste.
(Asai Bō)

Recollections

Hide my tears and outwardly smile
Sing a song that's missing in my heart
Merry and gay the *shamisen* and drum
But why must I work as a whore?

My loving parents in my home village
My sweet little brother and sister there, too
The word 'love' is there in that village, too
I am the caged bird who would fly but cannot
(Azembō)

Good Timing Song

Glaring at airplanes
Stamping my feet in frustration
Bayonet in my hand as tears trickle down
My, my! What great timing!
I hate, yes, I hate those fashionable high collar types
Their minds no more than turbo shells atop a fire and boiling
from within[12]

My, what great timing!

If sake its Masamune, for geisha Manryū[13]
If song, well then it's the 'Great Timing Song'
My, what great timing?
(Takeishi Muson)

The *I-ro-ha* Alphabet Apartments

I received a postcard from Tomomichi written in the katakana syllabary that read, 'Grandma says she can't possibly take care of me any longer. Please come back and take me with you.[14] My mother had at reached the limits of advanced age. She could no longer extend a hand to care for Tomomichi. I had to go get him.

First, I needed to prepare a nest. I went to Kobayashi's place. Harako Motoi lived nearby in the long, low, row of joined rooms, the *I-ro-ha* Tenement.[15] I asked him to rent a place for me there if something was open. It seemed that openings were hard to come by, but at last one became available and I moved in. It was a single four-and-a-half mat room.[16] There were forty-eight such units, thus the name *I-ro-ha* or ABC Tenement, a place with a room for each of the forty-eight marks of the syllabary. Fortunately, the former renter, Mr. Yamano, had been fond of cleanliness. I bought all his old furnishing for four and a half yen.

The place was located in an infamous slum. All sorts and types dwelled there. After moving in I witnessed a shocking scene. A small alleyway near the entrance to the longhouse opened onto a tiny vacant patch of land and there, straw mat spread on the ground and candle providing light, was an open-air gambling den. Many people crowded around the circle and it was not long before the place was raided. The police were rough in catching people. Fighting broke out, but at last the free-for-all died down and everyone got hauled in. I was asked to go assist in getting the group released. One fellow told me that when I go I should take this along and he pulled out a pocket watch. He said one of the police officers had perhaps dropped it during the dust-up.

189

I took the watch and set out. The Iriya Station was next to the Maeda mansion. A policeman who had trailed me on a previous occasion strongly urged me to talk directly with the chief constable. This was how I came to meet Mr. Arai. He had an agreeable air about him. As we talked, our conversation wandered into a discussion of poetry (and in this manner he became a haiku friend and took the pen name Arai Ifu). He and I agreed that it probably would be best for the *I-ro-ha* residents to cease their gambling if he was going to join the poetry circle.

Everyone at the I-ro-ha stayed up waiting my return. I was able to come back with many of the people who had been arrested. The relatives and friends who wanted them back came to bow and to say, 'Thank you for your good work, thank you.' I told them one and all to quit gambling and one and all promised that, 'We won't, we won't' and '"Right, never again, really we won't.'

This is how I started our life at the longhouse tenement and how I made friends with everybody. Year after year, the way of life among people in the tenements gradually got better. At the time of the gambling incident, the magazine *Ukise* or *Ever Changing World* ran an article that noted that, 'A famous man (literally "a reclining dragon") living in hermit-like obscurity instituted a poetry-based slum reform.' After this, I jokingly called our little nest the 'Grotto of the Reclining Dragon.'

A ragman named Kubota recommended that I remarry at any cost because having my son around without anyone to look after him was bound to lead to trouble. Of course, the only reason I had brought a child into the place was because I simply could do nothing else. Reflecting on that, I agreed with his suggestion and enlisted his help in moving in with a woman who once worked in a house called the Nakagome.

At first glance she did not appear to be a bad person. But in the morning when I went out to the public bath, I returned to find that breakfast was not yet prepared. I wondered what she was up to. Then I realized: she was just thick. The next morning I took a long leisurely time in the bath and, sure enough, returned to find that breakfast was prepared. I was relieved and sat down to eat when she said, 'You took so long I went ahead and ate without you.' There were no side dishes on the tray, just a bowl of rice. I picked up the rice bowl and went out into the street to the store that prepared various boiled dishes. I bought a main course there to go with the rice. On the way to

190

the store I came across Kuramochi who said, 'Hey, where to?' I answered, 'I am on my way to buy something to eat with my rice.' To which he responded, 'But don't you have a wife now?' And I said, 'No, I mean yes, but … .' Seeing that it wouldn't help to explain I just gave a resigned laugh and went on my way.

I took a half-gallon bottle of sake along when I later went to see the marriage go-between Kubota. He said that the current situation certainly would not do but he wasn't sure how he could help. The woman did have an older brother. But they had quarreled and she had no place to go. That was where things stood. Indeed, her circumstances had prompted him to plan for my ending up looking after the woman's welfare. He asked me to let her remain as is for the time being because she had nowhere else to go. After that meeting she stayed with us for fifteen more days.

I borrowed a dark blue *haori* coat with a white splash pattern and a kimono from Arai Ifū and began working, my son following along. Takazawa Kichisaburō came with us. Takazawa was to sing *enka* at the Yūgyōji temple in distant Fujisawa at a commemoration of the founding abbot's death day anniversary. It was a job for me, too, but I could not take the boy along.

So, once again, I set out to return my son to my mother's place. At Chigasaki Station, I made Tomomichi wait by our luggage while I went to the toilet. I somehow felt rushed. I did not have time to call at my wife's parents' home and felt as if someone was chasing me. I had become accustomed to being tailed by the police.[17] But this was different. It was as if some block of unease within me, something dark and heavy inside my chest, made escape impossible. I felt like Jean Valjean, child in tow, running away. I stayed in an inn in Fujisawa, still pursued by that dark, heavy sense of unease.

We were planning to stop off in Yokohama on our way back to Tokyo. But when we reached Kanagawa and got off the train to get into a horse carriage a fellow said, 'Oh, it's you!' It was Takechi Kohei. He worked as a *hakouchi*, someone who sells picture books and other items on the trains (the seller's usual refrain went, 'Sorry to trouble you again and again but … .') He said, 'I saw an article in the newspaper about that savage political party and someone with the same name as you was mentioned. Was that you?'

He meant the flyer written in opposition to higher streetcar fares. I thought it funny that he would use the word 'savage' to describe the group. I answered lightly, yes, it was me. He said only, 'You, you … .' I had my child with me, getting off the train that he was just boarding, and the exchange took but an instant.

Time passes. Back at the longhouse, people talked eagerly of nothing other than 'Gokurō, Gokurō' as they gave their reviews of this comedy actor and his work. I didn't have any interest in comedy and barely gave the craze any notice. Yet, I found that even over at Raidō's place the topic of conversation was the play 'Gorō of the Soga Clan' ('Soga no ya Gorō') and the actor Jūrō. Once in Yokohama I watched a comedy that starred Tsuruya Danjurō in a glossy wig and thought nothing could be so worthless. But I decided to reconsider and give it another try, so went to the Imperial Theater to watch *The Drum of Success*. The boy who played the role of the young lad in the drum shop was rather interesting and, on reflection, I decided that the form merited consideration and I began to look it with a different eye. I went to see another performance when the program changed. While I was waiting in front of the Imperial Theater and looking at the signboards there, I noticed a small man with a smooth face looking at the same board. He said, 'Soeda-kun.' Looking carefully I could see that the small fellow was Takechi. Thereupon he pulled out a name card. 'Here is my present affiliation.' The calling card reeked of perfume and was decorated with two butterflies that flitted across the paper. In writing it stated that the bearer was Soganoya Gokurō.[18] I said, 'What?! You are Gokurō?' And then I recalled the person who played the role of the lad in the drum shop. Takechi Kōhei was the fellow who had previously worked for Nihon-kan as an itinerant peddler of books and printed goods.

Murasaki bushi

I began to feel an interest in the meaning and content of 'New Popular Songs,' and suddenly threw myself into learning more. At first, the songs were tools used in the political movement. But soon I became dissatisfied with them as mere devices. I lost interest in using the music as no more than a means to shout; to express only anger, taunts, mockery, and curses. It was too superficial. I wanted to sing from the bottom of my heart. I wanted to sing of the hearts of our people; the way the masses lived, the way I lived. I wanted to find some way to more fully and more perfectly touch and express that. I again thought that one such path would be created by returning to the true song in the music. Past *enka* had been too dominated by the *sōshi* way of viewing the world and had become no more than shouting. I can best explain it as an experience that resembled the return of my artistic conscience, and it a sense that it was now circulating throughout my being. The desire it carried became expressed in the song 'Murasaki bushi.' I was happy when 'Murasaki bushi' neared completion because I found a way to express this fervent desire. At long last I felt I wanted to re-devote myself to *enka*.

As the music world developed, many *enka* singers contributed to an unhealthy atmosphere. They panted in desperation, wondering what to do next. A small number decided to march in step with me. At this time we attempted to spiritually advance our art. Through polishing and refining our talents we began to appreciate the undertaking and approached it with a new seriousness. The effort resulted in 'Murasaki bushi,' a song that took the world by storm. I, of course, enjoyed the commotion. *Enka*'s golden age had arrived.

Murasaki bushi

In your purple *hakama* kimono skirt and its rustling white ribbon
Where are you bound?
Ueno, Asakusayama, Mukojima?
A truly gentle, flower-scented breeze
Scatter, scatter, if you will scatter, scatter all at once
Choitone

Bitterly
Weeping while feigning sleep
Recalling, truly
Even treated coldly by you
As I cannot resign myself to leave you
The sound of regret welling into the night rain
Choitone

If you leave
I won't stand in your way
I will help you into your coat and embrace you
With tears in my eyes I will gaze at all the things in this house
And suddenly my boxwood comb will fall
Choitone

193

The night far advanced
Frost settling in the moonlight
My love sleeps just now
My love sleeps just now
Choitone
And now my love, are you caught in the rain in Komagata?
If it will fall, let it fall all at once, all at once, all night long
Rain without end, let it pour down
Then together one more night until tomorrow's dawn
Choitone

The *shamisen*'s song
Is that the slender sound of a *Shinnai* melody?[19]
Closing time is past
Moonlight shines coldly over the pleasure quarters
That, too, is because of love and speaks of love
The maidenhair coif now a little tousled
Choitone

I apologize with my eyes but the proffered cup
You refuse
Kneeling before you
You turn my sincerity to nothing
Indifferently you sit smoking
Choitone

Pointless, ahh, pointless, pointless
The hardships of a tenant farmer
The long awaited autumn arrives and I find
The landlord takes all my rice
My sweet wife and children cry from hunger
Choitone

Soaked by the wind-blown rain
I can raise no money now
It is all pointless
Truly hard to hit the road peddling goods
This line brings in not enough even for rice gruel
And there's no way to kill myself
Choitone

Again the cost of rice skyrockets
Babies made
Chased by the rent collector, no job
At home the wife and kids wail
It is terrifying to exist in this corrupt world
Choitone
(Azembō)

At the time, the price of rice shot up. For two or three months the newspaper the *Yorozu chōhō* carried a serialized article titled 'Rice is Expensive.' The series appeared after 'Murasaki bushi' had already become well known. For the longest time the popular songs had been 'Ah, The World Is a Dream' by Otoko Saburō and 'Paulonia Leaf' by Soeko. Their songbooks sold well. But now their voices were suddenly silenced, overwhelmed by the popularity of 'Murasaki bushi.'

The new life imparted by this song restored *enka* from the disgrace of the 'dissolute student' singers. Society lionized artists in our camp. We believed this was the result of our diligent efforts and the realization that unsavory elements had to be eliminated from *enka*'s ranks. My colleagues at the haiku meeting cooperated with me on this. The song, 'Treasury of Loyal Retainers Murasaki bushi' ('Chūshingura Murasaki bushi') was an exemplary effort. The song went through a process of polishing and polishing again until it was finally completed. I would say something like let's write a song along the lines of 'Lives of Loyal Warriors' and then we would divide up the work. Someone would write from the vantage point of Yasubee, someone else from that of Takadanobaba, and in this way the work was parceled out. People took it home, worked on it, and then would bring it to the next meeting of the poetry circle for additional polishing. I published the piece with the following prefatory note:

> On the occasion of pulling off the trick of publishing these lines and phrases, however off-putting some may find them to be, I must say that the effort is a sincere commitment to reforming and improving poetry as we seek a new mode of free and enthusiastic expression. A thousand men are blind, a thousand can see. In other words, many are wise and as many are foolish. In this respect, a common attitude has been 'Throw out some rubbishy verse and, sure enough, many will find a fondness for it.' This done, the world can become

the butt of one's private joke and that will be that. But we feel that attitude is unacceptable. It cannot be; the situation cannot be left as it is. We aim at sincere refinement and elimination of the coarse. Herein the intention is simple but elegant, reminiscent of a gift of pure salt sent by an old haiku poet. That salt from Ako has a distinctive flavor. It possesses its own slight pungency.

In the Cave of the Reclining Dragon

'Chūshingura' ('Treasury of Loyal Retainers') received a tremendous welcome. The 'Lives of Loyal Warriors' also went well. There were many songs dedicated to retelling the Chūshingura story. Among the most often sung were Raidō's 'Akagaki Genzō,' 'Nanbuzaka,' and 'Tamura no zashiki-ya;' Shumenshi's 'Takadanobaba,' 'Tagozake,' and 'Jūgyū;' and my own 'Ōtaka Gengo,' 'Kamizakiyogorō,' and 'Shikei no Ichiriki.' The success of 'Murasaki bushi' resulted in my being pressed to come up with new compositions atop new compositions. It was quite pleasant to be harried in that way. From the spring of 1911 through mid-year 1912, the songs maintained their standing as long-running hits.[20]

Meanwhile, rice prices continued to climb ever higher. The number of citizens who were falling into poverty became unimaginably large. With sales for foreign rice and the arrest of crooked merchants who used fraudulent measuring boxes, the situation was in an uproar.

After 'Murasaki bushi's' period at the top of the song world, the songs 'Wonder World,' 'Drifting Grass,' and the second a re-write of 'Shimoda bushi,' none of them really representative of any particular *enka* school, were published. In the wake of the surpassing 'Murasaki bushi' that was sung by the masses everywhere, these new songs became targets for laughter and soon withered away.

The economic crisis deepened. Material for *enka* was scarce. That was the state of things at the end of Meiji. Hard times, hard times, hard times. No matter where you turned, hard times and more hard times. Tomomichi was attending the Mannen Primary School in Mannen-chō.

Elder Brother, Younger Brother

My older brother who had moved to Yokohama tried his hand at various businesses but none went well. He then departed for Tokyo. Here he became a second-hand goods dealer. He had a night stall, too. Nevertheless, once again nothing worked out. Although he was a very steady person, he just was not cut out for business. He became acquainted with Harako Moto and while working together with him decided he wanted to relocate to Hokkaido. I tried to stop him but there was no way he would listen to me. Harako had recommended the move. It was absurd. Why was Harako, who had failed as a homesteading commoner farmer, now recommending just that course to my older brother?

I made my brother listen as I told him the actual conditions in the emigrant settlements. Indeed, it was true that if you went through all the procedures they would give you land, discount your travel costs, and make the whole thing sound like a marvelous windfall. But once you got there and took a look you would find things would not be at all as expected. Land had already fallen into the hands of others. True, in some cases, the land was still wild and uncultivated. Yet, even if vacant, it already belonged to someone. The only places left over were swampland and gravelly patches impossible to cultivate. Even if you wanted to sharecrop, you would have to pay something like a security fee for the privilege. On the way to Hokkaido, immigrants had to pay five *sen* for a single night at a no-meals-provided, 'sleeping only' inn. Once, I saw immigrants staying at one of those inns who had packed a wicker trunk full of *onigiri* cooked rice balls so that they might save a *sen* or two during the trip north. They sat in their room crunching on those frozen lumps to ease their hunger pangs. They continued to do that until they arrived in Hokkaido to find the conditions I have just described.

There were also thugs in *haori* jackets waiting for the arrival of newcomers. Even if you paid the fee and found work as a tenant, the landlord might change at anytime. And when the landlord changed, your deposit disappeared. Then the old tenants would be chased off or forced to pay yet another deposit. Land was bought and sold all the time. It was a plaything for the rich.

These were things that I had heard and seen in Hokkaido. They were the actual conditions in the settlements there. Yet, regardless of what I said, my elder brother would not heed my advice. He could not free himself from the pull of that wonderful offer he had heard earlier. Although I sincerely advised him until I was blue in the face, it did not change his mind and in the end he and his family, with Harako in tow, departed for the north (Harako's wife's father was also a member of one of the early immigrant bands.)

As I had expected, the plan flopped. My brother, his homesteading dream broken by an unscrupulous landlord, went to work in a match factory and after that labored as a timber sorter at a sawmill in Asahikawa. He said that one night he went out to the toilet and was terrified when he heard a bear rustling about nearby. It took only four months. After that, he realized that there was no future for him in Hokkaido. His life had been hollowed out. But on his way back, when he reached Otaru, he all of a sudden and quite unexpectedly ran into our younger brother Yoshigorō.

My elder brother, his home destroyed, met my younger brother, the home destroyer, under the open sky in a distant land. Although they had encountered one another without any planning or forethought, they were so happy that they embraced. My elder brother felt that he had fallen into hell only to land in the arms of a bodhisattva savior. In fact, this was exactly what had happened.

Yoshigorō worked as a porter aboard the *Kumamoto-maru* that had called at the port of Otaru. He asked his captain to allow our elder brother and family to board the ship and travel passage-free on its return trip to Yokohama. This agreed to, my hapless pioneering kinfolk managed to make their way back home. At the time, I received the simplest of messages from my elder bother telling me that they had arrived in Yokohama. His embarrassment before me explained the brevity.

The immigrant band that Harako had joined in a commoners' farm had failed, but many others had succeeded. There were those who had lost their lands in their ancestral homes, but had become outstanding landlords in Hokkaido. There was the Tokugawa Farm, the Iwasaki Farm, the Honganji Farm, and the Mitsui Farm. But these farmers did their plowing between silk sheets in the heart of Tokyo while holding a geisha's hand. The age of serious farming, when one could expect to succeed by simply gripping an iron hoe until blisters covered the hands, had passed. The new farmer went through the motions, fooling the authorities by scattering barnyard grasses in puddles and calling them rice paddies. Stories about tenant farmers who wept as their farms were sold out from under them, cultivation rights moving from owner

A to owner B, were well known. The old terms for settling the north belonged to a past that already seemed ancient. Now the term that remained to express opening new lands was no more than 'cosmetic cultivation.' My brother at last came to understand this. His trip had been a good lesson.

Well, I have dashed along with my story to this point. In the midst of writing, all kinds of memories have come bubbling up. Somehow I feel I have not been able to gather all of them. Now that I have expressed things that I never told anyone in the past, through that process of telling, I have come to think that there is so much more that I am leaving untold. Indeed, there is so very much more that can be said about the people with whom I was involved during the last years of Meiji. But now, we must quickly press ahead. I must not skip over the early Taishō years without writing something about them. But I will have to do it simply, as if stringing together newspaper headlines.

Notes

[1] Azembō based "Konjiki yasha," the song, on the wildly popular serialized novel by the same name written between 1897 and 1902 by novelist and poet, Ozaki Kōyō (1867-1903).

[2] The fishermen going for squid off the Izu Peninsula worked the coastal waters at night using hanging iron baskets filled with flaming firewood as lures to attract squid, hence the fiery lures in this song. Today they use brilliant electric bulbs.

[3] The *yamabuki* is the flower believed to have no seeds.

[4] Soeda Toshie drops out of the story here. It is unclear what happened to the second of the family's two children. One account states that she grew up with another family without ever again reuniting with Azembō and eventually emigrated to the US for marriage. After leaving Japan, her whereabouts are unknown.

[5] Tenrikyō or 'Teaching of Divine Reason' is a newer religion based primarily on the revelatory experience of Nakayama Miki, an impoverished farm woman. Her visions dating from around 1838 developed into a faith that combined elements of Shinto and Buddhism. Followers attempted to attain the 'joyous life' through charity and avoidance of avarice, arrogance, and anger.

[6] Most of the poets mentioned were minor lights in the Tokyo literary world around the turn of the century. Details beyond names are sketchy for the group. Members appear to have written poetry more as an avocation than a dedicated money-earning vocation.

[7] 'San' is the usual suffix placed after surnames, but Azembō is here addressed by his family name followed by 'kun.' 'Kun' is a suffix that functions like 'san,' but expresses a more equivalent and casual relationship. In addition to being used among peers, superiors, teachers and bosses, also use this to those at a lower place in the social hierarchy.

[8] Odake Kokkan (1880-1945) was better known as a painter and book illustrator than as a poet.

[9] Naito Meisetsu (1847-1926) was a leading haiku poet.

[10] Iwata's father is a transitional figure who straddles the worlds of Tokugawa and Westernized Meiji Japan, but never quite mastered all the changes from one era to the next. Here he is a single figure of fun, but surely he was not alone in his inability to master the onslaught of the new.

[11] The Tempo era lasted from 1830 to 1844; in other words, not far removed from the time period being described in the lyric.

[12] Turbo shells or *sazae* are fist-sized shellfish that are often cooked over coals with soy sauce poured into the top of the conical shell so that the meat is boiled in a combination of its own juices and salty seasoning. For Takeishi, the image of minds ablaze but unfocused, sizzling with fashionable ideas, resembled turbo shells atop a grill.

[13] The references are to a famous sake maker and an equally well-known geisha house.

[14] Tomomichi is still young and has yet to completely master the more difficult hiragana syllabary, so writes using the first-learned katakana characters.

[15] *I-ro-ha* is the first three designations of a 48-character traditional ordinal system used in a manner equivalent to the English language A-B-C system.

[16] 8.19 square meters, a typically tiny space in a tenement apartment.

[17] This was because of his political activities and provocative songs.

[18] The reference is to the comedian Soganoya Gokūrō.

[19] Although the *Shinnai* melodic style of narrative singing originally appeared in the *kabuki* theater, it eventually became established as an independent musical style. The *Shinnai-bushi* have been described as Edo-period prostitute's songs sung by men to the accompaniment of shamisens.

[20] Azembō is selectively showcasing his more militaristic songs, particularly ones that evoke images of traditional valor mixed with romance. There is no doubt that these songs were popular, but probably not as popular as his lamentations about the inequities of industrial capitalism. This chapter again reminds us that Azembō was writing with one eye trained on the wartime censors.

Chapter Six

Tasihō: an Abbreviated Record

Convenient and Cheap

The Plover's Song[1]

I write 'the forty-fifth year of the Meiji imperial era'
A slip of the writing brush
I rewrite: 'Taishō, year one'
Doing so brings such sadness
On this autumn morning
People walk the streets
Eyes that see mourning bands
Suddenly
Fill with tears

For fun, it is off to the Maiko shore
Look out over the water
Not too far away is Awaji Island

The plovers cry *chi, chi*
You can see a fluttering in the wind
Suddenly
The sails of a boat

The wind chime hanging from the eave and the greenness beneath
Suddenly a gust of wind
Behind their glass wall golden fish swim
Gliding almost silently *sara, sara, sara*
A middle-aged woman
Suddenly
Her just washed hair is blown by the breeze
(Azembō)

General Nogi's Song[2]

Ah, General Nogi is dead
His greatness inspired this transient world
His great prince having passed on
He follows after in death
Since the Restoration, the Land of the Rising Sun
Has relied on this true bulwark, always reliable
The very incarnation of the Japanese spirit
General Nogi is dead

Ah, the departed General
Reflecting on his blessed composure
Whose blood cannot help but be stirred?
Even the fiercest demon would weep for him
He who sacrificed for our sacred nation
His precious sword
Is stained with the General's own blood
A deep scarlet, like the sun on our flag
He never abused a weaker foe
Never feared a stronger enemy
His will like stone, like iron
He took to heart our Oath of the Imperial Charter

And never boasted of his victories
Indeed, he possessed the power to crush the wicked
And the heart to help the weak
Truly, such bottomless sincerity
Caused his sun to blaze ever brighter
No matter a rain of arrows or bullets beyond number
No matter a forest of swords
The fierce wind may storm and bluster
He did not bend before the dense thicket
That which does not waver is the Japanese Spirit
Ah, the General is dead

Recalling him brings forth an awesome crescendo
Trumpets sound and all at once
Asian skies stir
Praise for his hard battles, ever victorious
Calling out that Port Arthur will hold
The battle cry of our ever-victorious army
Behold the shores of the Far East
Flying high above in the pellucid blue
The symbol of the Rising Sun
Our flag's colors shine forth the light of honor
The clouds' ranks break giving way utterly to a clear sky
As the bright rays of peace shine forth
Cannons rain down fire
Blades of flame like scattered flower petals
Corpses pile up in mounds
Waves of blood to fill a sea
Blistering battle until nine months have passed
And in the end, Port Arthur does not fall!
Carve in stone this great feat
Ah, the General is dead

A winter day and the freezing wind cuts
And at a time when the fiery heat leaves you sweltering
Blades of ice and bullets of fire
These are traded back and forth on this killing ground
He forgets his family, he forgets himself
All with one mind: for the nation's sake
His resolve to the very end
Stronger than iron

203

Now as if knocked awake in mid-dream
Like a lamp suddenly put out
Transformed like dew and gone to another place
We beloved children recall
How great the General's capacity for compassion
When we the fifty million consider this
We know he is the very embodiment of the Yamato Spirit
General Nogi has passed on

Ah, the hundred thousand soldiers
On the piteous sacrificial altar
His bold shadow has vanished, has departed
But his greatness cannot be forgotten
Soldiers for the nation's glory
Until the sound of our bones pulverizing
Forever shall his testament be preserved
Ah, the General is dead.
(Azembō)

A clear difference emerged that set apart the Taishō world from that of Meiji. Until the last years of the Meiji period, the number of cafes and bars could be counted on the fingers of the hands. Then their numbers started to increase explosively. Moving picture theaters also began to be built one after another. Taishō geisha appeared. And the Taishō harp came into fashion.[3] The sound that it emitted was light and frivolous. And so was everything else. All that was 'cheap and convenient' made giant strides.

Jigoma gangster movies became popular.[4] *Nasanunaka* or relations not based on blood ties also became fashionable. *Enka* reflected these shifts in the social tides. *Naniwabushi* once again became popular as evident in songs such as 'Don-don bushi' and 'Nara-maru bushi'. Here are a few songs and excerpts that were popular through 1916 and 1917.

The New and Improved *Don-don* Song

Embrace a Buddhist priest and see how cute they are
Where are their heads, where their tails?
Priests today are a depraved lot

They eat meat, drink liquor
And women always appear in their sutra chants
Don, don
(Azembō)

The Wreck of the *Nara-maru*

The moon appears, the moon appears
It comes out above the cement factory
In Tokyo the smokestacks are many
No doubt even the moon is annoyed
(Azembō)

The 'Cousin Song' (Oitoko bushi'), 'Song of the Capitol' ('Miyako bushi'),
'I Will Go with You Anywhere' ('Omae to naraba doko made mo'), and
'Katushka's Song' ('Kachuusha bushi') were among the popular tunes. I also
wrote 'Doll's House' ('Ningyō no ie').

Around this period, a new dramatic form began to sprout. Of
additional note: the 'Pitch Black Song' ('Makkuro bushi') was in fashion,
the Empress Dowager Shōken had passed away, the Yamamoto Cabinet
dissolved, the Ōkuma Cabinet was installed, the Siemens naval scandal was
exposed, Sakurajima erupted, the Tōhoku region and Hokkaido experienced
major crop failures and famine, and finally World War I broke out. And a lot
more happened, too![5]

The Song of the Capitol

Parents, parents, and parental authority all puffed up
Don't be so haughty
Choito
Parents are but
Yare sore
Their children's' cast-off skins
That's it, isn't it? Isn't it?
Choito, choito
(Azembō)

The Pitch Black Song

The Hakone Mountains
In the past you crossed by packhorse or palanquin
Now in the space of a dream you cross by train
Smoke turns the tunnel black, black
The sound of strings strummed
It disappears, is heard, again disappears
Disappears, is heard, again disappears
That interfering wall
It is black, black

Sakurajima
Sakurajima of the old Satsuma domain
Smoke belches, fire spews, the mountain erupts
For miles in all directions
It is black, black

Rice, they cry
Born in Mutsu but unable to eat the grain grown here
It seems like a lie but come and take a look
Boiled grass and pine needle dumplings
It is black, black
(Azembō)

The Song of the Modern

'Newly patented product!'
But take a closer look
In tiny letters 'patent applied for'
That's what's written there
Hah! Now honestly!
Isn't that just utterly modern!

Before you even finish saying, 'This is my new girl'
All of sudden, hey!
You're a parent!
Hah! Now honestly!
Isn't that just utterly modern!

After you're dead
Instead of paradise
In this world comfy, comfy
That's the way I'd like to live
Hah! Now honestly!
Isn't that just utterly modern!

The preacher intones, 'Man shall not live by bread alone'
If that's true
Try not eating and see what happens!
Hah! Now honestly!
Isn't that just utterly modern!
(Azembō)

Leave Me Be

I saw my wife
I fell in love
Kitasaa
Me? Well ...
I strain and pull at freedom's oars
Leave me be
If we split apart, we'll be just like strangers
Kitasaa
Where to? Well ...
You have the right to go
Leave me be
If I became a bird on the company's roof
Day wages? Well ...
They're cheap, cheap I'd sing
Leave me be
(Azembō)

New Song of Nightfall

I stacked my rifle
Put up my tent, turned the pack into a pillow
Pulled the long coat over my head
And then
Choito
Ever so briefly
I met my wife
Yokkoriya
In a dream
Rain and officers
Hail and enemy bullets
Choi, choi

You and me alike
Neither of us has lived long enough
And perhaps only too few years remain
You don't have a wife
Choito
You have only your longings
You have what you lack
Pretending not to look
Yokkoriya
Why not take a peak?

Those faces again
Our eyes move over that scarlet crepe
Choi, choi

The Qingdao Song[6]

From the slopes of Qingdao looking down
Crossing that ocean will take you to Japan
Without a doubt they await our triumphant return
I have become Qingdao's guardian
Natchoran

Those big black hats and high coat flaps
That looks like a baby's bib on backwards
Sporting a *furoshiki* carrying cloth for neckwear
Spirited but innocent the sailors
Natchoran

Please hurry home
The tide that sent you away at the Zushi shore
I see a customer off
And stick out my tongue behind his back
Natchoran

The New Seashore Song

A white sail can be seen squarely offshore
The boat surrenders to the sail, the sail to the wind
And I
To you
Don't I give myself to your heart's whims?

The waves breaking at Point Miura
Test my darling's strength
Ride it out or go under
Your long, long oar will bend.
(Azembō)

The Poor and the *Enka* Association

Masuda Tarō's 'The New Song' ('Atarashii bushi'), Kaminaga's 'The Bet' ('Hitokake bushi') my 'Song of the Modern' ('Gendai bushi') and 'Hattose Song' ('Hattose bushi') came out and were followed by such new style songs as Misumi Suzuko's 'Vendetta at Hichiriga Bay' ('Hichigira hama no adauchi'), Yumeiji's 'Song of the Rose' ('Bara no uta'), Yoshii Isamu's 'Gondola Song' ('Gondora no uta'), and 'Danchone' ('Danchone'). There were also the *enka* 'Double Suicide at Sonezaki' ('Sonezaki shinjū'), and 'Double Suicide at Chiba' ('Chiba shinjū').[7]

209

After Takeda quit the song publishing business, Iwata monopolized the sale of *enka* booklets. He did this in a rather highhanded way, controlling singers by making them rent their bedclothes from him at six *sen* per night if they stayed in his second-floor room. He also made each of them pay a damage deposit every time they rented one of his violins. To have to rent the tools essential for doing business suggests the depths to which *enka* singers had fallen. If singers neglected to pay the 'roof fee' for two consecutive nights, Iwata would immediately bare his fangs. He also began to use a corner of the old dumpling shop for loaning small sums as he gradually expanded into other ventures. Some of the *enka* singers became his bill collectors.

Many singers resented Iwata's tyranny and in the spring of 1913 Kuramochi Guzen took a central role in organizing the Japan Folk Song Association (Nippon zokuyō kai) at 39 Yamabushi-machi, Shitaya.[8] At the time, I had published the 'New Oitoko Song' ('Shin oitoko bushi') and 'Nasanunaka bushi' ('Not Blood Relations Song'). I also wanted to fight against the music wholesalers and poured myself into helping to reform Japan's music world. Unfortunately, economic reasons forced the association to dissolve by the spring of 1914 and Iwata regained monopoly power.

While living in the *I-ro-ha* longhouse apartment, I began composing 'Living' ('*Seikatsu*'). I worked to help alleviate the problem of poverty. I got to know Sakamoto Ryonosuke, schoolmaster of the special Mannen-chō primary school, Salvation Army Lieutenant Katō of Airin Hall, Shimada Ichirō, Ichiba Gakujirō, and others.[9] Ichiba-san ran an orphanage and became a pioneer in researching prostitution as a social problem. He maintained the Freedom Club in Asakusa to pursue social work to reform unlicensed prostitution.

It was around the time when 'New Song of Nightfall' ('Shin kure bushi') became popular that Ichikawa Kyohō, Nagao Gingetsu, Gotō Koka, Miyajima Ikuhō, and others again began to advocate reforming the world of *enka*. And once again the campaign ended in failure. The outcome reflected the negative side of the *enka* life. It was a side that made it hopeless to expect that men inclined to wander and who together tended to be irresponsible idlers could unite in their common calling. There were notorious traitors to their own cause even among the movement's leaders. To the public they projected an image of unmitigated decadence, and this weakness was taken as one of the *enka* performer's characteristics.[10]

The *enka* artist's enemy was not only the music wholesaler, but also the bookstores that sold the cheap red cover paperback song collections. From time to time they sold pirated versions of these works at extraordinarily low prices. They completely ignored the *enka* professionals who had written the lyrics and composed the music. These were the people who had done the work that yielded the songs and made them popular. *Enka* underlings and traitorous insiders bought original songs at an incredibly low price for their own resale. At times, these frauds just stole work outright. In this manner, the cheaply produced song books went at a sharply discounted price. As the *enka* creators of these songs frantically sang on the streets, the results of their work appeared to be nothing more than scraps scattered in the wind.

A minority of purists existed among the *enka* singers. Their struggle was extremely wretched. Although these artists had created our nation's songs and stood out as performers in positions of leadership who possessed a genuine zeal for their work, even they feared getting pulled down in the wave of mud that had come to inundate the business side of *enka*. Some escaped the mire by becoming newspaper journalists, writers for magazines, opera composers, film directors, and arrangers of Western music. The tally of those who took this route comes to an impressively large number. As for me, I continued steadfast with *enka*. Yet, in the midst of worsening conditions, I also had to take a long, deep look at my own situation.

Kimura Hideo wrote the study *The Method of Free Dramatic Vision* (*Kan jizai jutsu*). Later his wife, Kimura Komako, created the *shingeki* or 'new school drama.' She joined Gokurō's troupe at the Kinryū Hall in Asakusa. Gokurō promoted her addition to the group by hoisting a signboard that proclaimed, 'Kimura Komako, the leader of the new true women's social group, has joined our company!' The group performed *Resurrection* (*Fukkatsu*), *Mona Bonna* (*Mona Bona*), *A Child of the Street* (*Machi no ko*), and *The Bear* (*Kuma*).

Komako asked me to bring Tomomichi to stay with her in her room in the theater even after she had ceased performing in *shingeki*. Gokurō also wanted Tomomichi to stay with him so my son ended up living in the theater. The time finally came for Tomomichi to graduate from primary school. Thanks to the good offices of the school's principal, Sakamoto, he was recommended to Matsuya Tenichibō and became one of the Matsuya's scholarship students. He was thus able to enter middle school. He also sold newspapers and worked at Baimon, a publishing company, to help with expenses.

In 1918, Kiyomizu Yojirō and Yasuda Toshizō, two *enka* performers, entreated me to help them create an *enka* performers association. I thus came to oversee the *Enka* Association Youth Friendship League (*Enka kumiai seinen shinkō kai*). I campaigned to enable *enka* writers to retain publication authorization rights over their creations, the general aim being to free themselves from an inferior position within the music world. The ultimate goal was to establish *enka* creation as a genuine profession (at the time, Kuramochi Gūzen in Osaka had also organized the *Enka* Youth Support Association).

New Smile Song

If with you, I will go anywhere
In the spring
To Ueno or Mukojima filled with blossoms
With your hand in mine
Your beautiful silhouette
If hidden by darkness how easy to part
I could find the will to sweep you from my heart
But the moonlight shines everywhere
(Azembō)

Isn't It Grand Song?

Hey, won't you take a look?
To be sure, it is beautiful spring rain
And it is watering the willow making greenness grow
In the shade a parasol with bull's-eye print, *chira, chira* glides by
Now that is truly something grand, isn't it?
(Azembō)

Carefree Song[11]

The school teacher is really great
So much so he can teach almost anything
The students so taught are so innocent
They believe all to be so
Ah
Isn't that just carefree!

In Western clothes, wearing leather shoes, he must be erudite
But without money you are, after all, just poor
Poor, poor, poverty
Poor but trying to look otherwise
Ah
Isn't that just carefree?
(Azembō)

These songs appeared at the start-up of the *enka* friendship association. The suicide by the Himoya railroad crossing guard, who took his life to accept responsibility for the accident there, occurred around this time. I was pleased that the *enka* I wrote elicited feelings that went beyond just interest in the gory incident itself. It did not take long for the song to be imitated and for those imitations to become popular, as was evident in the tunes used in the middle of the play, *Ikeru shikabane (A Living Corpse)*. These included 'The Wanderer's Song' ('Sasurai no uta'), and 'Watering Hole Song' ('Sakaba no uta'). Signs indicated we were entering a new musical age, that of the ditty-like *kouta* short song. This new era differed from the old days when a single song might be sung for several years. The trend reflected the easily changeable sentiment of the masses at that time.

The rice riots occurred. Prices for rice and other commodities shot up, the nouveau riche fever broke out, the ranks of the poor increased. Add to these: labor unrest, industrial paternalism, Mayor Amakasu, and Chinese rice imports. All kinds of new words came into existence, all manner of incidents flared up. New songs appeared, too. 'Tokyo Song' ('Tokyo bushi'), with its *paino-paino* refrain, and the '50,000 Yen Curse' ('Noroi no goman-en'), a song about the *Zuzu-ben* murder case became popular and sold five or six hundred thousand copies.

213

I began publishing a little magazine, *Enka*, that focused on popular songs and so doing began to lay down a new path for writing and publishing in the music industry. The effort was almost immediately copied by charlatan publishers. This led to many unhappy developments as individuals with motives that were less pure put their oar into the business. A number of songs, for example 'New Willow Song' ('Shinyanagi bushi'), 'The Song of the Swallow' ('Tsubame bushi'), 'Song of the Amakko Incident' ('Amakko jiken bushi'), and 'Dublin Bay' ('Daburin bee') followed the popularity of songs from Western opera such as 'A Woman's Heart' and 'Diablo' from *Rigoletto* and the 'Toreador Song' from *Carmen*. I also wrote take-offs based on these.

In 1921 the 'Hamada Eiko Incident' occurred as well as the affair in Ōiso in which Yasuda Zenjirō was stabbed by Asahi Heigorō.[12] Yasuda fled to his garden where he collapsed and died. Heigorō committed *seppuku* in the murdered man's living room. I recalled how the Atago Shrine had been pulled down to make way for the building of Yasuda's mansion. In November, close on the Hamada affair, Prime Minister Hara Takashi was stabbed to death by Nakaoka Ryō'ichi at Tokyo Station.[13]

I composed 'Song of Our Nation' ('Okuni bushi') and it was surprisingly well received. Before I knew it I had created eighty-five versions of new songs for distribution throughout Japan. After World War I, the 'Around the World Song' ('Sekai isshū no uta') also went over well. All of these were experiments with a new kind of *enka*. Each was a new creation and each was successful. In 1922, I changed the title of the *enka* magazine from *Enka* to *Popular Entertainment*. The revised version broadly treated the subject of mass entertainment. Yajima and Satsuki Shō joined me in the effort. Around that time, I also joined the Asakusa Society and met many people associated with it.

A Letter from an Old Friend

It happened around this time. Out of the blue, a totally unexpected letter arrived:

Dear Mr. Soeda,
Perhaps you know me. In any case, forgive me for intruding

with this unexpected letter. Through the *enka* society, I somehow feel that I have indeed met you. If I have, I would dare say that there is probably no need to describe my personal history, but if not let me say that I belonged to the Central Youth Club in Shin Tomi-chō and it was there that I composed *enka*. My maiden work was in the *yukai bushi* mode. I wrote lyrics about the late General Fukushima during his days as a colonel during the Siberian Expedition. My association with the club lasted through its period in Kanda's Jimbō-chō district right up until it fell apart. Well, Mr. Soeda, does this help you remember me?

I saw your name, Mr. Soeda, two or three years ago in a work put out by *Enka* Publishing. Thereafter I met Kubota Rokumaru, an old friend from the days of the Seinen Club. He now goes by the name Chiyoda Kanjō. He was sure that you are the very same Mr. Soeda from the days of the club. But we were both a little doubtful because the Soeda associated with *Enka* Publishing is said to have quite a long beard. The beard still raises doubts so perhaps you are not the Mr. Soeda in question.

Mr. Soeda, I have had *Enka* Publishing send me a copy of your magazine, *Popular Entertainment*. Reading through it I could not help feeling overwhelmed to the point of tears by memories of almost thirty years past and a longing for old friends. I have thus sent you this intrusive and impudent letter. I leave it to your pleasure to respond or not.

Jōshū Shinpō Editing Bureau
Maebashi-shi

Tonoe Suikyō

Dear Sir,
Yes, it has been such a long time since we have met. I am Soeda. I was deeply moved to read your wonderful letter and all the memories that it recalled about my dear *senpai* senior, Suikyō-san, a man of feeling overflowing. The people from

that time at the Shin Tomi-chō and Jinbō-chō have all but vanished. I suppose some have gone on to become worldly successes. Others have died.

Only I alone among them have persisted through thick and thin for more than twenty years as an *enka* artist. In 1902 (around the time of the Aomori 5th Regiment's snowy march to disaster) in all of broad Japan and Tokyo only I and my single follower, only the two of us, were performing *enka*. Furthermore, we walked the true path of *enka*. For those reasons I am today called *enka*'s originator.

Continuing to live this kind of life has meant that I am constantly recalling Tonoe Suikyō, Hisada Kiseki, Kubota, Eguchi, Ido, Tamura, Suzuki, and especially Mrs. Itō, the Club's housemother. I have found myself heading toward Maebashi on two or three occasions. At those times my class consciousness was quite clear. My heart blazed with a strong fire of resistance toward present-day society. I could not bring myself to call on you, but I did sometimes go to your company and stop briefly in front of it thinking, 'Tonoe-san works for this newspaper.' I also heard about you from Mr. Shioda (Tsukioka Shin) who was playing in a drama in Kiryū. Now my way of thinking has changed fundamentally and I would very much like to get together again.

By separate post I will send a back issue of *Enka* in which we published one of your old compositions. I wonder if you will remember it. Oh yes, I suppose I look fine in the enclosed photo, but the real thing is not as haughty looking as this image. In any case, please accept this as a response to you letter.

To Mr. Tonoe Hiroshi[14]
Soeda Azembō

Well, just as I expected you are Mr. Soeda! Thank you not only for answering but for even going so far as to send a magazine and photograph. I am so very pleased to receive both of them. I am glad that you are in such good health. Although you have long hair in the picture, your face appears just as it did in the past. Though the rumor circulates that you have a shaggy beard, I must apologize for working under a delusion as regards your appearance.

The title of the poem in the style of 'dissolute students' does indeed appear to be my work. As to the things I wrote then, well what can one say? I was pressed by circumstances and couldn't compose much that was worthwhile. What's more, I can't really recall much about the songs. I might have brought files of collected *enka* with me when I came to this place, but instead I left everything at the club. Now I regret having done that.

As for old friends, I hear virtually no news. Quite by accident, I did come across Kubo Roku. What I have learned about our old associates I have heard from him. I was surprised to learn that Ido Sawaei has become a loan shark working around Asakusa.

I visit Tokyo once a year. I will make it a point during my next visit to call at your office. I want to hear of your trials and tribulations since our paths parted nearly thirty years ago. I look forward to that opportunity. No, I intend to create the chance to make our meeting take place.

In closing, let me say that Endō Tomoshirō, a contributor to your magazine, appears to have been a colleague of mine when he had a position in our company some years back. Please give him my regards when you see him.

To Soeda Azembo,
Tonoe Hiroshi

The Great Earthquake

About this time the songs 'Ducks on the Green River' ('Ōryoko bushi') and 'Boatman's Ballad' ('Sendō kouta') could be heard all over Japan. And then the earthquake struck.

The Boatman's Ballad

I walk the river's dry bed
Pampas grass withered
It is the same with me
Pampas grass withered
It does not matter the two of us
In this world
No blossoms bloom
Pampas grass withered
(Noguchi Ujō)

'A Burnt-Out Diary'

On September 1, 1923, the earthquake destroyed my home. My house was in the very heart of Tokyo in the very center of a slum. It was the most rickety of those forty-eight run down rooms in the very middle of the *I-ro-ha* tenement in Shitaya, Yamamuro-cho. Despite all that, I had lived there for fourteen years. It was here that I had written and seen published so many popular songs and it was from here that I had edited and published *Enka* and, after that, *Popular Entertainment*.

The very day of the earthquake I had just completed the September issue of *Popular Entertainment*. By around nine that morning I had prepared everything to send to the workshop for binding. Every time I brought out a new edition, the son of Une Yoshito, an acquaintance, would come over to help distribute a certain number of issues. He came that morning and left with the amount allotted to his care. Satsuki Shō and Kuruma Misao, who together undertook editing work and mailing, were to come over during the morning hours to forward the latest issues, but they didn't show up. Left alone, I felt at loose ends and began to feel hungry. I thought I would combine breakfast and lunch and took out some cold rice and leftover side dishes and lined them up atop the table. I lifted my chopsticks to eat at exactly twelve noon.

At that moment, I heard a rumbling and felt the ground shake, then crashing sounds, *battan*! Things on the shelves came clattering down. The shelf boards themselves broke into pieces and fell on my head and shoulders. The bowl of cooked rice and everything else on the table were smashed to pieces. Without a moment's pause, there was a terrific vibration and the sounds of *mire*, *mire*, *do*, *doon* and then half of the house just tumbled down.

I was amazed at the sight and just continued sitting as I had been. For a moment I did not move, but just observed the scene. I was not at all petrified with terror. After a while, I got up to try to look out the back window of the house that now suddenly sloped toward the rear. From behind me, a boarding house had collapsed over part of my place. The pressure from the neighboring building had caused my house to cave in. I piled up the bundles of magazines to improvise a stool to enable me to climb out through the window and escape to the roof of the boarding house that had come down atop my own.

Then the shaking started again.

Kuramochi and his family from block 38 sought refuge by climbing onto the roof of my collapsed house. Everyone went up on the roofs. Soon fire broke out. We could see smoke rising from the direction of Asakusa, Kanda, and in Honjo from seven or eight directions. Gradually the flames spread. The wind blew. With conditions like these there was no way that the fire would be contained in far-off Honjo. By two or three in the afternoon, the original fires had spread and now smoke rose anew from other sections of the city. The fires most easily seen were those that engulfed soaring twelve-story buildings. People from the longhouse tenement, young and old, fled to the grounds of the Maeda mansion in Shinsakamoto-chō. Satsukii Shō and Kuruma climbed up on the roof of my place. It was five or six o'clock and night was falling as plumes of red and black swirled and burned in the sky. Some people had made preparations and were ready to flee; others argued that it was best to stay put. That the issue could be discussed suggests that we still had some time before the fire would reach us.

Looking at the wide boulevard that ran from Asakusa to Ueno, I saw great numbers of excited refugees streaming down the street. There were many pushcarts. People passed in succession, some carried the sick, others carried a child on their back and pulled another by the hand. Along came men in their prime, the elderly, people shouldering bundles and carrying goods, men bearing iron tea kettles, and the wounded - in a ceaseless flow they all pushed on to Ueno, to Ueno.

I climbed back on the roof. I figured that in the end it would not do to stay here. We didn't have a single grain of rice to eat so the three of us made do by sharing a watermelon. Later, Satsuki Shō, Misao, and I joined

219

the stream of fleeing refugees. We advanced toward Ueno. Well, not really advanced, we were pushed there. After somehow managing to get to the Shimokurumazaka bus stop, the crowd came to a standstill in a human traffic jam. Worse yet, the people in back were being pushed by the people to the rear of them. The crush was unbearable. There was no way to go forwards or move back. I could see Misao's face in the crowd some ten feet behind me, but had lost sight of Satsuki. The fire gradually came nearer and nearer. I felt terrified. A space near the train tracks; there was a little opening there. Maybe that would provide some safety. Each and every face was completely clouded by fear. At last, Satsuki and Misao came along. Together we followed the railway tracks until we came out at a place near Uguisudani.

We saw the weird sight of the flames rising from the huge tiles of the Honganji Temple. Soon the sky began to lighten as night gave way to dawn and the sun appeared above the flames.

The second of September. The fire grew ever fiercer. I stood on the tramline tracks and stared unmoving at the deep red of the rising sun. The culture of half a century had been so easily destroyed. How flimsy science. How weak humanity. How small I am. These are the things I thought. I turned to look toward the hills of Ueno and saw a mountain of people there. Some appeared at the edges of precipices on the verge of falling, others clung to the edge. People clustered below the ridge near the railroad tracks. Some sat on bundles of belongings, others leaned against their bags. Some just looked dazed and vacant, while others wept, maintained a stony silence, or kept repeating to themselves, 'What do we do now?' 'What will happen?' Such people filled the area to overflowing. A great number of them then tried to break free to move in the direction of Nippori and Tabata.

Misao, who had been beside me, lying on his side, then got up and craned his neck to look around at all the refugees. He then laughed like a mad man as he shouted, 'There are no rich, no poor! How funny! Now everybody has to sleep outside! Ha, ha!'

Before long Misao, Satsuki, and I made our way to my younger brother's place in a rear section of Nippori. I called on Uchiyama, a friend of Makaya Moto. By then it was around seven in the morning. Uchiyama gave us a warm welcome. I washed my face, arms, and legs at his well.

I talked with Mr. Uchiyama. His wife told us that the breakfast she had prepared would be ready soon. As we sat before the wooden trays I drank a little sake with Uchiyama. On this day, at this time when many people had been burnt out of their homes, I thought how fortunate I was to be able to drink sake and eat warm rice. I imagined that I was perhaps the only one to be so lucky. Mr. and Mrs. Uchiyama also intended to abandon their house and flee. The secondary shocks and the falling ash made staying here unsafe. On Uchiyama's urging I slept for a couple of hours.

Sometime after noon, my younger brother and his entire family abandoned their place and fled to Uchiyama's. Everyone from the neighborhood had fled to the Ueno hills. They had only water to drink and nothing to eat. Many showed sickly pale faces. The children were especially pitiful. Today they might die under the brightly shining sun. Many people had gone missing; others were so exhausted they could no longer move. Satsuki and Misao worried about the plight of these people and carried them *nigiri* rice balls.

In front of the police box, a signboard stood bearing a message that had all the marks of the stiffly formal but very sensible policeman. It read, 'An earthquake has hit Tokyo and Yokohama only. Other places are unaffected.' 'XX tons of rice will be shipped from Osaka.' I read the text and realized that I could not possibly survive on these meager words alone.

Evening. I pushed for getting out of harm's way, favoring relying on our legs to make a long-distance trek to safety. Those who agreed with me and decided to go along included Mr. and Mrs. Satsuki, my brother's wife and their children, and Misao. Night came. We seven bid farewell to Mr. and Mrs. Uchiyama and set out in the direction of Ogu-machi. We marched along a narrow road dodging an unbroken stream of carts and horse-drawn wagons. We went on until we reached a vacant lot near the Ōji Electric Railway station on the outskirts of Ogu where we made camp. Even from there the sky above Ueno still appeared red.

We tried to sleep but mosquito attacks made this impossible. As an added bonus, members of a group that appeared to be a local young men's association kept up a steady din. They created a constant ruckus yelling, 'Last night we got paid twenty yen to catch a thief,' and noisily announced news such as the arrival of this fellow and the departure of someone else. Life

221

outdoors was not easy. Late at night one young fellow rushed to our camp to tell me that, 'If a certain Mr. X shows up here it will be dangerous. You should move to a safer place two or three blocks away.' He then directed us to the rear section of a field. Even now I recall that the local youth association members demonstrated all of the confusion one might expect at the outbreak of a war. It reminded me of nothing other than a poorly performed Sogonoya comedy farce, but several times we met with real danger.

Trains were leaving from Kana-machi. Our group got off in Abiko in Chiba Prefecture. One of Zenjirō's old friends lived in nearby Kazahaya village. We found temporary refuge there (just the month before, we at the magazine had set up a branch outlet for Popular Entertainment and had attended a meeting here). I decided to leave the group and go ahead on my own.

I got off the train at Mito. A rest shelter for refugees had been set up in front of the station and many were working there. I was worn out and asked them to direct me to some place where I could stretch out my body and rest. They sent me to a hall in Mito Park where Mito Kōmon once studied.[15] The view was wonderful and the place quiet. I plopped down in the big hall and then a student from the work group appeared to tell me that he was firing up a bath for me. I felt as if I had come to a villa on vacation to escape the summer heat. Of course, I could not arbitrarily enjoy all that serenity just by myself. That night about a hundred additional refugees noisily crowed into the room to share the accommodation.

The next day I went by train directly to Aomori. At the each station, relief food and other goods were thrust through the windows of the cars. From Aomori I went on to Hirosaki. I stopped at the Chata-rō as a first stage of my flight. It was here that I composed 'Earthquake Ditty' ('Jishin kouta') and 'Song of the Great Earthquake' ('Dai jishin no uta'). I pressed on to Ōwani, Ōyu, and then to an acquaintance's Wainai Hotel in Towada. I then went to Sendai and it was there that I published on a provisional basis through the offices of Takazawa Yoshisaburō the songs I had just composed. I sang these tunes with Takazawa on the streets. Some people commented, 'My gosh, what an old *enka* singer.'

I settled down at Satō Genkai's place in Aizuwakamatsu and performed *enka* there. After a separation of three months, Tomomichi came to visit. He had gone home, walking through the ashes, and was building a barrack-style shack among the burnt-out ruins. He had the frame already up and asked me how I felt about going back.

I continued to wander around Tōhoku for a while singing my own compositions. My 'Great Earthquake Song' ('Dai shinsai no uta') and 'Reconstruction Song' ('Fukkō bushi') had come out in Tokyo and were now being sung throughout Japan.

Earthquake Ditty

My Tokyo place
Burned out
And you, just the same
Burned out
Any how, both of us
Homeless

Burned out
Right, friend?
But our will to live
What's changed about that?

Me and you, too
From here on out
Let's hit the road
Suffer the travails of travel
And live

The plains of Musashino
From ancient times
Radiant in the moonlight
I will wander these
Suffer the travails of travel
And live

223

Song of the Great Earthquake

Ah disaster, disaster
The time: 1923
September 1, noon
Heaven's pillars and Earth's axis pulverized
The ground rumbled, houses shook and quivered
Destruction's mad din horrific
Buildings collapsed, hills crumbled
The land cracked, the sea roared
People accustomed to peace
Turned pale and their eyes became bloodshot
And where the earthquake had run riot
Fires broke forth everywhere
Explosions heard far and near
The fire spread and scorched the sky
In a moment a horrific scroll unfurled
Carnage and cries, scenes from a living hell
How pitiful these people
Their greed and fear and misery
They carry rattan woven suitcases, clothes boxes, chests of drawers
They load these on carts and become frenzied in their flight
And so easily do they lose their own lives
They fall in flames, burn to death, die in madness
Parents call their children and children their parents
In the midst of the fire, in the midst of the water
Where's the husband, where the wife?
Where the older boy, the younger, the sisters?
Where are they? Are they alright?
The fleeing run in all directions
Those that survive torture by fire and water
Get buried alive when the bridge collapses
Others are swept away when their boat burns around them
The number drowned is beyond count
A wind fans the inferno
Clueless as to escape they sink down into the pond's mud
Trying to keep the fire's flying sparks at bay
Their bodies sink deeper and deeper
But relentless the approach of those tongues of flame
So many are steamed to death

And atop their corpses tread still others
Submerged in smoke and flame
Those who had somehow managed to escape with their lives
Show wounds unbearable to behold
Half alive or more likely half dead
Their wretchedness insect-like
And those who survive
Have nothing to eat, nothing to drink
They sleep outdoors with the clothes on their backs
Days and nights more dead than alive
Indeed they have nothing left, only their lives
Parents dead, husbands dead
Nothing left to live for
At this weeping mother's side
A child watches as emergency rice relief
Prepares to treat her to a rice ball or bread
She suddenly breaks into a brave smile
Laughter at the limits of utter misery
Ah the horror of those who fell victim
In greater Tokyo and Yokohama
The Bōsō Peninsula, Izu, and Sagami
Only once the shaking that rocked all to fall
The people so proud of their culture
Life's arrogant dreams
All pulled down to where not a trace is left
Ahh, in one stroke all smashed
And the ruins of the fire hardly visible
We cannot turn our eyes to behold our compatriots
Their corpses in the tens of thousands piled into a mountain
A scene from hell more terrible than hell itself
Older brother, younger brother, parents, children
Men or women
One cannot differentiate faces
Some are festered, others swollen
Heads crushed, stomachs ripped
Bones smashed, guts flowing forth
The sharp stench sticks in the nose
Pile the corpses as they are
Pour on the oil and watch the burning sight
Choke on the smoke from the pyre

The people who have survived
Hold a tearful memorial
Those who watch cry silently
Those who hear of it bite their sleeves as they weep
Ah, horrific calamity
Ah, the horrific calamity

Reconstruction Song

Though fire destroyed the houses
The Tokyoites'
Spirits will never dim, just watch us
Arama, *oyama*
Standing in a row
Barracks shacks
At night we recline to sleep and gaze at the moon
Eezo, *eezo*
The Imperial Capital rebuilds
Eezo, *eezo*
(Satsuki Shō)

In 1924, thoughtful people tended to frown at songs such as 'Bird in a Cage' ('Kago no tori') and 'Suton Song' ('Suton bushi'), both of which were popular at the time. Satsuki Shō in Suton sang of life in the barracks housing. 'Bird in a Cage' came from a hit movie and marked the arrival of the golden age of movie ditties. 'Suton,' 'Water Blossom' ('Mizu no hana'), 'Love Ditty' ('Renbō kouta'), and 'Carefree Song' ('Nonki bushi') were all used in the movies. Later, the use of ballads in films conversely brought about the central role of theme songs in movies. This was also the period of the golden age of the *yasuki bushi* songs. In addition, the situation on the continent was reflected in *enka* such as 'Song of the Horseback Bandits' ('Bazoku no uta') and 'Song of Korean Defense' ('Chōsen keibi no uta'). Thus the Taishō era came to an end.

Notes

[1] The death of an emperor meant a change in the name of the reign period. The poem marks the transition from the Meiji to the Tasihō period.

[2] Nogi Maresuke (1849-1912) is probably the best-known military figure of the Meiji period. During the Sino-Japanese War, he led troops in the successful capture and occupation of Port Arthur, a feat he repeated but with heavy losses in the Russo-Japanese War. Despite the heavy costs of his victories, he achieved the rank of general in 1904. On the day of the Meiji Emperor's funeral that Azembō describes in the preceding poem, Nogi and his wife Shizuko committed suicide together.

[3] The Taishō *koto* that resembles a dulcimer with keys is a Japanese musical instrument invented by Morita Goro in the first year of Taishō, 1912. Its sound resembles a mandolin.

[4] The Zigomar films were a series of gangster adventures imported from France.

[5] Most of the events listed are self-explanatory. The Siemens Scandal of 1914 involved bribes made by the German firm to secure Japanese naval contracts. It hastened the collapse of the Yamamoto government and the installation of a new administration; Sakurajima is a still active Kyushu volcano that erupted in 1914.

[6] In 1914, the Japanese, as World War I allied soldiers, seized the Chinese port city of Qingdao that had previously been held by Germany. The song is from the perspective on one of the occupying troops and his love, who awaits him at home.

[7] In 1917, Masuda Taro released *Korokke no Uta* of 'Song of the Croquette,' the deep-fried French-inspired dish. The others names mentioned in this section refer to the songwriters Kaminaga Ryōgetsu (1888-1976), and Misumi Suzuko (1872-1921); and poet, Yoshii Isamu (1886-1960). Yoshii was a poet who achieved instant fame with his hedonistic poems collected in *Sakahogai*; (*Revelry*, 1910), and he continued in the same stylistic vein for the rest of his career. Nakayama Shimpei and Yoshii wrote Gondora no Uta, or 'Song of the Gondola' in 1915.

[8] Kuramochi Guzen was one of Azembō's close associates, who also composed lyrics for the 'Democracy Song.'

[9] Mannen-chō was a Tokyo slum district and the site of reformist activities by the Salvation Army and other groups.

[10] This may have been self-criticism, albeit unintended. I am grateful to Gary Jung for pointing out the significance of this paragraph.

[11] Azembō wrote a more complete and biting version of this song. The lyrics for this more popular version went:

Showing magic lantern images of the plundering *narikin* nouveau riche
A teacher at a broken-down school tells his pupils
With honest work this could be you!
He's teaching them success
Ah, aren't we carefree!

It's because we are poor, we Japanese are great!
Atop that, our patience is first-rate
Prices know no ceiling as they rise
But supping boiled water and rice gruel
We somehow survive
Ah, aren't we carefree!

Eating Nanking rice, being eaten by Nanking bedbugs
Living in the likes of pig sties
Japanese citizens don't have voting rights
But we are proudly arrogant nonetheless
Ah, aren't we carefree!

Swell, swell, our nation's might swells
The tyranny of the capitalist swells
My wife's belly swells
The ranks of the poor swell
Ah, aren't we carefree!

[12] Yasuda Zenjirō (1838-1921) began his rise to leadership of the Yasuda *zaibatsu*, one of Japan's big five prewar financial and industrial conglomerates, as a money changer in the last years of the Tokugawa period. At the time of his death by a right-wing assassin, he was known as Japan's richest person.

[13] Hara Kei (or Takashi, 1856-1921) served as a journalist, government official, and party politician before attaining his highest post as Japan's Prime Minister. He cooperated with Ito Hirobumi to form the Seiyūkai (Friends of Constitutional Government Party) at the turn of the century, after which he was elected to the Lower House in 1902. After becoming Prime Minister in the wake of massive civil unrest over high food and other prices in 1918, he created a cabinet that relied heavily on party politicians, a first for Japan. In 1921 an assassin cut him down on a Tokyo Station platform.

[14] First names can be read in two ways. A variation of a name can indicate an especial closeness in the relationship, the idea being that the name is known to friends and not to the world at large. Here Azembō is writing to the same Mr. Tonoe, known as 'Tonoe Suikyō,' but addressing him as 'Tonoe Hiroshi' to express the intimacy of his relationship with his old friend.

[15] The former is well known among Japanese people as Mito Kōmon, or Tokugawa Mitsukuni (1628-1700), the second lord of Mito clan. Knowledge of his life and accomplishments has also spread to modern audiences through the long-running TV drama, 'Mito Kōmon' that began in 1969 and is still broadcast today. Statues commemorating this local hero can be found throughout Mito City.

Chapter Seven

Spiritual Life

On April 18, 1925, I began living in the mountains of Kiryū, where I devoted myself to mental and physical training.[1] I stopped eating cooked rice and begin a diet that included pine needles. Here is a message of greeting that I sent at that time.

> Dear Sir,
> My apologies for the long silence. I, Soeda Azembō, deeply appreciate and thank you for all the troubles you took on my behalf. My move this time is to the location noted below. Perhaps you think I have started to live the life of semi-hermit. But please understand: I am not running away, but entering into a truer form of human life. I undertake this course with a new and strengthened sense of conviction.
>
> I would appreciate receiving your views and advice about my new direction. In haste I am sending you this notice to let you know about my move. In addition, I recognize that as a matter

of course I may tend toward being remiss in keeping in touch hereafter. I offer my apologies in advance for my neglect. (I have not given up my former address at 37 Yamabushi-chō, Shimoya.)

April 25
Kosone, Kiryū City, Gunma Prefecture, (In the precincts of the Takejirō Inari Shrine)
From the Tenryūkyō
From Soeda

Let me try to make an abstract of Tenryūkyō precepts.

A face with a fresh luster and skin that smells pleasant gives a person a sense of pleasure. Yet, this is a point of pride only among those people who are overflowing with vitality and possess a healthy spirit. The face is the heart's mirror. Eyes are windows on the heart. Do not allow your heart to become clouded. The beauty of complete health is born in the heart.

Corpulence symbolizes degradation. The fat person is not truly a healthy person. This is especially the case after one becomes middle-aged. From the standpoint of general health and longevity, to fatten beyond your normal weight is not a happy occurrence. On the contrary, it is better to be thin. For long life, it is safer to maintain a weight below one's average. This is borne out in statistics maintained by health insurance companies in every country.

In recent years the number of people making noises about the importance of nutrition has increased. Nevertheless, these erstwhile nutritionists themselves do not possess healthy bodies. Conversely, people apparently unconcerned with the issue appear to have healthy bodies. 'Nutrition' is not simply a matter of food.

A large amount of food means a large amount of excrement. This has nothing to do with human nutrition. If humans are not eating machines neither are they devices for producing feces. All food is poison, all are drugs. It won't do to err when it comes to ingestion. The sick are countless in number. Most of the ill suffer from abnormal 'sickness phobia,' 'reckless medication,' and 'excessive nutritional intake.' All are end products created from an unnatural civilized life.

Nothing is more difficult to contend with than being human. Humans prayed to their first gods seeking special dispensation to allow them eternal life. As the years pass, their backs gradually become bent, eyes cloud, and hearing fades. They become miserable, old and infirm, and greatly embarrassed by it all. Their 'special dispensation to never age' has been completely revoked. One must not enter the gate of believing in never aging.

To face nature with the eyes wide open is the beginning of wisdom. The removal of existing practices not in complete accord with the principle of nature's nourishment is the basis for great personal happiness and the wellspring of society's benefit.

We must mutually reflect on this: the moral thought of Japanese people conforms far too much to the life of society. We are too bound by external standards. This causes the individual personality to contract and wither. In turn, this causes the withering and contraction of society itself. Don't misunderstand; I am not calling for the perfection of individuality, but simply recognizing the importance of emphasizing the vantage point of the individual in society.

Wherever one goes, Japanese social life is thoroughly fixed. Fixed is dead. Originally, life flowed through ceaseless activity. Externally and internally, the state was one of ceaseless activity.

If you are faithful to your own life, you can sensitively respond to external stimuli, approach them on your terms, and chose to accept or reject them. This is by far the best way. One should affirm one's own existence. One cannot afford even for a moment to neglect this principle. Nothing is harder to bear than a life unfulfilled. Far more bitter than life without money is life in which the spirit is unfulfilled.

The next year, 1926, I began 'Lectures on the Abolition of Superstition' in Maebashi City. I had hoped to abolish old traditional superstitions and get rid of new scientific superstitions in seeking a kind of truth. Truth must be pursued to be grasped. To do this, one must first begin by getting rid of the aforementioned superstitions, old and new. Living in the midst of superstition and chaos, we can grasp nothing. Nothing can be realized.

Seeking sponsorship for the lectures I called at the office of the *Joshū Shinpō* newspaper to visit Tonoe Suikyō. I found that he had already retired. A company car was provided for the drive to his home. Although we had exchanged letters for the last time three years earlier, it had been more than thirty years since our last meeting. It was an emotional reunion. At the train station in Ueno he had said, 'I'll be back soon,' and those words caused me to recall his image at that time.

At our meeting this time, I said 'It has truly been a long, long time, hasn't it,' and smiled as I added, 'you really put one over on me.' Rain began to sprinkle lightly when I departed.

'Soeda-kun, Soeda-kun,' Tonoe had dashed out of his house following after me with a pair of wooden clogs suitable for the wet weather and an umbrella. 'You can just toss these when you are done with them.' His expression looked just as it had so long ago.

The lectures were a great success. (Tonoe passed away while I was gone on a pilgrimage. Ah, my mentor and friend Tonoe Suikyō!)

Some time before this I submitted to the journal *Reconstruction* (*Kaizō*) a piece on 'The History of Popular Song' to be published in serialized installments. This became an opportunity for Hisada Kiseki and Itō Tomojirō to meet with my son Tomomichi at Yamabuse-chō.

In the early summer of 1927, I was living temporarily in Gifu and sang 'Fate's Prophecy' ('Unmei yogen'). Ishida Shikibu was there in Gifu, too. In midsummer I moved to Rokkaku-dō in Shinō Ōmachi. In the fall, I was at Toyoshina at the Takayama Temple. People at the newspaper *Azumino Nippō* sponsored me. This was the year of 'Fate's Prophecy.'

In 1928, the first general election under universal male suffrage was held.

They say labor is holy
Why don't they give us the right to vote?
Yooi, yooi
Democracy!

Kuramochi Guzen belted out this song in Osaka. Upon returning to Tokyo he took command of the *enka* world. Meanwhile, he also gave rise to a new movement in the world of *tekiya* charlatans by putting himself forward as a candidate for office once that long awaited universal male suffrage was implemented. Yes, this was the way universal suffrage went into effect. Unfortunately, it arose from electoral conditions that were already deeply corrupt. Consequently, nothing changed in the slightest. Kuramochi, who had started from scratch, lost the election. Yet, during the next year, 1929, he was elected to the Tokyo Municipal Assembly. Since then, the city of Tokyo witnessed an unprecedented display of artful deviousness.

The *I-ro-ha* tenement house had been rebuilt as a barracks only to be torn down during the reform of the ward system after the Great Kantō Earthquake. Tomomichi moved outside the city to Nagasaki-chō. I sent this New Year's greeting in 1931.

Felicitations on the New Year.
New Year's Day, January 1, 1931.

This year I wish to publish booklets on the Seishō Seitai movement to cultivate the maintenance of physical and spiritual health so that the methods can spread throughout society. I seek and appreciate any and all support you might lend to this effort.

After that I added,

It may seem a little odd for me to give my age, but this year I will be sixty. It has been seven years since I gave up rice. I am continuing my special work on 'Research on the Human Body' and 'Food Research.' My mind is refreshed, my body is very healthy, food tastes wonderful, and I haven't a cent.

Seishō Seitai Cultivation School, Tenryūkyō, Soeda Azembō
2566 Nishimukai, Sotonagasaki-chō, Tokyo

233

The development of my spiritual state that brought me to the point of beginning my pilgrimage is complicated. A few words won't sufficiently explain it. Nevertheless, I think that my desire to enter a completely transparent mental state by literally taking the Buddhist path was a remarkably natural transition.

I began preparing for my pilgrimage first at the Yūya Tengai and then at the Yūya Otojirō, both temples in Fukagawa. The priest Itō Kaijun of Shō-ji Temple in Horikiri provided guidance.[2] Teacher Kaijun had a pen name, Gyūho ('Ox Gait'). As it turned out, another of my haiku friends, Awaji Kochō, had also received guidance from Teacher Kaijun. Awaji had started on his pilgrimage before me.

I received lots of parting gifts from friends and acquaintances. Haijima Kenjōbō came to see me off from Machiya where I began 'a new journey' on the pilgrim's road.

I arrived alone at Muya and for the very first time placed my feet on the soil of Shikoku. My immediate impression of that moment of landing in Shikoku is powerful. I jotted it down on a scrap of paper by noting:

> Strong impression. I could not help getting excited by the emotion welling up in my breast. That overwhelming sensation! To describe it is beyond my power. But at the very least I can imagine that everyone has shared this very same feeling. After all, the pilgrimage itself has to be a very emotional experience. How could I feel other than moved beyond description at this moment?

In Shikoku I made a pilgrimage to the eighty-eight holy places in three and a half circuits of the Island. I also went once around both Kyushu and the Chūgoku regions. Along the way, I happened to come across Hisada Kiseki in Shimonseki. He was living in Shinshi-chō and pouring his efforts into public service. I visited the Shunpan-rō, a hall where the Shimonseki Peace Treaty negotiations took place. I saw the chairs in which Itō Hirobumi and Li Hung-chang sat. The room had been left exactly as it was at the time. I stood there, momentarily overwhelmed with the fullness of my heart and reflected on my past.

Notes

[1] Kiryū City is located in Gunma prefecture, which forms the northern part of the Kantō Plain on the main island of Honshu. Kiryū is approximately sixty miles from Tokyo. The mountains that can be seen to the north of Kiryū include the distinctive shape of Mount Akagi. Kiryū is sometimes referred to as 'the Eastern Kyoto.'

[2] The 'ji' in 'Shō-ji' actually means 'temple.' Although including 'ji' or the variant *'tera'* or equivalent term, 'in,' along with the English term 'temple' is redundant (in English, the literal translation becomes 'Shō Temple temple'), it is a standard convention and I have used it in this chapter and the next.

Chapter Eight

A Pilgrim's Account

Shikoku on Foot

In the middle of autumn at about three in the morning, I stepped off the boat to set foot on Shikoku.[1] I keenly felt a marvelous freshness in the clean, cold air, a sensation that reached into the corners of my heart, and then I sensed something like a powerful force from afar that seemed to be pulling my body in its direction. My legs moved as if on their own. As I left the passengers' waiting room, a woman approached and asked encouragingly, 'Do you need to hire a car? If I can get another rider we can go right away.' I promptly declined saying, 'I will walk.' I felt in my own clear words the power of my own strength. In the form of a pilgrim, with only the strength of the pilgrim's staff, I stepped firmly on the earth, and strode through the long, long town of Muya in the darkness. Dawn was at last beginning to break at last when I drew near the Shūhandaishi Temple.

After I dedicated sutras at Ryōzen-ji, the first temple of the old Awa Domain in Shikoku, I picked up a pamphlet on 'Instructions for Pilgrimages to Shikoku's Holy Sites.'[2] It urged that the guide be read carefully after the pilgrim checked into lodging. Before leaving Tokyo, Itō Kaijun (better known as 'Gyūho') the chief priest at the Shō-ji Temple in Horikiri, had already kindly and elaborately instructed me along these lines. Now I was on my own, experiencing the pilgrimage in the actual place for which my training had been intended. As I read I noted that Gyūho had instructed me well on each point. I had received good guidance in the basics of conducting a pilgrimage and again felt grateful for his help. I walked and walked thinking about how deeply I appreciated him.

The pattern for pilgrims is that one can stop at ten sites within a distance of something shy of twenty-five miles.[3] All of the holy places are close to one another so the further you go the more sites you can visit. But I took a serious approach and decided that for my first night I would stay at an inn near the third holy site, the Rinsen-ji Temple. Three other *dōkō-san* (the expression used by fellow traveling pilgrims to refer to one another) had arrived at the inn before me. After briefly greeting each other, we began to chat among ourselves.

One person had come from Iyo in Ehime Prefecture seeking to cure a sickness. 'I have been sick since the very start and because of this weak body I will have to go back by car,' he sighed. Another man complained that during his stay at the Daikoku-ya inn in Muya the previous night someone had stolen his purse. It didn't have much money in it but it was an inconvenience nonetheless. Another pilgrim, a man of about forty who had worked somewhere in Tokyo, told how his wife had taken off with her lover and he had come to Shikoku on this pilgrimage to assuage his sadness. On his way, however, he came across four friends in Osaka and after talking things over with the group settled on going along with them to Muya.

They all loved sake and drank a lot. When they began to feel in high spirits, they decided to put up in a brothel where they used up almost all of their money. At the end, the four of them together had a grand total of only five yen left. Although the other three said they would return to Osaka, one fellow said that no matter how hard, he would go on with the pilgrimage even if he had to do it as a begging mendicant forced to sleep out-of-doors along the way. It was that determination that had brought him this far. Later, I came across him again and again at holy sites and inns along the pilgrimage route.

The Second Day

'Now as in the past, when it comes to travel, early to bed and early to rise is the soundest course.' As the guidebook advised, I departed early the next morning. Signboards stood within the precincts of sacred places and along the roadside. They bore advertisements by a newspaper company proclaiming to be supporting 'Shikoku Pilgrimage Cultural Promotion.' In fact, the ads were really pushing guidebooks and maps for using vehicles to make the trek. So much for the painful efforts of the civilized man. I had no use for such things.

From the start, I believed in a primitive trip. I was absolutely dedicated to making the pilgrimage on foot. A pilgrimage is not in any way play or a jaunt. In the course of the pilgrimage, I met people who boasted of walking around Shikoku more than ten times and others who took pride in claiming to have done it a hundred times. Many spoke of the number of treks, how many days they took, and the speed of their travel. They were especially self-satisfied with their speed. One heard all manner of such things. They were no use to me. The pilgrimage is never a marathon race.

Before moving forward to the most dangerous place on the Shikoku pilgrimage, the twelfth stop at Shōzan-ji Temple, I found a 'Free Rest House' and decided to stop briefly there. The proprietor asked me, 'Shall I have your bags sent ahead to the sixteenth station?' It turned out that forwarding luggage was the establishment's real business. Looking around, I saw a young man getting ready to depart on a bicycle laden with pilgrims' bags. Other luggage stood in rows ready for later shipment.

At the time, the shipping fee was a mere fifteen *sen*, but I still thought I should ascend carrying my own bag on my own back. This is the point of this religious practice. It is the true way. But people are people and to my resolve the proprietor convincingly answered back, 'From here on it's all mountains. People don't usually carry anything more than their sutras. That way they can make the climb easily.' I listened but in the end firmly refused his offer. Reflecting on it now, I think my resolve was commendable.

Fortunately, it was only three uphill *ri* to the Shōzan-ji Temple and a downhill path that went on for five more. I got through it without my feet hurting. I also believed I had gradually become used to trekking along. Unfortunately, this led to overconfidence. I not only went too far at a single stretch but on the uphill ten-*ri* segment to the twenty-first site at Tairyū-ji Temple, I made matters worse by rushing the climb. Night was closing in and I did not want to rest just because of a pair of sore feet. I thought that if I coddled my feet now they would just begin hurting again at some other hard stage of the journey. In short, I thought I could use mind over matter to create a regimen for my feet. Each and every day, no more than two *ri*, all the while with a grimace on my face. I also proceeded as a begging priest.

After a stop in Awa at the twenty-third stop in the procession I went on to the twenty-fourth in Tosa. According to the old *ri* measurement, I had covered a distance of about 21 *ri* (or about 30 of the new *ri*).[4] The pain in my feet gradually subsided. At an extra stop, an addition to the pilgrimage at Sabadaishi, I became acquainted with an old fellow-traveling *dōkō*. I fell into step with him and we proceeded on the trek together. As we walked, our conversation touched on the destinations that awaited us, the holy sites, and all manner of other things. I was able to learn much and felt my spirits rapidly reviving.

I thought the old man was someone of many abilities. And well I might. In the past his uncle had been the abbot at the seventy-second holy site, Mandara-ji Temple. My traveling companion had served as an apprentice there and he talked about the temple's affairs from that time in his life. It was a conversation that revolved around events during 1876 or 1877.

At that time, rice cost just 3.5 *sen* for a half-gallon measure. The fee to dedicate a sutra was just half a *sen*. Although the cost of living was low, robbers and thieves often set upon temples. Not long after he had become an apprentice priest, three robbers burst in and tied up the abbot and his assistants. The thieves made tea and ate all the cooked rice. After that, they swaggered off, but not before taking the sutra dedication offerings and uncooked grain. Our apprentice had witnessed the terrible scene from start to finish from his hiding spot inside a large cauldron. From time to time I remember the smile on his face as he related the story.

In those days, many people frequented the Zentsū-ji Temple so it did not suffer such losses. But sites such as Shushaka-ji, Mandara-ji, Iyadani, and Kōyama-ji were lonely places where few ventured and each of them was hit repeatedly.

On a fall evening the thread of one's memories has no end.

Walking Alone

After reaching Tosa, my *dōkō* and I went our separate ways. I followed a road that was completely free of houses. I walked alone along this long, long stretch. On the right were mountains, on the left the sea. On and on, to the right mountains, to the left the sea. I reached the twenty-fourth site, Hotsumisaki-ji Temple (commonly called Higashi-dera or East Temple) and continued on to the twenty-fifth, the Shinshō-ji Temple at Hōshuyama. I did not encounter any pilgrims walking back from these sites and so proceeded entirely alone. Traveling together with someone can be interesting to a degree. You walk and share stories. But I liked it best when I walked alone. Traveling and living are activities that are best done with a companion, so goes a proverb that is considered something akin to commonsense in our world.

But during a pilgrimage one is dressed as if dead. During my journey I accordingly gave myself over entirely to concentrating on the sutras. I chanted and chanted, without self, even without the Buddha. I soaked myself in solitude and single-mindedly pursued what I considered to be the right path. To forget everything and be bound by nothing, calmly walking, letting my feet show me the way. That is the way it should be. Legs are for walking, the heart is to be free. There is no reason to rush but neither is there time to fool around. Continue the journey. Adopt the attitude of the priest. The heart freed from all entanglements is like a cloudless sky arching over the earth melting into it naturally at some invisible point. My silent walking was much like going into meditation. There the Great Teacher exists. One person but not one person; two *dōkō* on a single path. *Namu Daishi Henshō Kongō*, Save Us Great Teacher Henshō Kongō.

Ever deepening silence. I cannot express the feeling of that silence. In its indescribability is the ineffable flavor of the infinite. It is a taste that one cannot experience when traveling with someone else. I could call it the flavor of Zen or the refined taste of haiku, but neither adequately captures the silence's mysterious quality. That deeply mysterious flavor. Analyzing it is impossible.

I was grateful to have made the pilgrimage this far. Nothing can be more settling than this.

Before I knew it I was standing before the gate of the twenty-fifth holy site and resting for a moment. Looking about me I could see that this was a lonely mountain temple. Not a soul was to be seen in its wide precincts. Around the main hall were dilapidated wings that looked as if they were temple ruins. Here and there the gate pillars had been defaced by graffiti. Among the scribbling I picked up two verses from a poem:

> Far more than the compassionate heart
> There is nothing more than the Buddha nature
> In this world even we shall return to the soil
> We possess nothing

I prayed before the principal Jizō stone image and then moved off to the place for dedicating sutras.[5] This, too, was a lonely spot. A boy who looked to be a middle-school student was in charge of the temple office. I offered the sutra and he politely and silently received it. Somehow I felt deeply grateful. He then carefully drew me a detailed map to the next holy site, a sketch that pointed out the false turnings that might lead me astray.

The twenty-sixth site was in the center of a bustling town known for its prosperous fishing industry. I visited Kongōchō-ji, its main object of worship, the Yakushi Nyorai bodhisattva statue, an image associated with medicine and healing.[6] After worshipping at the main hall, I visited the Daishidō Hall and then stopped at the place for dedicating sutras.

In the dedication room, I found three letters that had been sent there awaiting my visit. These were the first messages I had received since leaving Tokyo. I felt a pang of yearning. I immediately read them on the spot. The card from the priest Itō Kaijun of the Shō-ji Temple read in part, 'I have worried about you. You have traveled so far so quickly.' I was pleased to read his card. Being reminded of Kaijun's solemn little smile made me feel happy.

While observing the manners of the local townspeople in a rather haphazard way, I walked slowly to the west, to the west. There were fishing women. There were women day laborers. The fact that women worked remarkably hard made a powerful impression. I found the Tosa dialect fascinating. '*Samuyakunatta nou shi,*' '*Mokkoto nou shi.*' This is the way they expressed 'It got cool, didn't it' and 'Yes, it truly did.'

I sought lodging at an inn called Omi-ya. The woman owner of the place was away but there were four or five fishermen from Korea who were

242

boarding at the lodge. They sat about working on their nets. One of them had started the kindling for the bath and he said, 'Go ahead and stay here.' He added, 'The mistress of the house said if it's a clean pilgrim then it's okay to put him up.' I guess I retained a part of me that still looked clean or at least sufficiently so to satisfy my hosts. In any event, I felt relieved that the problem of housing was solved.

There were no other guests. I was shown to a clean room. Shortly thereafter the lady of the house herself came to my room to say hello as she shouldered a bundle of freshly dug devil's tongue roots. This was a region where the women really work!

I began a note to Priest Kaijun saying:

Thanks to you I am proceeding safely on my pilgrimage. I have at long last become accustomed to things. Once I had injured my feet but they are healed now. I had planned on going to Tsurusan-ji Temple and staying there, but instead pushed on toward Tairyū-ji Temple. This was one of my mistakes. I had no problems when I started out walking but as you know the approach to the place is a steep slope that goes on for ten *chō* and as day was coming to a close I got into a confused rush.[7]

Then I thought, if I write this kind of thing the Priest Kaijun will envision me as suffering because I was unaccustomed to the mountains, breathing hard and drenched in sweat. I would appear feeble in his eyes, with my back bent under my belongings, shaking, no time to wipe my sweat-dripping face, climbing five or six steps and then finding that my leggings had come undone, stopping to tie them, again bending under my load. Truly, I would seem a complete weakling and immature to boot. When I recalled myself at that time I felt ashamed.

Coming out of the bath I found the electric light lit. A dinner tray had been brought in. After saying prayers, I turned to the dishes, and as I ate I thought about tomorrow and the mendicant's rites I would perform in this town and the possibility of perhaps staying here another night. I registered my name in the lodger's log and for a while meditated in silence.

In the lamplight of an autumn night
The shadow of a solitary silhouette

Ascetic Practice

I started early in the morning. Although I had no money, I was keen on going forward, ever forward. At a tea house near a town on the Kira River, bean jam dumplings were displayed in a row. I rested there, sipping tea as I spoke with an old woman. She told me of the disaster that befell the area when hit by a huge tidal wave that smashed into the coast and snatched away houses and families. Listening to the old woman's stories I felt the hardness of this world.

After passing through the town of Nahari, I crossed over the Nahari River to stay at the Awa-ya Inn near the entrance to the town of Tano. As I approached the twenty-seventh sacred site my purse became lighter; in fact, it was almost completely empty. No matter. I must stop here to perform ascetic begging practices. The weather, however, was getting worse and worse.

Eight or nine *dōkō* pilgrims were staying at the inn. Among them was a pilgrim family including a woman and her son of no more than seven years of age. The man of the family wore a beard. There was something sharp about the look in his eyes and sure enough, I learned that he had evaded a dragnet in Osaka aimed at catching gang members. He had simply shut up his house and taken to the road disguising his family as pilgrims. I understood as much after speaking with him a bit. Another of the guests was a military officer who had been pensioned off, a *naniwabushi* balladeer, an unemployed narrator of silent films, and what was left of a former coalminer. I thought what a rich variety of people travel about Shikoku.

During my Shikoku sojourn, while sitting quietly in a corner listening, my knowledge gradually increased. The rumors that circulated around the inns, the behavior of pilgrims, the state of ascetic practices at the sacred sites - the conversation about these and other topics went on endlessly.

Once more the fellow with the beard who had assumed the role of our commander spoke, 'Near the border of Tosa and Iyo, deep in the Shikoku interior, there is this encampment where they give out rice by the measure-full. The population isn't large and there aren't many houses, but it is a very popular valley. One time I went by the entrance to the settlement where seven or eight pilgrims had camped out in a tent. Most of your average *dōkō* pilgrims don't know about the place, but I have gone there twice to perform rites. This time I walked by that outdoor camp in my normal dignified manner. That was my first pass in front of them and one of the guys among the pilgrims shouted, 'Hey, cheeky bastard, you think you've come here to practice rites?!' He acted as if he had exclusive rights and this was his own territory. I took my pilgrim's staff, walked directly up as if to give him a good thrashing, and stared him in the face. I asked him who do you think you are you lousy son-of-a-bitch. He backed off completely. And the next time I went there, the guy was all smiles, wishing me good morning, and carrying on like a perfect coward. 'Ha, ha, ha!' The bearded one laughed. Everyone laughed with him.

When the lively stories ran out, everybody went to sleep. I listened to the sound of rain. So, it had at last started to fall. The next morning the cold rain continued to come down. After breakfast the talk began again. At about ten, a little sunlight began to break through the clouds. It was at this time that I left to perform my practices. At one o'clock in the afternoon the rain began again. I got a little wet and decided to seek refuge back at the inn. The other *dōkō* returned completely soaked, too. Despite that, each of us had returned having received just enough money to pay each of our bills. It was odd. If we went out to practice the art of the begging mendicant we received just what we needed. We shared our happiness at being provided for.

At around four, a pilgrim in a straw cape raincoat came in seeking to be put up. Glancing at him I recognized his face. He was a pilgrim I had lodged with in the Shishikui and Kannoura inns in Kannoura. I asked him, 'Where are you coming from?' In a vigorous voice he answered, 'From the Kira River and I am beat.' I recalled that first time I met him he made the same complaint of being 'beat.' On that occasion, he had given me stern advice, 'In Shikoku inns if you are even a little short on paying the bill you'll be in trouble. They won't advance you a *sen* in credit.' Today he seemed to be in trouble again. But things were generous at this inn. Arrangements had been made so that if you were short today, you could carry out your begging practices tomorrow and pay the amount owed then. He ended up staying, but for all that he was a pitiful old man.

The bath was heated. The order for bathing was that the lodgers who had stayed longest at the inn got to bathe first. While waiting my turn I spoke with the old man. I urged him to remain there for two or three days while he tried his mendicant practices. But he shook his head and said, no, that it wouldn't do. He added that he would have to go hungry because there was no way that he could match someone like me, so skilled in ascetic practices.

It was a forlorn conversation. After all, regardless of the person, there really wasn't much difference in what we did.

As for ascetic practice or living as a petty beggar, people in society perhaps consider that a foolish thing to do. But for pilgrims it is an important act that must be done. Even a person not in need of money must stand at a person's gate and beg. That is the true pilgrim's way. He accepts whatever is given. In short, the rule is: although not formally a priest, with a priest's heart. And 'from life taken to life received,' that is the first step of ascetic practice. Furthermore, and needless to say, without money the only way that a pilgrimage can be made is by resorting to this method. A beggar, a beggar. The Zen priest Dōgen said, 'There are the poor. If you are poor you have compassion for the Way. If you become poor the Way has compassion for you.' The great teacher Denkyō Daishi also said, 'In food and clothes there is no piety, but in piety there are food and clothes.' To the extent that one practices asceticism it is to that extent you will find what you need. All the great teachers, the Ōdaishi-sama, proved this to be true. But the old man could not escape his unease about practicing and therefore could not be cheerful. It was as if he was constantly pursued by his fear and this caused him to shrink. His reduced state made him try all the harder, putting so much more unneeded effort in taking pains to do what other people do quite simply. I sympathized with him to a point. But this is a pilgrimage, a pilgrimage. Be poor!

Tosa's Demon Country

> The morning breeze from the sea
> Bites to the marrow
> Winter has come

At the bottom of my purse I had sixty *sen*. From what I had earned from begging, I had 1.58 yen after paying my bill at the inn. This meant that I was rich with more than two yen to my name so I bravely set out for the next lodging at Tano.[8] On my way, I encountered a new *dōkō* fellow traveler from Osaka. We fell in together and performed ascetic practices as we made our way toward the Kōnomine-ji Temple.

The mistress at the Hashimoto-ya, an inn at the foot of the mountain, called out from her garden inviting us to lodge at her place. We silently assented to staying by together removing our packs and resting our backs as we sat on her porch. After taking a brief break, we vigorously climbed up to the sacred site. I took along a small notebook for copying sutras. The slope was quite steep and the round trip meant traversing a distance of sixty *chō*. I was reminded of the proverb that defined difficult tasks. It went, 'Mastering the three Buddha spirits, the summit of the gods, and the bladed valley of hell - these are challenges that cannot be overcome.' I was more tired than I expected to be. It grew late. In the dusk as we hurriedly returned down the sloping road, we encountered three or four children collecting nuts from the trees. Their faces could not be seen clearly. The light at the inn had already been lit. I took a bath, rinsed away the sweat, and felt carefree in mind and body. Soon the dinner tray was brought out. I felt grateful.

During my pilgrimage in Shikoku I often heard my fellow *dōkō* speak ill of Tosa by complaining, 'Tosa is the land of the demons. There's no place to put up' or 'In Tosa be prepared to use stones for your futon.' I had resigned myself beforehand, but it was not that way at all. There were folktales and country wisdom that spoke of the advantages of making a rock your pillow. But as for me, I found that in all things I was much more comfortable in Tosa than I had been in Awa. I was particularly impressed to find the sleeping mattresses at the inns were so large, lovely to behold, and plump. They were not at all like the bedclothes one finds in flophouses. And the room charge, one that included meals, was such that if you paid fifty *sen* you could expect to receive change.

We slept two in a row in an eight-mat *tatami* room. As we talked before falling off to sleep we could look at the moon through the translucent paper panels of the *shoji* sliding doors. All was comfortable and I was glad to know that according to local custom the heavy outer shutters were not used even in winter.

I stayed at the Tokushima-ya in Aki-chō, at the Wajiki-ya in Wajiki, and the Sakura-ya in Teii before finally arriving in Noichi. There were two inns in this town. I had heard that the Asahi-ya had an excellent reputation as the best place of its kind in Shikoku but that it was full-up year round. As I would only be in the town for one night I decided to put up at the Akaoka.

The next morning was clear. After worshipping at the twenty-eighth sacred site, the Dainichi-ji Temple and carrying out my ascetic practices, I went to visit the Cave of the Reclining Dragon, which had only been discovered a few years earlier. I just looked in from the cave entrance without venturing deeper. I was not interested in seeing the fantastically shaped rocks and strange stones, so once again made my way toward the town of Yamada.

The town had no inns for pilgrims so I stayed in an ordinary flophouse. It lacked any sense of warmth. I keenly felt that while on a pilgrimage one must stay in a lodge for pilgrims. I felt a categorically different and disagreeable sense of loneliness and unease at the flop. I did not feel like carrying out my ascetic practices, but simply waited for the light of day as I enjoyed the place's cold comfort.

After visiting the Kokubun-ji Temple, the twenty-ninth site, and walking 15 or 16 *chō,* I found an inn. The place was called the Dōkō-ya and it was the real thing, a genuine inn for pilgrims. Although it was too early to check in, I decided to stay here. The treatment was first-rate, the sleeping mats the best, the bath pleasant, and what's more, the host was a man of refined accomplishments. I felt quite comfortable.

Here I met and became friendly with a married pilgrim couple from Tokyo, the Tanakas, who had arrived a few days earlier. The couple was truly fond of cleanliness and both husband and wife were constantly doing their laundry, airing the futon, and surveying the place for signs of lice. They said, 'It is quite a task to walk all over Shikoku in these white starched clothes and not get them dirty.' The wife had a habit of reading magazines whenever she had a free moment. Although she was born in Kochi, she had wide experience walking in many places. She was frank, interesting, and a very shrewd woman. Whenever it got cold, lice would attach themselves to pilgrims. She said every pilgrim has at least a few lice and she even kindly removed the ones from my shirt.

The delousing reminded me of a story about Ryōkan and I told this to the Tanakas.[9] Ryōkan carefully raised lice and never killed them. When he was bored, he would place his lice in a row on a board and take great delight in making them run. He would whisper to one or another of them, 'My, you are slow, aren't you!' Then he would pick up his bugs and neatly return them to his pocket. Mrs. Tanaka squealed with laughter at the story. From that time forward she persisted in calling me 'Ryōkan-san.' As I liked Ryōkan and the sound of the name, I accepted the title and it afterwards became another of my nicknames.

The Pilgrims' Inn

The three of us moved to the Ōzaki-ya at the foot of Mount Godai outside Kochi City. The end of the year was approaching and the place was convenient for visiting the thirtieth, thirty-first, and thirty-second sites. There was also a wide area for mendicants to beg. For these reasons we planned to remain there to send out the old year and welcome the new.

There were many inns and guests in the Enoguchi section of the city. Among them were places like Yamanishii and Beni-ya, both of which could accommodate more than fifty lodgers under their roofs. The guests were not only pilgrims. I heard that entertainers, vagabonds, peddlers, and all manner of others stayed there. During my time in Shikoku I had never stayed in such a large-scale lodge and I was keen to set foot just once in a real center for pilgrim travelers. I asked the Tanakas about the prospect and Mr. Tanaka answered that at the end of the year the inn's regular customers, who customarily spend the New Year holiday at the place, book ahead by mail. He was sure that if we tried to stay at the place we would be pouring in atop all the visitors already there. It would just be impossible to get in. On the seventh day after New Year's Day, a certain number of guests leave, but until then all the inns in the city are full to the gills. We could not find a place there at year-end. As Mr. Tanaka had made the pilgrimage before, he was quite well informed and I followed his lights on the matter.

We welcomed the new year at the Ōzaki-ya. For pilgrims on the road there is no special celebration of the day itself. Furthermore, although a new calendar is in use in the city, in the region surrounding the foot of Mount Godai, the holiday is still celebrated according to the old calendar. On New Year's Day, I and my *dōkō* friends went sightseeing and shopping in Kochi City, enjoyed a hike up Mount Oshirono-yama, and then returned to the inn.[10]

January 8. We four, the Tanakas, a pilgrim from Iyo, and I, formed a *dōkō* group that settled in one room at the Beni-ya inn, a three-story building in front of Kunteki Shrine and Anraku-ji Temple in Enoguchi in Kochi City. Mr. Tanaka was fond of singing Buddhist pilgrim's songs and with his fine strong voice sang quite well. He took pleasure in going out to perform winter night ascetic practices but did not have the proper attire. I lent him a cape that I had along with me. The four of us, along with other chanters, went out into the winter night to perform. During the day, he went out with his wife in the same sedge hat and white clothes he usually wore. Both of them appeared to be somewhere on either side of forty years old, small in stature, and of refined appearance. Indeed, they were the very image of cultivated pilgrims. They were known at every inn far and wide for being pilgrims of the best sort, refined and clean.

In Shikoku, with more than too many pilgrims wandering the roads in horribly tattered rags, it was quite natural that the clean ones would stand out. This inn also swarmed as if infested with virulent germs, not only with fairly unclean pilgrims, but with dirty, wandering street artists, sneak thieves, cobblers, wooden clog restorers, blade sharpeners, tinkers, and people all too familiar with the ways of the world. A man might look pretty good in a fine set of clothes, but then you might spy a tattoo on his wrist peeking out of his sleeve and you would realize that this fellow with the malevolent look was an evil priest and sham ascetic.[11] He might boast that he himself was in fact greater than the 'Daishi' great teacher. Many of this sort would get drunk on cheap sake or *shochū* distilled spirits. Then they would start blowing the old conch shell, talking big as they looked down on, mistreated, and otherwise sought to intimidate the new faces among the serious pilgrims. Yes, there were rascals in the pilgrims' midst and it was difficult to maintain one's patience. It was a trial to not get angry, keep a composed heart, and continue from start to finish pressing on with the pilgrimage. It was indeed a truly difficult undertaking.

In this confused inn, only the third floor was quiet, especially the single room in which we four resided as if a single family and in which Mrs. Tanaka played her ever-sensible part with grace and confidence. In appreciation, the clerk at the inn was particularly considerate. Everyone in our room was treated as a lodger deserving special treatment. We were very comfortable with everything.

First thing in the morning the clerk came to light the hibachi brazier and put a kettle atop it. After this, we got up to clean our room after which the breakfast trays would be brought in. To have to climb up and down, to constantly dash between the first and third floors, was not easy. But the chief clerk appeared unperturbed. He did everything. He not only looked after the customer's needs, but also cooked pots and pots of rice, cleaned the baths, prepared kindling and the fires beneath the tubs, and kept the books. And he did it all on his own. The master of the place had promised to put him in charge of his own branch inn and the prospect made him quite happy. He was an unusually hardworking and honest man.

The fifth morning of our stay. While we were eating breakfast, Mr. Tanaka turned to me and asked, as if the idea had just occurred to him, 'Ryōkan-san, shouldn't we be moving on?' I responded that yes, it sounded like a good idea. Mrs. Tanaka laughed and said, 'What? Again?' I suppose she was well used to her husband's habit of suddenly changing plans. She also said there were plenty of good places left for performing our ascetic practices. The fellow pilgrim from Iyo said nothing but gently scratched his chin and looked into my face. I told him there were places everywhere where we could do our practices.

Racing clouds, flowing water - to take life as it comes. Marvelous weather! I felt invigorated.

Passage of Exemption

We remained at the Beni-ya inn at the entrance of Kochi Enoguchi and on the fifth morning set out for Nagahama, where we would stay, after carrying out our ascetic practices at the thirty-second sacred site, the Minen-ji Temple.[12] Nagahama was the location of the thirty-third stop, the Sekkei-ji.

We walked slowly along the foot of the mountain, talking among ourselves. The weather was good, the view splendid, and all were in good spirits. At the gate marking the beginning of the climb to Minen-ji Temple, two refined-looking old women said, 'Hey pilgrims, let us treat you' and gave each of us five *sen* from their purses. We handed out pilgrim cards, thanked them, and began to walk on. Mr. Tanaka said laughing that all we need do is walk and all will be provided. So saying, he scooted out about ten paces ahead of us at a brisk pace. His wife followed trotting along and with her stick playfully poked at the bags slung from his back. It was a cheerful trip.

All of a sudden, I recalled Tanaka Tsugutarō and the visit to his home district. After conducting our practices in Niida and Tanezaki, we crossed the prefectural highway and entered the town of Nagahama. Once we had settled into the Sanuki-ya, we all went off to wash our clothes. The inn was not crowded and made us feel at ease. I was relieved.

After completing a call at the thirty-fourth stop at the Tanema-ji Temple, we enjoyed a view of the sea and the light breeze from Fukushima in Usa where we lined up to wait for a ferryboat at the landing called 'Gomen,' which means 'Exemption.' The Gomen crossing today does not mean anything special, but it was once taken seriously by dedicated pilgrims traveling about Shikoku. It reminded pilgrims on the approach to the thirty-sixth site at Seiryū-ji Temple that this ferry was the only conveyance in Shikoku permitted for their use.[13] Hence the place name 'Passage of Exemption.' For today's pilgrims who use trains, cars, and steamships to go round Shikoku, the name makes little difference.

I remember the recollections of an old woman with whom I shared the road for a few hours as we walked together in Awa and conducted ascetic practices in a dozen places. She remarked, 'One time I was invited by my grandchild and friend to accompany them on a visit to the eighty-eight sacred sites. But they forced me to ride in a car and travel by steamship. It was like making me drink vinegar. I had a terrible time.' No matter what anyone says, the Shikoku pilgrimage should not be done in a vehicle. No excuse will do for the Great Teacher Ōdaishi. No, it would be an insult to the high priest and Great Kobō Daishi who toiled so hard to open the mountain and provide havens for traveling pilgrims. I firmly believe that if we genuinely yearned to trace the path of the true penitent on a sacred journey we must never ride in or on a vehicle. *Nanmyō Daishi Henjō Kongō*, the Dainichi Buddha! We were amazed to find that the old woman was such a true believer. Shortly thereafter she announced that she would strike out on her own separate way.

We went to perform ascetic practices at the thirty-sixth site, the Seiryū-ji, and worshipped its main image, the Nimikiri God of Fire, then stayed at Usa. We set out the next day to double back to the thirty-fifth stop at the Kiyotaki-ji Temple located in the direction of Takaoka. Along the way snow began to fall. The Tanakas had their straw capes but I did not have any rain gear.

In Takaoka there was a store that provided all manner of equipment for the pilgrim, including raincoats of its own manufacture. The town itself was famous for paper production. We all ordered raincoats and heavy rubber-soled *tabi* outer socks. At that point we also discussed the prospect of having to find somewhere to spend the old lunar calendar New Year holiday. We decided to seek lodging at the Yoshimatsu-ya.

I had heard that it was a good place but its owner a little high-strung. In this region 'high-strung' in fact meant quite mad. It was bandied about that the owner was confined to one of the inn's rear rooms, but upon seeing a guest he sometimes went berserk. A *dōkō* from Iyo who had gone to the well for a drink of water returned saying that it tasted terrible and asked the old man why. The fellow's eyes filled with tears and he began to rave, 'You've all come to eat me out of house and home!' We can call that madness born of greed. A man's madness is often born of greed, a woman's madness of lust - or so goes an old saying.

On a snow-free day, clear and bright, we left Takaoka and headed for the thirty-seventh site, Iwamoto-ji Temple. It was quite a distance to Kubokawa. We planned to stay at two places in Suzaki and Kure. On the first day we would walk the six *ri* on the prefectural highway leading to Suzaki. There were so many steep stretches that we could not take time to perform our ascetic practices. Mr. Tanaka was now able to walk atop the snow in his new rubber-soled *tabi*. He was delighted to find that the footprints he created looked like the Asahi Company's mountain logo. He looked at the imprint, his innocent face smiling. His wife laughed and teased him for acting like a foolish kid. A child. For me, those footprints were priceless. They were beautiful.

Running Pilgrims

In March at the beginning of spring the 'running pilgrim' season begins. This is an annual custom. It is peak season for those on the road and inns everywhere fill to capacity. Farmers often make renting out short-term lodging one of their seasonal sidelines. Everything is exceedingly lively. The sacred sites are, of course, especially busy; indeed, it is their busiest time. But 'running' is probably not understood by many people. The expression is an old one used by veteran pilgrims, people who make their pilgrimage throughout the year, to describe the pilgrim inns and the sudden influx of wanderers who stay at them. As for the identity of past 'runners,' present-day owners of inns themselves are unclear. The expression isn't formal or even widely used. The word seems to have originally meant something similar to expressions used for countrified visitors on a quick tour of the capital, words like 'red blanket,' and 'country guest.' Clerks and touts at Tokyo inns spoke ill of such customers declaring, 'What?! Are you from Nagoya or what?' and the like. This meant that the bumpkin was stingy and, in accord with the reputation that Nagoya people were tight-fisted, one could not expect anything extra for serving them.

The 'runners' usually formed groups, small bands of five or six people or larger ones of fifteen or sixteen. Couples traveled together. In any case, the one feature common to all was that they always rushed about in a hurry. Where they could run they ran and ran fast. If there was some sort of conveyance available, most of them rode. From early morning to late at night, from start to finish they rushed about. 'Run, run!' But I also felt that 'run' also meant something like the first product of the season, such as the run of the first bonito of the season or the run of the first mackerel pike, or perhaps the first run of the early ripening eggplant.

I enjoyed making jokes, laughingly commenting to Mr. Tanaka, 'There's a runner,' 'Another runner,' 'Here comes a runner,' over and over again. He would laugh and say, no, no, 'runners' wouldn't come swarming out until the sun warmed things up a bit. Then he would add, Ryōkan-san, you can say 'runner, runner' all you want, but remember that at first we were runners, too. It wasn't until our second pilgrimage that my wife and I gradually got to where we could walk it easily. The first time we ran about, flying here and there, isn't that right, Shizuko, he would ask his wife. She commented that we could run about now if we had a mind to, but as they were on the road with Ryōkan we would not run. The first Ryōkan-san, the priest Ryōkan, was not a runner and we won't be, either! From the get-go we shall not run! She answered me teasingly, 'No, our current Ryōkan-san is certainly no runner.' The *dōkō* from Iyo burst into laughter at the riposte. While walking along we all felt guilelessly carefree. We were all children. Mrs. Tanaka began to sing:

> Not to boast of my homeland
> But the fish spout water
> As they swim in the ponds
> *Yosa koi, yosa koi*

This was a genuine '*Yosakoi bushi*.' It was a merry pilgrimage.

We arrived at Asahi-ya inn in Suzaki at three in the afternoon. It was overcrowded, but they arranged rooms for us. There were four in our group and they gave us one room to share. We appreciated that. Mr. Tanaka practiced his Buddhist pilgrim's songs. Mrs. Tanaka borrowed some old magazines. I took one to flip through and caught her habit of reading magazines. Thinking about it, I realized that since coming to Shikoku I hadn't felt the urge to read a single line of print and my desire to write had vanished completely.

At this inn there was a fellow who claimed to be a follower of Gaigo Saba Daishi - a believer in the 'Great Teacher of the Extra Edition Mackerel' or something like that - and two or three *dōkō* fellow travelers of the same unusual persuasion. Mr. Tanaka observed that when they had met Ryōkan-san for the first time, they had thought I was a little out of the ordinary, too. But now that you have completely settled down, your deportment and intelligence are unsurpassed, he said with a laugh. Perhaps it was so.

We carried out our practices there for three days, in Kure for a single night, at the thirty-seventh site of Iwamoto-ji for another night, and at last approached the thirty-eighth stop at Cape Ashizuri. Along the way, we ourselves, acting like 'runners,' neglected to perform our practices. It took us four days to fly from one spot to the next. The roundtrip visit to the site required traveling seven *ri*. This was close to following the set route, but we did not make the return leg but went on to Matsuo, Ōhama, and Nakanohama before arriving in the town of Shimizu.

A *Settai* Reception

Shimizu was one of Tosa's renowned fishing ports. Although there were no sacred sites here, the town was famous from olden times for hosting the lively *settai* 'Great Reception' during the spring season.[14] Pilgrims from everywhere converge on the town to take part in the reception. Every year the inns are jammed full. In some inns more than a hundred people put up and it gets so crowded that there isn't room to sleep. Even if you can stretch out there is no way to nod off. It is an extremely confused and noisy affair. Thanks to Mr. Tanaka's guidance, we travelers who had arrived just at the time of the great reception found a place to stay at the Buriki-ya on the outskirts of town. The owner of the place was quite selective and only allowed fifteen or sixteen guests to stay so it was a quiet place. It was a kind and restful lodge.

In the morning we set out to follow our customary practices and perform our rites. We took part in the reception and returned. It was before one o'clock. Shortly thereafter, the Tanakas returned. We had naturally come to synchronize our schedules. We would perform rites until before noon and then, even if carrying out our practices at different locations, it became our unbreakable mutual custom to return about the same time.

From Mr. Tanaka I had heard an account of 'driving out the pilgrims' and just as I was imagining a scene of lean and hungry ghosts, three *dōkō* pilgrims returned to the lodge. Mr. Tanaka winked at me and whispered in a low voice saying that the real pilgrims in that story have just turned up. They yelled, 'We've arrived,' and as they came up the stairs grumbled complaints among themselves.

'My, my, didn't we step into it today! We heard that a reception would be at Shimizu at noon and we thought we would join in one at Nakanohama until then. Thinking we could do both we poured on the horsepower to run down the mountain to Nakanohama but it was over by the time we got there. Then we turned around at full speed and went back to Shimizu in a great hurry, only to find that the reception there had finished, too. He who hunts two hares catches neither. And we didn't get to perform ascetic practices, either. Looks like we will just have to eat the cost of staying at this inn.' And they sighed at the end of this tale.

Mr. and Mrs. Tanaka looked at each other with a grin. And Mr. Tanaka teased the newcomers saying, 'Chasing two hares won't do. It tired you out, didn't it? And none of the pilgrims here at the Asahi-ya were much help, none of them made a peep.' I thought to myself, 'What a greedy waste of effort, just like machines with their gears spinning to no end,' and I shut my eyes.

We stayed at the Tanaka-ya inn in Misaki, the Seto-ya in Kotsukushi, and then proceeded to Sukuma, where we put up at the Tokiwa in Wada for two days. We went to the thirty-ninth site, the Terayama Temple.[15] I came across Awaji Kōchō who was staying in the inn. I had heard of this pilgrim when I was in Tokyo and it was deeply moving to have the opportunity to meet him now. It was especially good to find him so full of vitality. On that night we lined up our pillows to talk about Shikoku and had one those rare talks that last until dawn.

Early next morning, our group started out from the front gate of the inn in the direction Mr. Awaji had indicated to reach the forty-first site, the Kanjizai-ji Temple.[16] He himself stayed behind to perform his practices, but being a strong walker soon caught up. We chatted with him as we crossed the

Kashiwa incline. He also shared a room with us at the Kado-ya in Wakamatsu. We happened upon him again at the Ryūkō-ji Temple in Uwajima and on the final approach to the forty-third stop, the Meisiki-ji Temple. I am not sure if he had gone ahead of us or had followed behind. Most likely he arrived first.

It was twenty-one of the old *ri* to the rear area of Mount Iwoyama. It took several days to traverse the distance while we punctuated the trek with stays at the Fumoto-ya inn in Ōshū, the Daigoku-ya in Hatakenokawa, the Ogawa-ya inn in Uchiko, and the Konishi-ya inn in Umezu. From there we went to the forty-sixth site, Jōruri-ji Temple, and then doubled back to visit the forty-fourth, Taihō-ji. There were difficult stretches all along this course, but the mass of 'runners' took a relaxed approach to them by traveling aboard a bus. This was, of course, quite different from what we were doing

Our fellow *dōkō* decided to leave us to return to Iyo, his hometown. In his place, the pilgrim Ishii Densaku joined our group. He took lessons in singing Buddhist pilgrim songs from Tanaka-san as he walked with us. He was a good person, too. We were as happy as ever. We went to the forty-fourth site, Taihō-ji Temple. Here I received a postcard from the Priest Kaijun with a prayerful wish that my aims would be fulfilled.

Mountain after mountain, we walked continuously for several days and came to the beginning of the downhill stretch at Misaka. The sloping road went on a great distance but we found relief in looking down it from above and seeing in the distance nothing but level ground to Matsuyama and Dōgo. We all said let's take a break as we rested our backs beneath a pine tree. Mr. Tanaka, his face tired, wordlessly took out his lunch tin and finished off the leftovers therein. I ate a *mochi* rice cake that Mrs. Tanaka had received at a reception and then given to me. Ishii-kun, who did not smoke, nibbled on parched peas.

As we sat there resting, a group of seven or eight *dōkō* came by saying, 'Thanks for your efforts!' as they rapidly set off down the sloping trail.[17] Mr. Tanaka got to his feet and said with a laugh, 'Ryōkan-san, perhaps we should spend five or six days in Dōgo. At the fifty-first stop at Ishite-ji Temple they have lots of receptions and many at Taisan-ji, too. But this year, well I just don't know ... .' His wife was the first to start walking again.

The *settai* receptions seem to become fewer with each passing year. In the past, when things were done according to the old lunar calendar, there

257

were more *settai*. The season lasted from the third month, at the start of early spring, through the middle of the fourth month. During this period, people from poor settlements swarmed out onto the roads as they suddenly became newly made pilgrims. The participants in the organized 'pilgrim drives' could easily be distinguished from the others on the road.

The sacred sites with the most receptions were temples that enjoyed thriving economic conditions. The *settai* were sponsored in fishing ports and farm villages by both individuals and community groups. Some of the Daishi were considered so efficacious and powerful that their followers even provided bales of rice from far away Kyushu. Inside the temple grounds, stalls were set up resembling those seen lining the street in a shopping district. Bags of rice rose in stacks high atop tables and stands. There was also *mochi* rice cakes, postcards, coins for making offerings, hand towels, toilet paper, sweets, yams, red bean rice, fish-free *gomoku* sushi covered with various vegetable toppings, sweet red bean soup, fat *udon* noodles, and lots of other items. The goods offered were not for sale but, as a sign made plain, 'Provided for the reception of our pilgrims.'

From as few as three to as many as six or seven people might run one stall. Pilgrims came one after another to receive these bounties. In return, they handed over sutra cards and intoned the chant 'Save them Great Teacher Henshō Kongō.' There is another song-chant called '*Settai kankin*,' but when places are very crowded there is no way it can be sung as pilgrims behind pushed and jostled those in front.

Although some of the sacred sites did not have *settai*, in other places you might run across them even on streets and byways outside temple precincts. All of a sudden you might be hailed, 'Hey pilgrim, come over to our *settai*.' This was truly an occasion for which one felt grateful and happy. Above the entryway of houses that provided *settai* you could see the pilgrim cards stuck on the large sacred straw hawser that hung over the doorway. You could also find them on the gateposts or *torii* gates marking the entrances to various villages as well.

Even during this hectic season, our group continued to be in our usual good spirits. We got along as ever, walking along together down roads barren of houses and into towns and villages where we performed our ascetic practices. After our rites we would wait for each other, regroup, and begin walking once again. Clouds would come and go. We were embraced in nature's sweet bosom as we walked calmly along. Before our eyes, nature provided stories, poems, and pictures. We ourselves became one part of it. Arriving at an inn, it was as if we had become a single family and had decided to stay there. We lacked for nothing and felt perfectly free.

Other *dōkō* groups appeared to share the same feeling, but some members in 'runner' groups sometimes spoiled the scenery. When they started out from their home places they did so in shared high spirits and feelings of friendship. They even had things just as they wanted at the lodges and sacred places. But somewhere along the road, one way or another, many of the runners began to have words with their fellow sojourners. The confrontations worsened to the point that people ended up parting after quarreling. What a shame. They had come to make amends for the sins accumulated during the course of their humdrum lives and paradoxically ended up creating new sins during their Shikoku pilgrimage. Of course, there were some among the newcomers who maintained a dignified silence from start to finish. Although they traveled among the 'runners,' they did not whip themselves into confused activity. But those types were rare.

'Returning the reception' was also practiced. According to the Great Teacher's sacred way, this meant the practice of former pilgrims themselves sponsoring receptions. After visiting the eighty-eight sacred sites (and sometimes even more in on top of these) and returning safely home without mishap, one's happiness with so many blessings would culminate in this generous act. This was the true way of the pilgrim and it was one of Shikoku's beautiful customs.

Somebody said that our departed fellow sojourner from Iyo was probably holding a 'return reception' right about now. Indeed, what had become of Awaji-san? Scraps of memories, stunning scenery, the nightingale's song, the frog's croaking. We gradually saw fewer and fewer 'runners;' it seemed that the *settai* receptions had ended. But we continued our pilgrimage - no matter how long, no matter where.

An Inn of Good Works

Along with the pilgrim from Osaka who had replaced our friend from Iyo, we proceeded to Sakade where we lodged at the Wakamatsu-ya inn. We performed our practices there for three or four days. We agreed to put our feet in a row and walk together. On the second day I went about as a begging priest on the edge of a salt field.

At eleven o'clock in the morning, I was called from the latticework doorway of a house that stood near a postbox and was attached to a tobacco store. I was invited to rest there for a while. I talked with the occupant and learned that he and I were born in the same year. His name was Takagi Yukitsugu and he had been a soldier until he was wounded and retired. Instead of 'pilgrim' he called me 'Great Teacher' or 'Ōdaishi-san.' He repeatedly entreated, 'Great Teacher, by all means stay here tonight. Although it is early now, do return later. You'll find that you won't be treated shabbily. Please, please accept this invitation.'

I thought that I would pass along the invitation to my fellow pilgrims and that we would all return to this house by the postbox at around five in the afternoon. The tobacco shop was Takagi's wife's family's home. Here an old couple lived in quiet retirement. A bridge-like passageway connected the houses so that one could come and go freely between them. It was a nice house.

The old man's emphatic 'I will be waiting for you, waiting for you,' still ringing in my ears, I went off to work as a begging priest. Afterwards I returned at around one o'clock to the inn where we had originally taken a room. The others had not returned. I told the mistress of the inn the situation and asked that she convey this to my fellow sojourners. Although it was still before the appointed time, I then set off to Takagi's, taking a route that allowed me to see a bit more of the town.

The master of the house was happy and so was his wife. They had prepared a welcome by lighting incense of the Buddhist altar and turning on lights throughout the house. They were Shingon sect believers and very pious. They said that soon my hot bath would be prepared so please enjoy it, Great Teacher. The bathing area was in the main house so I had to cross the connecting bridge. The tub was of some kind of manmade black granite. Once I finished bathing I was immediately called to return to my host's place. I found that they had prepared sake and snacks. The host had started to drink and I was in a fix. I refused his offer to join him by explaining that I was in the midst of a pilgrimage. But the old man loved drinking. Not only that, his wife also offered saying tactfully, well you will be going to sleep soon anyway.

To this the master of the house added, it really isn't a problem because this is *gomazu*. In other words, he said he was offering only vinegar made from sesame seeds. But the expression was just the way people in Shikoku jokingly referred to sake (much like Zen sect believers have a custom of calling drink *wakayu*, or 'the first water boiled on New Year's day'). I said I would have some, but must wait a bit. And so I sat in front of the Buddhist altar to officiate a simple ceremony. My host sat nearby and his wife fanned both of us.

After the rites I drank *gomazu*. It was the first alcohol I had had since arriving in Shikoku. The next morning sake was offered again, but this time I refused. I did a little laundry and rested for the remainder of the day as I chatted with my host. He was an old salt field boss who had worked hard from an early age. He told me about changes in the cauldrons used in salt manufacture and described his plans to go to Akō to sell one of the old cauldrons and many other things besides. His wife once again brought out sake.

Sitting there, I could clearly see men working in the salt fields. The old boss said to his wife, 'Order up a sea bream for tomorrow.' He tapped me on the back and pointed to a direction somewhere over my left shoulder saying that at the base of that hill we can land sea bream with golden scales. He added that the house belonged to them and I was welcome to stay just as long as I liked.

The 'fire boiled method' for producing salt is a specific method used worldwide. It requires a site blessed with an excellent climate. More than 160 years ago, during the ninth year of the Ansei period (1780), Kume Michitaka, from Sanuki in Kagawa, studied mathematics and surveying under the teacher Magoroheibee Shigetomi in Osaka. When Kume returned to his home district the local daimyo lord, Matsumoto Noriyoshi of Takamatsu, ordered him to work as a surveyor. The lord was keen on enriching his domain, which suffered from a lack of anything but the poorest industries. He thereupon relied on Kume to work out a plan to develop the Sakade salt fields, which Kume did by making plans to construct the project and supervising countless workers. After struggling for many years, he successfully produced salt and thereby made the Takamatsu samurai clan rich. Since then there had been many changes in the cauldrons and ovens. I was made to understand that these improvements now enabled my host to go to Akō to sell one of the old cauldrons soon.

261

The boss finally drank himself under the table.

The next morning as I was preparing to leave he sad here is an offering and took out something wrapped in paper. Despite my refusal he pressed it into my hand.

As I walked I thought to myself, 'Well after all, the "Great Teacher" ate a lot of fish and drank a lot of *gomazu*.' Repent all, Repent!

Upon arriving at the Wakamatsu-ya, I found my fellow *dōkō* had already left the inn without me.

The Pilgrim Lodge Late in the Year

Glory Be to the Great Teacher Henshō Kongō! I follow in the Great Teacher's footsteps, from sacred site to sacred site, today travel, tomorrow travel, the penitential tour continued. This is the way of the pilgrim. But at the end of one year and the beginning of another soon at hand, one must resign the self to thinking ahead, to securing lodging for some place to stay. At this time even many flophouses will not allow pilgrims to stay. And even the rare flophouse that allows pilgrims will not accept new guests if the place is full at the end of year. (Some pilgrims attempted to struggle along by sleeping outdoors, but for most camping out was all but impossible without any preparations or equipment.)

These full-up lodges might have been thought to hold only pure pilgrims, ones who uncomplainingly went on with their lives. But there was no law against one lightly calling oneself a pilgrim. In fact, all manner of people used the title. There were the pilgrims who were street artists, lion dancers, puppeteers, scissors and blade sharpeners, tinkers, umbrella menders, repairers of rubber soles, vagrants, the lame and deformed, fake orphans, bad drunks, and habitual kleptomaniacs. And that was why staying at such places was so troublesome. In this respect, Shikoku was no different than Kyushu.

December 30. Four in the morning. The sound of the tinkling bell of a peddler of boiled beans. I opened my eyes. I arose from my corner in a ten-mat room that had been set aside for use by single travelers and threaded my way through the sleeping forms to the toilet. I washed my face. A fire had already been lit in the kitchen. Rice and soup were boiling away. I returned to the second floor. People there were still asleep. I alone quietly folded my futon and completed a simple morning meditation. I then took a brief rest at the side of the brazier downstairs. The master of the place and his counterman were having their morning tea. They offered me a cup, too. I accepted it with thanks. They used leaves that cost two yen and although it was a bit watery, it tasted better than the coarse *bancha* variety of tea that was offered to guests from the big common metal teapot. At five I went to the dining table. I ate before the others.

This inn generally adhered to a set of faithfully enforced military-like rules. At the call of 'Mealtime,' twenty-four or twenty-five guests would come clattering down to the dining hall. Those who came late would not leave happy. Yesterday a ragged pilgrim was driven off after suffering a tongue-lashing for taking to many liberties with the rules. The old man was from Iwakuni Suo in Yamaguchi. I felt sorry for him but it couldn't be helped. Even in a flophouse, I suppose when in another country one must follow the local rules. But the old man seemed to have become accustomed by long years of experience to sleeping outdoors and was strongly disliked by everyone at the place. When forced to leave, he left without a word of good-bye to anyone with whom he had shared a common room. Ten mats and eight people, take away one made seven. The ones remaining gathered around the brazier and chatted heartily, content for several hours.

Although I said I was staying there, this does not mean I was staying inactive. The pilgrim has a pilgrim's daily work. Performing ascetic practices, mendicant begging. For the sake of paying for the flophouse room, for the sake of the sutra devotion fee, for the sake of the straw sandal fee - one could not take even a single day off. Mending torn leggings and washing clothes, these chores should be done at a time other than that for performing ascetic practices. Ah, the weather looks bad, we're in for it; no money; my legs hurt; the rubber on this sole is about gone, this won't do - as the pilgrims mumbled their complaints they made their preparations.

In the room there was one man who went out to buy used and discarded articles. He spent all of his time drinking and was already an alcoholic. His habit was to drink everyday at the sake merchants and then come back to sleep. But he didn't drink much yesterday and this morning he is up, clean and sober, before anyone else. He went out wearing an arm strap reading 'Yahata City Salvage Goods Employee' and wearing an apron emblazoned with the message 'Ōno Merchandizing - Everything in Salvage' and carrying a hanging scale. He would be gone for a few days.

Not long afterwards others departed. Out went the old man, one of neuralgia's orphans, Mr. Yamada; the asthma suffer, the old pilgrim Ejima who worked for forty years in a coal mine and at the age of 73 has become an ancient pilgrim. And in another room, there remained the couples. Soon the blind street performers and all the rest departed. I left last.

In the street there were banners advertising goods on sale and banners put out to send off soldiers. They all flapped in the wind. The wind at a time of crisis: cold, cold. Two o'clock in the afternoon. A half day of ascetic rites performed, I went back. But not a soul had returned yet. The charcoal in the brazier had gone out. A snowy wind set the glass door rattling. Cold.

I received a letter from Haijima Kenjō in Tokyo. 'At this time of national crisis the imbalance in the economy is extraordinarily large,' and 'the vice-minister of the Ministry of Finance was shocked by the massive sales figures for luxury items sold at year's end at the department stores,' and 'even workers in the defense industry, right down to the factory laborers, are drunk on luxurious living' and 'a neighborhood kid, only nineteen years old, is earning more than 200 yen a month while others are suffering by being thrown out of work or having to change trades - as you know the family running the Harako Shoe Store is one sad case in point, I feel especially sorry for those compatriots,' and other comments similar in tone. The wind that blows through this world is harsh. Everyone appears to be suffering considerably.

After a while, all of my roommates returned, one by one. That jolly orphan Yamada came in saying he was hungry. I felt empty, too, but we had plenty of time before dinner. He immediately took out the *go* board to play the simple five stones in a row game. He asked me if I could stand to lose a few more games. I told him that this time I would not lose. If I don't win one game out of three I will be shamed before my ancestors. He made a wry face and laughed saying that he didn't have a father or any ancestors so it didn't bother him. He really was a happy orphan.

Four-thirty in the afternoon. As we lined up at the dinner table, five or six fellows shaping the rice into glutinous rice cakes came in saying 'Sorry to be late' by way of greeting. The master of the inn joined in saying that even he didn't have time to eat. By the time we had finished dinner, the workers were beginning to complete the pounding of steamed rice into *mochi* cakes. Their work seemed to be humming along.

The old man Ejima came into the room cradling lots of kindling coal in his kimono skirt. He held his shirt, a rag that was really no more than a nest for lice, over the hibachi brazier and I could hear a popping sound like someone parching nuts as Ejima burned his pests. Things were humming with him, too. In a corner of the room, the asthmatic old Kojima spoke as if to himself, 'You need hot water for that otherwise it won't do any good.'

To which the elderly Ejima responded as he paused from roasting his peas, 'Kojima-san, don't speak to me like you are talking to a child. I know that hot water would be better. But then the shirt will get wet. And it is impossible for a man without a spare to have his clothes get wet.' He raised his voice in anger and as he pulled at his beard in irritation. For all the world he looked exactly like that minister on a one-yen note. The old man Kojima said no more. I went to the medicinal baths with the old orphan, Yamada. That night my pillow was lined up with the orphan's and I listened to his unusual life story until I dropped off to sleep.

The thirty-first. Morning, half past six. Shortly after breakfast, the master of the place came in to make up the room as usual. When he put the bedclothes into the closet, he found that old Ejima had wet his blankets. He threw them onto a drying rack as he grumbled about how the old guy was already entering his dotage, even wetting his bed, and continued his cleaning. After he had finished his chores he confronted Ejima. 'You can't stay here anymore. You must go. You trouble the other guests, it's a problem for this house, it is unbearably smelly. Here, I will give you this, so go.' He took out thirty *sen*. The old man accepted the coins and for a long time sat stock still as if deep in thought.

Soon the other pilgrims had made their departure preparations. Some of them were penitents who would depart to do their practices even on New Year's Eve. I had considered taking the day off to go out and do a little shopping - maybe buy new *tabi* socks and a shirt.

Again the host came in. Old Ejima had at last made his preparations. It was sad but could not be helped. I gave him ten *sen*, he smiled, said thanks, and descended from the second floor. The most lost of the losers. It was pitiful. The orphan Yamada-kun said he was going to bed after doing his laundry.

The snow falls lightly.

A Cheap Inn

The second day in Bitchū in Okayama. Along a hot, hot road that never seemed to end I walked drenched in sweat and caked in dust. I trudged from an inn in Yorijima as far as the town of Tamajima. They say it is about three and a half *ri* but I felt like I walked more than four. Perhaps it was the heat that made me feel so tired. I entered the town well after noon.

I worshipped at a shrine, the Haguro, located on a rise in the center of the town. I received a red seal in my notebook containing my collection of stamped impressions from holy sites. I rested in the shade of a tree within the shrine precincts. Just then a group of traveling worshippers arrived. Students, teachers, girls who worked in a restaurant, the owners of the establishment - various people filled the place to overflowing. It was the seventh day of the seventh month, the anniversary of the second full year since the 1937 China Incident. Perhaps that is the reason there were so many visitors. And then there is me. I, too, went slowly down the stone steps to the post office near the shrine to get a rubber stamped impression to commemorate the anniversary. The office was quite near the shrine and inside it was standing room only. I came out and looked around the town and the signboards about its various stores. My eyes all of a sudden came to rest on the sweet shop.

'Tamajima's Special Ryōkan Rice Crackers' it read. And then five or six paces on 'Tamajima's Specialty Ryōkan Steamed Dumplings.' The Priest Ryōkan and dumplings - I wondered what the holy connection was. But immediately my memory was refreshed. This was where Ryōkan had stopped. Indeed it was in his middle years during his time of mental training. He would now and again pause from his travels to listen to what people were talking about. I had completely overlooked that fact. Today traveling, tomorrow traveling. Day after day I walk in a strange land. I may have forgotten the thrill of traveling; perhaps I even lost my taste for it, even while still absentmindedly staying on the road. This must certainly be 'travel intoxication' or something similar. I was amused at myself. The priest Ryōkan set foot in this temple, the Entsū-ji of the Sōtō sect of Zen. Now the surrounding hills were called the Entsū-ji Park and had become a famous attraction in Tamajima. Within the temple precincts the Ryōkan Hall still remained. As I killed time in the park, I asked one of the local old folks, 'Is there still a priest at Entsū-ji?' I was told, 'I think there is one, but he's not around. Why don't you take the job?' I rested on a rock beneath a tree and ate the tomato I had brought along for lunch. I thought of Ryōkan and the past.

Memories of Ryōkan in the cool shade of Entsū-ji
On all sides beautiful scenery of an unknown spot in the
summer haze
The water in the reservoir pond shriveling beneath the
drought clouds

That day I just walked, the time for mendicant begging having already passed. But I didn't feel right if I didn't do at least a little something by way of performing the rites. I begged. Yes, a little in the way of ascetic rites. I felt better. At a last house on my way someone called to me, 'Hey pilgrim, have some tea.' If one just does a little in the way of performing the rites then one day you are bound to come across two or three special houses like this one. It is truly a wonder. It is the grateful path of Buddhism. Our talk over tea at this house led me to understand that even now there were still many believers in Ryōkan in Tamajima. In fact, local people became prominent in sponsoring the various gatherings such as the 'Meeting to Discuss the Hidden Anecdotes of the Priest Ryōkan.' Among them were the old artist Nakanishi Yōdo, who now lived in Kyoto, and a former teacher at the local girl's school, Hanada Kazue. Hanada had written a series on 'The Child Mind of Priest Ryōkan' for which Nakanishi had drawn the illustrations. This was published in a newspaper intended for children and contained some of Ryōkan's cherished poems and calligraphy. Soma Gyōfu disputed the authenticity of some of the items.[18] But it was clear that local people in this region, even children, were quite familiar with Ryōkan. In fact, I even saw a photograph taken to commemorate the 'Meeting to Discuss Anecdotes.'

Tamajima town extends over a wide area. Although a walking pilgrim like me had no use for it, Tamajima Railway Station (on the San'yō Line) is a full *ri* and a half away from the town. On my way to Kurashiki, where I was headed the next day, there was the very long Kasumi Bridge, a famous Tamajima sightseeing spot. There was also a point with the extraordinarily long name of 'the small cape much beloved by late Tokutomi Rōka.'[19] There were also many lovely places with no names at all. It was a rather nice region. And I came to like Tamajima very much.

With the tide's fragrance there's coolness atop the bridge
Fresh leaves on the giant tree reflect the sunlight as they
drink dry the marsh
Beneath clipped rushes

Bitchū and Higo stretch out below the glow of evening
clouds
Light of the persimmon tree
Leaves dyed red in the sun's last blush

I walked along the outskirts of town wondering how the evening's inn would
be. In Kure and Hiroshima I had heard that the Akama-ya was a good place.
But according to my experience, places that were said to be good were lousy
and the lousy places were surprisingly good. It depended who was doing the
talking and when they were reporting. Furthermore, an inn, no matter how
adequate, could be rotten if one had to put up with poor-quality roommates.
The mood could be and was frequently wrecked. And mood is everything in
a flophouse. I had stayed in countless cheap inns during my pilgrimage in
Shikoku and travels about Kyushu. I had been wandering; four years of non-
stop travel.[20] The inns had become my home. My nerves had gotten tougher.
I was no longer surprised if a place was good or bad. That place is the place
designated by god - and I would leave it all to the spirits. I had become simply
grateful to be allowed to stay the night. After all, a common man is a common
man. If one is lucky enough to hit upon a good inn that is just fine.

I could see a big signboard reading Akama-ya Inn sticking out about
a block away. I entered the courtyard and called out 'Hello' and 'A little
help please.' An older couple who looked to be in their sixties and shared a
peaceful countenance answered, 'Come in please.' It was easy to recognize
that these were indeed good people. In the corner of the courtyard stood a
pile of antique tools. Originally, this had been a tool store. The *tatami* rooms
were also interesting, with other curios laid out in various arrangements.
The master of the place came in saying, 'Your bath will be ready soon,' and
he showed me a smiling face. The years had aged him but he seemed to
have shed himself of desires and found a calm heart in simply pursuing the
uncomplicated life of an innkeeper.

Three people who appeared to be traveling peddlers were staying
in the ground-floor *tatami* room. The room looked spacious and I thought
it would be fine for me, too. But the owner said, 'This room is hot. A nice
breeze blows through the upstairs and it's better up there.' He showed me
upstairs where there were three rooms but not a single guest in any of them. I
chose a ten-mat room with a window that looked out on the front. It was the
coolest place. As was the custom in this inn he immediately handed me my
bedclothes once the room had been decided upon. This saved him from doing
the chore later.

He chose good futons for me and provided a brand new white mosquito net suitable for draping over eight mats. It was a joy to sleep by myself in such a spacious room. Last night's place had been caught up in the middle of an air raid drill practice and had been noisy. Today the drill had been lifted. At five o'clock I took a bath. It was a moxa bath.[21] After getting out of the bath I ate dinner just as I was, in the nude. The couple who ran the place and the other guests were kind to me and I felt quite comfortable. It was truly a peaceful, cheap inn.

One day's affairs finished. All that was left now was to sleep, but it was still early and my fatigue had vanished. I put on the summer kimono and went outside to walk around the streets a bit and enjoy the evening coolness. There was not the slightest breeze.

I returned and got directly dead center under the wide canopy of the mosquito net. I was tasting 'paradise' sleeping alone in this big room. I thought I would write a postcard. It was ten o'clock and the master brought up another guest. Oh boy. On top of that, he was drunk. I thought my paradise was going to fall to ruin. The master showed the newcomer to a room next door, fished out another mosquito net, and then in a quiet voice said, 'Good night.' I was grateful. The master had preserved my 'peaceful retreat.' It was a gift of consideration. For a cheap inn, this was treatment that was almost too kind. It was remarkably generous.

I turned on my side and shut my eyes. I had no idea what the new guest looked like nor his trade. Someone who shows up late and drunk is probably bad business. Most inns would turn him away. Perhaps he was a regular here. Troublesome guests always fail to show consideration and often beckon you with a loud 'Hey, neighbor next door,' but this fellow was comparatively quiet. Rather than talking to his mates or anyone else, he simply said a few words to himself before falling off to sleep.

Merciful eyes behold the life of all
Bounties as full as the endless sea

I felt at peace and had realized my 'paradise.' And from that state went in to the paradise of dreams.

Return

After five years of pilgrimage I returned to Tokyo. And now I am on the second floor of the used goods warehouse from where I look out on a new world. I thought I would die. To die would have been fine. But I did not die. In fact, I didn't even come close. I now think that the trail of my life will go on without end.

A bright hopeful world will emerge. If I had not converted to Buddhism, I would have lost the light needed to see the world and might not have been honored to participate in the great work of the nation and shine in the Emperor's light. I will follow the way of Buddha and to my posterity bestow a taste of life. That is a delightful way to live, I think.

Notes

¹ Azembō's account of his Shikoku pilgrimage compresses time and in a few instances blurs space. In fact, his wandering lasted for approximately five years beginning in 1935 and included trips to places beyond Shikoku to Kyushu and the Chūgoku region of central Honshū. For additional details see the 'Chronology' in Soeda Azembō, *Azembō Ryūsei-ki*, Tokyo: Nihon Tosho Senta, 1999 (reprint, originally published in 1941) pp. 305-9.

² Here again the 'ji' in 'Ryōzen-ji' actually means 'temple.'

³ Azembō gives the total distance as ten *ri*. The traditional or old *ri* was equivalent to 2.44 miles.

⁴ The old *ri* was a traditional Japanese unit of distance equal to 2160 <u>ken</u> or 12,960 *shaku* (the *shaku* being the Japanese equivalent of the foot). This is about 3927 meters or 2.44 statute miles. See Measures and Money at the beginning of this volume.

⁵ *Jizo* is an important bodhisattva, an incarnation of the Buddha that has voluntarily renounced Enlightenment in order to guide lesser beings through the realms of creation. *Jizo* is thought to take particular pity on the souls of dead children, who wander as lost souls (*munebotoke*) between the worlds. *Jizo* usually is depicted in the form of a bald Buddhist monk with simple features; at times dead children are shown climbing up him or seeking shelter from demons in his robes.' http://people.brandeis.edu/~eschatt/ImmortalWishes/jizo.html.

⁶ This is the *honzon* image placed in a central hall or other central location in the temple.

⁷ A *chō* is about 300 meters so Azembō had climbed about two miles over steep terrain.

⁸ Azembō is poking fun here. He is by no means rich, but at least he is a bit ahead of his usual hand-to-mouth condition.

⁹ The Zen priest, Ryōkan (1758-1831) also affectionately called the 'Great Fool,' was a popular poet and Azembō's alter-ego. In a manner similar to Azembō he wrote with directness about life's simple pleasures and hard challenges. He also lived as a hermit, maintaining himself by begging.

¹⁰ Note the failure of central calendars to penetrate into the countryside even as late as 1939, despite the central government's mandated use of the Western calendar from January 1, 1873.

¹¹ Then and now, tattoos are generally associated with criminality. This is not only because of gang markings but also because tattooing was used to punish criminals. Among younger people today, a new fashion sense is neutralizing the stigma.

¹² Azembō appears to have misremembered the temple's name. The thirty-second stop in the pilgrimage is actually Zenjibu-ji.

¹³ Azembō's text indicates that the temple is called Seiryū-ji, but recent guidebooks call it Shōryu-ji.

¹⁴ The *settai* or, more politely, *osettai*, was and is any gift given to a pilgrim. It may range from lodging to money. Although the practice of giving to gain merit for the giver is the same today as in the past, the large community receptions have largely been replaced by individual acts of charity.

¹⁵ The temple is better known as Enkō-ji.

¹⁶ This is actually the fortieth, not forty-first stop.

¹⁷ The group of pilgrims greeted Azembō's group with the phrase, '*Gokurō sama*.' In thanking fellow travelers for their efforts the intent is not to express gratitude for anything specifically done for the party uttering the greeting. It simply recognizes in a friendly way that both are engaged in something that might be arduous or perhaps troubling.

¹⁸ Soma Gyōfu (1883-1950) spent decades studying the life of Ryōkan and published books

for adults and children based on his research. These appeared in the late 1920s and mid-1930s.

[19] Tokutomi Rōka (1868-1927) was a novelist best known for his novel *Hototogisu* (1898). He was also the younger brother of the journalist and historian Tokutomi Sohō.

[20] It appears that Azembō has been on the road for five years of non-stop drifting. Most chronologies indicate he returned to Tokyo and took up his life in the junkyard in 1939.

[21] Moxa is a flammable substance derived from Japanese and Chinese wormwood plants. It is often used in acupuncture treatments by placing moxa atop a needle. The herb can also be used directly in moxibustion, a treatment where a cone of moxa is ignited on the skin to cause a favorable if painful reaction. Azembō's hosts are using moxa in the bathtub, where it is heated by the steaming water.

Bibliography

Adachi Hideya. *Warau kado ni wa chindonya*. Tokyo: Sekifū Sha, 2005.

Anzai Kunio. 'Uta ni miru jiyū minken ki,' *Rekishi chiri kyōiku*, 656 (July 2003): 16-21.

Arima Takashi. *Jidai o ikiru kaeuta kō*. Tokyo: Jinbun Shoin, 2003.

Atkins, E. Taylor. *Blue Nippon: Authenticating Jazz in Japan*, Durham, NC: Duke University Press, 2001.

Azembō no Kai, eds. *Azembō no kai* (mimeographed pamphlet), Tokyo: 1959.

Bowen, Roger W. *Rebellion and Democracy in Meiji Japan*, Berkeley: University of California Press, 1980.

Brink, Dean Anthony. 'At Wit's End: Satirical Verse Contra Formative Ideologies in *Bakumatsu* and Meiji Japan.' *Early Modern Japan* (Spring) 2001:19-46

Czarnecki, Melanie J. http://www.aasianst.org/absts/2005abst/Japan/j-87.htm.

Gramsci, Antonio. *Prison Notebooks: Selections.* Translated and edited by Quintin Hoare and Geoffrey. New York: International Publishers, 1971.

Groemer, Gerald. 'Singing the News: Yomiuri in Japan during the Edo and Meiji Periods.' *Harvard Journal of Asiatic Studies* 54(1 [June]) 1994:233-61.

Hunter, Janet E. *Concise Dictionary of Modern Japanese History.* Berkeley: University of California Press, 1984.

Hutcheon, Linda. *A Theory of Parody: The Teaching of Twentieth-Century Art Forms.* New York: Methuen, 1985.

Itoh Akira. 'Gramsci Study in Japan: Achievements and Problems.' http: www.italnet.nd.edu/gramsci/igsn/articles/a12_5.shtml

Kanagawa Bungaku Shinkō Kai, eds. *Soeda Azembō, Tomomichi bunko mokuroku.* Yokohama: Kanagawa Bungaku Shinkō Kai, 1994.

Kawabata Yasunari. *The Scarlet Gang of Asakusa.* Translated with Preface and Notes by Alisa Freedman; Foreword and Afterword by Donald Ritchie; and illustrated by Ōta Saburō. Berkeley: University of California Press, 2005.

Kimura Seiya. *Soeda Azembō, Tomomichi.* Tokyo: Riburopōto, 1987.

Kōdansha, ed. *Kōdansha Encyclopedia of Japan,* 9 volumes. Tokyo, Kōdansha, 1983.

Komata Nobuo et al. *Nihon ryūkōka shi,* 3 volumes. Tokyo, 1994.

Kurata Yoshihiro. *'Haryari uta' no kōkogaku: Kaikoku kara sengo fukkō made.* Tokyo: Bungei Shunjū, 2001.

Lee, Gregory B. *Troubadours, Trumpeters, Troubled Makers: Lyricism, Nationalism, and Hybridity in China and Its Others*. Durham, NC: Duke University Press, 1996.

Malm, William. 'The Modern Music of Meiji Japan,' In: Donald L. Shively, ed. *Tradition and Modernization in Japanese Culture*. Princeton, Princeton University Press, 1971:257-300.

Miller, J. Scott. 'Lost Melodies Rediscovered: Recordings of the Kawakami Troup at the 1900 Paris Exposition.' Liner notes for music CD, *Yomigaeru Oppekkepee: 1900 nen Pari banpaku no Kawakami ichiza*. Tokyo: Toshiba-EMI Limited, 1997.

Mizuno Takashi. *Tatakatta 'Nonki bushi': tarento gi'in dai'ichigo, enka shi, Ishida Ichimatsu*.Tokyo: Bungei Sha, 2002.

Nihon Rekishi Gakkai, ed. *Meiji ishin jinmei jiten*. Tokyo: Yoshikawa Kōbunkan, 1981.

Nishizawa Sō. *Nihon kindai kayōshi*, 3 volumes. Tokyo: Ōfūsha, 1990.

Paine, S.C.M. *The Sino-Japanese War of 1894-1895*. Cambridge: Cambridge University Press, 2003.

Rōdō Undō Shi Kenkyū Kai, ed. *Osaka Heimin Shinbun*. Tokyo: Meiji Bunken Shiryō Kankō Kai, 1962.

—— *Shūkan Heimin Shinbun, I, II*. Tokyo: Meiji Bunken Shiryō Kankō Kai, 1962.

Ryōkan. *Dewdrops on a Lotus Leaf: Zen Poems of Ryōkan*. Translated and edited by John Stevens. Boston: Shambhala, 1993.

—— *Ryōkan: Zen Monk-Poet of Japan*. Translated by Burton Watson. New York: Columbia University Press, 1977.

Sawamura Sadako. *My Asakusa: Coming of Age in Pre-War Tokyo*. Translated by Norman E. Stafford and Yasuhiro Kawamura. Rutland, Vermont: Tuttle Publishing, 2000.

Seidensticker, Edward. *Low City, High City: Tokyo from Edo to the Earthquake.* New York: Alfred A. Knopf, 1983.

— — *Tokyo Rising: The City since the Great Earthquake.* New York: Alfred A. Knopf, 1990.

Shimane Kiyoshi, ed. *Nihonjin no denki 23: Yokoi Kinkoku, Osaki Tatsugoro, Soeda Azembō.* Tokyo: Heibonsha, 1982.

Soeda Azembō. *Azembō Ryūsei-ki.* Tokyo: Nihon Tosho Senta, 1999 (reprint, originally published in 1941).

Soeda Azembō and Soeda Tomomichi. *Asakusa teiryūki.* Tokyo: Tōsui Shobō, 1982 (reprint, originally published in 1930).

Soeda Azembō Tsuikai Danshō no Kai, ed. *Soeda Azembō tsuikai danshō no kai* (mimeographed pamphlet). Tokyo: 1950.

Soeda Michio. *Ryūkoū uta gojyū nen: Azembō utau.* Toyko: Asahi Shinbun Sha, 1955,

Soeda Tomomichi. *Enka no Meiji, Taishō shi.* Tōsui Shobō, 1982.

— — *Enkashi no seikatsu.* Tokyo: Seikatsu Sōsho, 1967.

— — *Kūshū ka no nikki.* Tokyo: Tōsui Shobō, 1984.

— — *'Meiji, Taishō ryūkōka rekishi ni tsuite.'* Liner notes for LP sound recording, *Shōji Tarō Meiji Taishō ryūkōka shi.* Tokyo: Japan Victor, 1967.

— — *Ryūkōka no gojyū nen: Azembō wa utau.* Tokyo: Asahi Shinbun Sha, 1955.

Statler, Oliver. *Japanese Pilgrimage.* New York: William Morrow, 1983.

Suzuki Yūko. *Heimin-sha no onnatachi.* Tokyo: Fuji Shuppan, 1986.

Takahashi Chikuzan. *The Autobiography of Takahashi Chikuzan: Adventures of a Tsugaru-Jamisen Musician.* Translated and annotated by Gerald Groemer, Warren, Michigan: Harmonie Park Press, 1991.

Takahashi Shin'ichi. *Ryūkōka de tsuzuru Nihon gendai shi*, Tokyo, Ayumi Shuppan, 1985.

Tokyo Asahi Shinbun. 11 March 1892.

Waley, Paul. *Tokyo Now & Then: An Explorer's Guide.* New York: Weatherhill, 1984.

Yumoto Kōichi. *Bakumatsu Meiji ryūkō jiten.* Kashiwa Shobō, 1998.

—— *Meiji jibutsu kigen jiten.* Tokyo: Kashiwa Shobō, 1996.

Index

For Product Safety Concerns and Information please contact our EU
representative GPSR@taylorandfrancis.com
Taylor & Francis Verlag GmbH, Kaufingerstraße 24, 80331 München, Germany

www.ingramcontent.com/pod-product-compliance
Lightning Source LLC
Chambersburg PA
CBHW060143280326
41932CB00012B/1620